THE
Empty Nest
COOKBOOK

recipes • menus • revelations

THE
Empty Nest
COOKBOOK

JOY SMITH

CUMBERLAND HOUSE
NASHVILLE, TENNESSEE

Published by
  Cumberland House Publishing, Inc.
  431 Harding Industrial Drive
  Nashville, TN 37211

Cover design: Unlikely Suburban Design
Text design: Lisa Taylor

Library of Congress Cataloging-in-Publication Data

Smith, Joy, 1942–
    The empty nest cookbook : recipes - menus - revelations / Joy Smith.
        p. cm.
    ISBN 1-58182-376-2 (pbk.)
    1. Cookery. 2. Cookery for two. 3. Menus. I. Title.
    TX714.S58887 2003
    641.5'612--dc22

                                                            2003017613

Printed in the United States of America
1 2 3 4 5 6 7 8 — 08 07 06 05 04 03

For the loves of my life: my husband, Gil, who rode into
our lives in a brown Pontiac and took on three babies as
his own; and for my children, Meara, Lisa, and Richard,
who have brought me untold joy.

Empty Nest Syndrome: A depressed state felt
by some parents after their children have
grown up and left home.

---

*Look for the silver lining in every cloud and those
revelations will create the thread to weave the fabric
of a renewed and joyous life.*

Contents

ACKNOWLEDGMENTS

Many thanks to all you fabulous folks who helped make this book a reality. Without the publishing prowess and personal attention of the Cumberland House staff, especially Ron Pitkin, Julie Jayne, and Lisa Taylor, *The Empty Nest Cookbook* wouldn't be in your hands right now. I couldn't have produced these tasty recipes without the discriminating palates of my family—my husband Gil, Rich and Marianne Anderson, Meara and Joe Kirsch, and Lisa and Mike Poole—and the tolerance of all my friends. My writing pals (a.k.a. The Ya Yas) Pat Sheehey, Mary Ann Libera, Rita Isaacson, and Marge Mehler offered critical wisdom that helped mold this book, along with their warm friendship and support.

INTRODUCTION

After all those years of trying to stay out of the kitchen, who would have guessed that cooking would become a catharsis to help me through one of the most difficult times in my life? Maybe it will help you as well. A piece of me was ripped away each time a child moved out of our home. They went off to college, and then got married. How I missed the bustle, the urgency, talking to them, seeing them. I took to wandering through the house searching for a way to drive away the emptiness inside me; invariably, I wound up fiddling with food. But I suppose there's nothing strange about that, for it is in the kitchen that the heart of our family beats the loudest and through the recipes and cooking that our family is bound.

As I cook, I feel the familiar warmth of us all gathered around preparing and enjoying meals—and each other. Our family tradition was to set aside at least one day a week to sort through recipes and plan a meal together, nicknamed FD's (Family Dinners). Often, friends would join us, and we'd all sit at the table for hours retelling family stories and cackling over bad jokes.

When marriages were in the making, the kids hounded me for our favorite recipes; so I got busy and wrote down ingredients and techniques as I cooked—a habit I can't seem to break. This released my culinary creativity, and before long I had developed a cookbook's worth of new recipes to pass on. Doing this kept me involved enough to work through my loneliness and get over the self-pity thing.

I came to my senses. Why mourn loss, when I have truly gained the best of both worlds. At last, I have time to think, to plan, to pursue my own interests and to enjoy my home, my marriage, and my friends. And I really am not alone, because my children are still here, although no longer underfoot. Perhaps the revelations that have carried me though this transition will help you discover, as I did, that the pain of separation is short-lived, and that your empty nest is very full indeed.

THE
Empty Nest
COOKBOOK

Who needs a recipe, anyway?

Once you have mastered doctoring bought goods and proven recipes, you will have developed the confidence to create recipes of your own. Again, begin with the more forgiving recipes, such as salad dressings and dips, before graduating to more complex fare. At our house, we've always made dressing right on the salad by pouring and sprinkling a bit of this and that until it tasted "right." There's a certain freedom to this, but understand that your dressing will never come out the same way twice, unless you measure and write down ingredients as you add them. One trick I use to capture measurement without giving up the fun of sprinkling with abandon is to lay out a sheet of waxed paper and pretend it is the bowl or pan. After each spice is added, I gather it up, measure it, and write down the amount.

You'll find that common condiments like mayonnaise, catsup, soy sauce, hot sauce, and barbecue sauce (which you can easily make from scratch) can be the basis for many interesting marinades and sauces. For a flavor boost, add an unexpected ingredient—fresh herbs, a tangy pepper sauce, or a squeeze of lime juice—to a routine combination. Make a game of discovering new ways to use a favorite dressing or sauce. If it's creamy, spread it on sandwiches or use it as a base for a dip. Spread chunky blue cheese dressing on a roast beef sandwich; use it as a dip for celery or spicy chicken wings, or stir it into mashed potatoes. I put an open jar of mango chutney to work by adding it to guacamole and by using it as the base for a sauce that complements a chicken or pork entrée.

Lighten up on exactness

Once you have treaded sacred ground by doctoring recipes, you'll find your inhibitions about measurement drift away. It's okay to ease up on the measuring cup habit when creating dishes that won't suffer from a little more of this and a bit less of that. You are, after all, an artist creating a masterpiece. The majority of entrées and side dishes—casserole, entrées, dips, and marinades—are forgiving; but bear in mind that more delicate mixes, such as soufflés, cakes, and breads, depend on exact measurements to rise properly and have the desired texture. Here's how you can train yourself to judge dry and liquid ingredients.

Spooning

If you don't already use the cupped-palm method of estimating dry ingredients, teach yourself to do it. Start by understanding how specific amounts look. Fill various-size measuring spoons with dry ingredients, such as salt or parsley flakes, and then empty each spoon into the curved palm of your hand. Note the fill level for each measure. Once you've done this a few times, you'll be able to differentiate between teaspoons, tablespoons, and portions thereof. An eighth of a teaspoon is one or two finger pinches. Ordinary dinner teaspoons and tablespoons can be used in lieu of measuring spoons but wavering between heaping versus level spoon measures may affect the consistency of a dish.

Cup size

Once you know which of the cups or glasses in your cupboard hold eight ounces (one cup) liquid measure, it will be a snap to figure the percentage of the cup that represents ½ cup, ¼ cup, and ⅓ cup. One-eighth (⅛) cup is two tablespoons.

Good seasonings

If you are exercising your creativity with herbs, a good rule is not to mix two very strong herbs, such as oregano or rosemary, within a dish; but rather add one or more mild herbs, such as parsley or sage, to complement the dominant flavor.

Popular combos

Certain combinations of herbs and spices work together to give dishes their distinct flavor. Some blends are so common we don't think of them as combinations but as seasonings in themselves. You can make yours from scratch as you go or buy them ready-made.

Italian:	parsley, basil, and oregano
French:	rosemary, tarragon, and thyme
Mexican:	chili powder, cumin, cilantro
Indian:	coriander and curry
Chinese:	ginger and soy

But don't overdo it

We all have an inherent sense of what works and what doesn't. For example, a tablespoon of black pepper will be too much for most recipes, six cloves of garlic will fight off werewolves, and one-quarter cup chili powder will send anyone hopping up and down in agony. And sometimes, we go crazy and either overseason a dish or manage to have such a laundry list of ingredients that we don't care to make it ever again.

The trick is to figure out the ratio of one seasoning to another in order to obtain the best flavor; salt to pepper, and oregano to parsley, as examples. When doubling or tripling a recipe, adjust the seasonings in lesser amounts:

> 2 times the recipe: use 1½ times the amount indicated
>
> 3 times the recipe: use 2 times the amount indicated
>
> 4 times the recipe: use 2½ times the amount indicated

Oops! You've added too much of a good (or bad) thing? Try these ideas to save your soup (or whatever):

- Strain out bits of herb and spices, or scoop off any that has not yet dissolved.
- Simmer a raw, peeled, quartered potato in the mixture for 10–15 minutes to absorb some of the excess flavor. Remove and discard the potato afterwards.
- Reduce the amount of salt, if it has not already been added in, and stir in a little sugar.
- If a mixture is overly sweet, sharpen the flavor with a teaspoon (small squeeze) of lemon or lime juice or about a teaspoon of vinegar.
- If possible, serve the dish well chilled, as cold numbs the palate.
- Prepare a second batch, omitting the seasoning, and combine it with the first.

Well, there you have it, the wherewithal to be Queen of your kitchen. We never did talk about cleaning up though, did we? Maybe you can rouse your King from his TV chair to help with the dishes. Fair is fair.

Part 1: Appetizers to Entrées

RECIPE FOR BEING A GOOD FRIEND

Never borrow money

Keep in touch, no matter how busy you are

Be a good listener

Don't offer unsolicited advice

Honor your commitments

Help others feel good about themselves

Don't gossip

Don't flirt with your friends' husbands

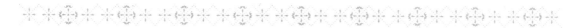

COCKTAILS TO SHARE

Why is it that when we finally enjoy the companionship of our children it's time for them to move out and on to the adult phases of their lives? Once our kids stumbled through the teenybopper years, they actually became human. As parents, my husband and I were thrilled to trade the odious job of disciplinarian for that of advisor. Joyce Brothers has nothing on me! I've heard problems with boyfriends, got excited over good grades and high-scoring games, and tried not to show shock when the subjects of contraception, drugs, drinking, and smoking arose. With many of the conflicts gone, our family of five began to enjoy being together. So much so that, during that wedge of time before dinner, the cocktail hour, whoever was home could be found ensconced at the kitchen table sharing the smiles and woes of their day. These days, it's more common for my husband and me to share the cocktail hour with each other and often with our friends, good friends.

Good friends are like old slippers . . .

Friendships take on a new meaning once our kids move out. Who but a dear chum will put up with all our complaining? Many of them are missing their kids, as we are. We get together and commiserate. We sense when one of us is down and suggest a day of shopping, or stop over for a glass of wine or to share a pot of coffee. We goad each other to try new things, to set goals, and to progress through life's good and bad times. We help fill the gaps in one another's lives as our kids move on. With old friends, we can dine in the kitchen on paper plates or eat on TV trays in the family room. There's a relaxed feel of family; it's being together that matters, not the where, when, or how.

The sad part about friends is they're almost as bad as our kids are; they leave us, too. Their lives change as do ours. They suffer job relocations, retire and set up house-keeping in a warmer climate, or go on to other phases in their lives where we may no longer fit in. When a friend moves on, we never know if we'll remain good friends from afar, or if our lives will become so separate that our contacts will dwindle from phone calls and emails to that dreaded Christmas card with no note.

When I look back, I see my life in chapters, like a book. In each "chapter," I've relied on friendships to carry me through various plateaus. I had wonderful work friends who I all of a sudden had nothing in common with once I switched jobs. When the kids were small, I consulted other mothers for information on anything from pedi-atricians to toenail clippers. During my divorce, when I needed a shoulder to cry on, I sought friends with marital problems like myself. But here again, once I remarried and life was good, the camaraderie was gone. I feel a sense of failure each time I think of one of these special people. How could I have let them go? I wonder how they are doing and where they are now. Would we still be good friends if the changing circum-stances of our lives hadn't twisted us apart?

I have managed to pick up a few kindred souls along the way who I'm convinced will remain lifetime friends. No one stays in one place anymore, so whenever distance separates me from one of these precious gems, I feel as if a piece of my security blanket has been torn off. While these golden friendships fade a bit with the distance, when-ever we talk it's as if we've never parted. Good friends are as important to me as my family, and the nice part is that when we get together they pay their own way.

It seems that as we get older, we spend a lot of time coping with losses and transi-tion, doesn't it? You would think we would be old pros by now, but it always hurts. I've been driven to go out and solicit new friendships when I suffer losses. Making new friends is like starting to date again after a divorce. It feels fake and uncomfortable, like a brand-new pair of shoes. Those same old insecurities pop up, and I find myself trying to impress them with fancy hors d'oeuvres and company meals on the good china. Then, I wonder *why?* Do I fear people won't like me as I am? My cheeks hurt from smiling, trying to make small talk with lovely folks I don't know well enough to ask probing questions or confide in. It's such a strain to prove all over again that I am a person worth knowing. Oh I've made some wonderful new friends and I cherish them; but I'm not sure how long they will stick. What if we move or change our lifestyle? Will we still have enough in common to remain friends? Only time will tell.

I look down at the floor and wiggle my toes. My feet feel good in these comfortable, old, bedroom slippers. I smile and think of how much they remind me of my lifetime friends. Like my slippers, my friends are always there whenever I need comfort or just need to keep my feet firmly on the ground. Yes, I'll always want to make new friends, but in the meantime, I'll wear my comfortable, old pair of slippers. They are already broken in, and I know for certain that they fit.

APPETIZERS

Cajun Shrimp Cocktail

While there's nothing wrong with shrimp served with purchased cocktail sauce, I've found that a little extra spicing makes it even more popular. When prepared this way, my guests stand over the platter of shrimp and don't leave until it's empty. The sauce is easy to make and keeps well. No Cajun seasoning on hand? See Gravies, Marinades & Seasonings for a recipe.

1	pound fresh or frozen cooked shrimp
½	teaspoon Cajun seasoning

ZESTY COCKTAIL DIP:

½	cup catsup
1	tablespoon jerk sauce
1	tablespoon lemon or lime juice

Place cooked shrimp in a plastic bag along with the seasoning and shake until coated. Chill until ready to serve. Mix the dip ingredients. To serve, place the shrimp on a platter atop lettuce leaves, if desired, and offer the dip on the side.

Note: for peel-and-eat shrimp, simply leave on the shell.

SAUCE MAKES ½ CUP

SERVES 4

ABOUT JERK SAUCE

Jerk sauce is a complex combination of herbs and spices unique to Jamaica and the Caribbean. Most commonly it is used to season meats. It's easy enough to find recipes for jerk marinades and dry rubs, but the laundry list of ingredients can be rather intimidating and I have found many of the flavors too pungent for my taste. I routinely order ready-made jerk sauce from Sunny Caribbee, a popular spice company based in Tortola in the British Virgin Islands (www.sunnycaribbee.com), but other brand bottled jerk sauces are available at supermarkets next to the catsup and mayonnaise. For a similar flavor in these recipes, substitute either bottled A1 Bold® steak sauce or use regular A1® sauce and add a few drops of hot sauce per tablespoonful.

Disappearing Crab Bites

Prepare these luscious little cakes ahead and pop them in the oven to bake just before serving. Feel free to substitute all or part of the canned crab with fresh crab meat—they will disappear even faster. Serve with Louie-style Seafood Sauce.

1	egg, slightly beaten
2	tablespoons mayonnaise
1	teaspoon Worcestershire sauce
1	teaspoon Dijon mustard
1/4	teaspoon black pepper
	Dash hot sauce
2	6-ounce cans lump crab meat, drained (or the equivalent in fresh crab meat)
1/2	cup Italian-seasoned breadcrumbs
	Cooking spray

Preheat oven to 450 degrees. In a medium bowl combine the egg, mayonnaise, Worcestershire sauce, mustard, black pepper, and hot sauce. Stir in the crab meat, then the breadcrumbs. Shape the crab mixture into 1-inch patties. If the mixture is too moist to form cakes, add more breadcrumbs. Spray a baking sheet with vegetable oil. Place the patties on the baking sheet and lightly spray the tops of the cakes. Bake at 450° for 4 to 6 minutes, turning once halfway through. Serve hot with a dipping sauce. May be reheated.

MAKES 18 ONE-INCH CAKES

Louie-style Seafood Sauce

I developed this sauce for leftover lobster, but it also works well for shrimp and crab meat. It makes up easily using ingredients I normally keep on hand and is a refreshing change from traditional seafood sauce.

1/4	cup (4 tablespoons) mayonnaise
2	tablespoons catsup
3/4	teaspoon pickle relish
3/4	teaspoon fresh chopped oregano leaves (or 1/4 teaspoon dried)
1 1/4	teaspoons lime juice
1	teaspoon bottled jerk sauce

Mix the dip ingredients.

To serve: Line a serving platter with lettuce leaves. Pour dip into center and spread toward the sides. Distribute seafood evenly over the top, leaving a ring of dip showing. Serve with wheat or plain crackers.

MAKES ABOUT 1/2 CUP

Shellfish Spread

1/2 cup cooked, chopped lobster or crab meat
1 tablespoon minced onion
1/2 teaspoon minced jalapeño pepper
1 teaspoon fresh lime juice
2 tablespoons mayonnaise
1/2 teaspoon dried cilantro

In a small bowl place the lobster or crab meat and stir in the remaining ingredients. Chill for at least 1/2 hour before serving to allow flavors to meld. Serve as a spread with wheat crackers or pumpernickel cocktail bread.

MAKES ABOUT 1/2 CUP

Leftover Salmon Spread

Ever wonder what to do with leftover fish from the previous evening's dinner? Turn it into an appetizer like this one. I used salmon, but any boneless cooked fish will do.

1/2 cup cooked salmon
4 teaspoons mayonnaise
1 tablespoon minced onion
1/8 teaspoon liquid smoke
1/4 teaspoon jerk sauce
1 teaspoon fresh lime juice

Mash salmon with fork in a small bowl. Add remaining ingredients and mix well. Serve with pumpernickel cocktail bread sliced in triangles.

MAKES 1/2 CUP

Dried Tomato Baked Brie

DRIED TOMATO TOPPING:

2	cloves garlic, finely minced
1/2	cup or 1 small jar sun-dried tomatoes preserved in oil, cut up fine
3	tablespoons finely chopped fresh basil
2	tablespoons finely chopped fresh parsley
1/2	teaspoon dried oregano
1	8-ounce ring Brie, skinned if desired

Mix all topping ingredients. If you wish, do the chopping by whirling topping ingredients together in a blender or food processor.

Center the Brie on a heatproof or microwave-safe serving platter and coat with topping. Place in a preheated 350° oven for about 10 minutes or in the microwave for 1 to 2 minutes. Heat until the Brie begins to soften and melt, but holds its shape. Serve immediately with crackers.

Curried Chicken Paté

This really is more of a spread, but "paté" sounds more exotic. Mix it up using leftover cooked chicken, and you're done. Serve with crackers or sliced apples and pears.

1 1/4	cups chopped, cooked chicken
1	4-ounce stick of butter or margarine, cut up into chunks
1/2	medium apple, peeled, seeded, and diced
1	small onion, diced
2	tablespoons walnut pieces
1	teaspoon fresh lemon juice
1/2	teaspoon salt
1/2	to 1 teaspoon curry powder
	Pinch black pepper

Put all ingredients in a food processor and mix well or mix by hand, blending in the butter well. Chill until ready to serve.

MAKES APPROXIMATELY 1 1/2 CUPS

Raspberry Brie Puff

This airy, oozing treat garnished with fresh raspberries is a sure bet when you're looking for something different to wow the crowds. The fresh raspberries are essential, so be prepared to pay extra for them if they are out of season.

1   8- or 10-ounce round of Brie
1   10-ounce jar raspberry preserves
1   pint fresh raspberries
1/2 package Pepperidge Farm Puff Pastry

Preheat oven to 350°. Lay out puff pastry on a breadboard and allow to thaw. Roll out to make a square. Place the Brie in the center of the pastry. Spread the preserves on top of the Brie. Fold the pastry over the Brie to cover, and seal all edges. Place on a baking sheet or ovenproof serving platter and bake at 350° for 20 to 30 minutes. Garnish with the fresh raspberries and serve warm with plain crackers.

SERVES 8 TO 10

Cranberry-Pecan Cheese Ball

Serve this for a special occasion, and then roll the leftovers back into a ball and wrap tightly with plastic wrap for another time.

2   8-ounce packages cream cheese, softened
3   tablespoons confectioners' sugar
1   teaspoon curry powder
2/3 cup flaked coconut
2/3 cup dried cranberries
2/3 cup chopped pecans

In a medium mixing bowl place the slightly softened cream cheese. Add the remaining ingredients, reserving 1/3 cup of the pecans. Form cheese into a ball and roll ball in the reserved pecans to cover. Chill well before serving.

Serve on a platter surrounded by sliced red and green apples or crackers.

MAKES 1 BALL ABOUT 5 INCHES DIAMETER

Rosemary Pecans

*This combination of seasonings is amazingly comple-
mentary. The last time I brought these nuts to a party,
I was confronted by three women who forbade me to
leave without giving them the recipe.*

4	tablespoons ($^{1}/_{2}$ stick) butter or margarine
1	tablespoon dried rosemary leaves
$^{1}/_{4}$	teaspoon dried basil
2	teaspoons seasoned salt
3	drops hot sauce
3	cups pecan halves

Preheat oven to 325°. Melt the butter, and
then stir in the rosemary, basil, salt, and
hot sauce. Add the pecans and mix until
coated. Cook for 8 to 10 minutes, until
pecans are aromatic and slightly dried, but
not burnt. Let cool and serve at once or
store in a tightly covered container.

MAKES 3 CUPS

Island Guacamole

*When we stay aboard our boat, the cocktail hour is an
every-night affair that challenges me to create using
limited ingredients. This basic guacamole can be
quickly tossed together, and it tastes fine even if you've
omitted the chutney. Serve within a day.*

1	California avocado, peeled and mashed
1	clove garlic, minced
	Juice of half a fresh lime
$^{1}/_{4}$	teaspoon salt
	Dash black pepper
$^{1}/_{8}$	teaspoon hot sauce, or to taste
2	tablespoons mango chutney

Add the remaining ingredients to the
mashed avocado and mix well. Serve with
pita chips.

*Note: if using a Florida avocado, double the recipe,
as they are nearly twice as large as California avocados.*

MAKES ABOUT $^{1}/_{2}$ CUP

Quick Dip

Use this all-purpose dip for vegetables.

2   tablespoons mayonnaise
1   teaspoon Dijon mustard
1/4 teaspoon red pepper flakes (or dash of
       hot sauce)
1   squeeze of a lemon or lime wedge

Mix and chill for about half an hour before serving. Good with veggies or seafood.

MAKES ABOUT 1/4 CUP

Strawberry Salsa

This recipe is a product of my strawberry experimentation era. What do you do with 10 pounds of strawberries? Use as a chip dip or as a topping for fish, chicken, or pork.

1   cup (about 10 berries) diced fresh
       strawberries
1   jalapeño pepper, seeded and minced
4   scallions, finely sliced
1/2 teaspoon grated lemon peel
2   tablespoons fresh lemon juice
1   teaspoon dried cilantro (or 1 tablespoon
       chopped fresh)

Mix the strawberries, jalapeño pepper, scallions, lemon peel, lemon juice, and cilantro. Serve immediately as a dip with tortilla chips, or refrigerate until ready to use. Do not prepare more than one day in advance or the strawberries will become mushy.

MAKES 1 CUP

Fruit Dips

These are so obscenely delicious that you'll want to sample them with a spoon. Serve with seasonal fresh fruit.

Apricot Walnut Dip: Combine 1 cup sour cream, 1/4 cup apricot preserves, 1/4 cup shredded coconut, and 1/4 cup chopped walnuts or pecans.

Marshmallow Yogurt Dip: Combine 4 ounces fruit-flavored yogurt with one 7 1/2-ounce jar of marshmallow fluff.

Honey Anise Dip: Stir together 1/2 teaspoon anise extract, 1 tablespoon honey, and 1 cup sour cream.

TIME TO WINE

Wine has bound our family for generations—my dad used to make a year's supply of red wine each fall from California grapes, using the family's built-in wine press in our basement. So when I talk about wine lovingly throughout this book, it's not for its alcoholic qualities but for what it symbolizes. To our family, a glass of wine means celebration, the prospect of good times and good cheer. Your "wine" may be a cup of herb tea, a tall glass of iced water with lemon, or a can of diet Coke. In this book, I also cook with wine and liquors. The alcohol in these beverages cooks off, imparting a sophisticated flavor to the recipe.

The recipes in this section are primarily alcoholic, which can be a problem for pregnant daughters, menopausal friends, and those on special medications. Treat guests who can't imbibe with a dollop of perception. Serve them virgin look-alikes in beautiful cocktail glasses—nix plastic or paper cups and water glasses or soda cans, and don't forget to plop in a wedge of lime or a strawberry for garnish.

Golden Shaker Margaritas

A Margarita has always been one of my favorite drinks, partly because it's not too sweet. Normally, I omit the salt—who needs to retain water? A virgin Margarita is precisely limeade on the rocks.

1	cup Rose's Lime Juice or reconstituted limeade
1/4	cup water
1/2	cup Cuervo Gold tequila
1/4	cup Cointreau or Triple Sec orange liqueur
2	cups ice cubes
	Lime wedges for garnish

Place all ingredients in a drink shaker or in a 1-quart plastic container with a secure top and shake for 30 seconds, until foamy. Pour into Margarita glasses and serve. Garnish with a wedge of lime.

Note: If you use reconstituted limeade, eliminate the water from the recipe. Avoid the temptation to use fresh lime juice. The drink will be too tart no matter how much sugar you add. If you wish, salt the rims of the glasses by wetting them with a wedge of lime, then dipping them into coarse salt.

To make an Orange Margarita: Substitute fresh orange juice for the water and garnish with orange slices.

To make a Grapefruit Margarita, my personal favorite: Substitute grapefruit juice for the limeade and garnish with a maraschino cherry.

MAKES 3

Pink Vodka Lemonade

My daughter and I started with simple vodka and lemonade but found it too tart. The cranberry juice cuts the tartness without making this refreshing drink sweet.

1½ cups vodka
3 cups seltzer water
1½ cups lemonade concentrate
¼ cup cranberry juice
   Mint leaves or strawberries for garnish

Mix all ingredients in a pitcher or covered juice container and serve in tall glasses over ice. Garnish with mint leaves or a strawberry.

SERVES 6

Mojito

This classic Cuban rum spritzer is fast gaining popularity. Authentic Mojito calls for sugar cane and Cuban white rum, but it will also taste fine if made with granulated sugar and any white rum.

   Fresh mint leaves removed from one sprig
1 teaspoon sugar or to taste
   Juice of half a lime or about 1½ teaspoons bottled lime juice
1 ounce white rum or to taste
   Seltzer water

Place the mint leaves, sugar, and lime juice in the bottom of an 8-ounce glass and mash them together with the back of a spoon to release the mint oil. Add the rum, and stir to dissolve sugar. Fill glass with ice, and top with seltzer water. Stir once more. Serve.

MAKES ONE 8-OUNCE DRINK

Passionate Mimosas

These go down more easily than orange juice–based mimosas, as the juice is less tart.

1 cup chilled champagne
1 cup chilled tropical fruit juice blend, such as guava, passion fruit, or mango
2 fresh strawberries for garnish

Pour half a cup each of champagne and fruit juice into 2 champagne glasses. Garnish with a strawberry and sip slowly. When you're finished with this one, make everyone another round. For a virgin Mimosa, substitute ginger ale for the champagne.

MAKES 2 GLASSES

Caribbean Rum Punch

We discovered the best Rum Punch in the Caribbean at a beach bar on Silly Cay, a small isle off the coast of Anquila in the West Indies. A delectable combination of dark rum and Caribbean punch base loaded over ice into a tall glass, topped with Amaretto and nutmeg, kept us sipping for an entire afternoon. Caribbean punch base isn't the simple combination of fruit juices it appears to be. To duplicate the Silly Cay drink I remembered, I began with a standard island recipe, and then adjusted ingredients and proportions until it tasted "right." Although any dark rum will do nicely, Mount Gay is the choice of sailors. This punch even tastes good without the alcohol. Spike it with dashes of rum and almond extracts and a sprinkle of nutmeg.

PUNCH BASE:

2	cups unsweetened pineapple juice
1	cup grapefruit juice
1¼	cups orange juice
1	cup Rose's Lime Juice*
1	cup water
½	cup grenadine syrup
	Nutmeg for garnish

MAKES 48 OUNCES OF BASE

FOR EACH DRINK:

½	cup (4 ounces) punch base
2	ounces (¼ cup) Mount Gay or other dark rum
1	ounce (2 tablespoons) amaretto
	Dash fresh nutmeg

Mix punch base and refrigerate until ready to use.

For each drink: Fill one 10-ounce glass half full of cubed or crushed ice. Add rum, then punch base. Pour the Amaretto on top and garnish with a sprinkle of nutmeg. Drink at once, slowly.

*To substitute limeade concentrate for the Rose's Lime Juice, mix up the limeade as per the directions, and then measure out the 1½ cups of the reconstituted juice called for in the recipe. Omit the cup of water. Make sure that whatever form of lime juice you use, it is sweetened; otherwise, the punch will make you pucker.

Joy Juice

Here's a simple version of Rum Punch.

8	ounces Mount Gay rum (or other dark rum)
48	ounces guava juice
4	ounces lime juice (fresh squeezed limes, Rose's Lime Juice, or limeade concentrate)
	Crushed ice to fill remainder of container

Mix all ingredients in a 64-ounce plastic jug and shake well. Serve over additional ice with a dash of nutmeg, if desired.

By the glass: Fill a 12-ounce cup or glass with ice. Add 1 part rum to 3 parts guava juice. Squeeze in a wedge of fresh lime.

BY THE JUG

Strawberry Mint Party Punch

Everyone loves this nonalcoholic punch because it's not too sweet. Good for bridal and baby showers.

1½ cups orange juice
1 48-ounce can pineapple juice (1½ quarts)
¾ cup lemon juice
½ cup lime juice
1¼ cups sugar
½ cup mint leaves
1 48-ounce bottle ginger ale
1 32-ounce bottle seltzer water
½ pint fresh strawberries

Mix the orange, pineapple, lemon, and lime juices with the sugar and mint leaves and refrigerate until you are ready to assemble the punch.

To assemble: Pour fruit juice and mint mixture into punch bowl. Add ginger ale and seltzer and stir lightly. Add the ice block to the punch. Garnish with fresh strawberries.

Make Ice Block: Prepare one day in advance. Fill a gelatin mold pan with water. Garnish with slices of fresh fruit, such as oranges or lemons. Cover with foil and freeze until solid. To unmold, place briefly in hot water. Put ice mold into punch to keep punch cold.

MAKES ONE PUNCH BOWLFUL

Fruit Slush Punch

Share cups of this wonderful, sherbet-like punch with friends, and then store the leftovers by refreezing them in small containers—serve as a sorbet.

1 12-ounce can frozen lemonade concentrate, thawed
1 12-ounce can frozen orange juice concentrate, thawed
3 cups cranberry juice
4 cups vodka
2 cups cold water
1 quart 7-Up or ginger ale
1 lemon, sliced thin, for garnish
1 orange, sliced thin, for garnish

Mix everything except the 7-Up in a large container and freeze at least 24 hours or until mixture is the texture of sherbet.

To serve: Scoop frozen mixture into a punch bowl. Pour in the 7-Up. Garnish with lemon and orange slices and ladle into punch cups.

MAKES A PUNCH BOWLFUL

Sun-brewed Tea

There's been some controversy about the safety of drinking sun tea. A study done by the University of Colorado indicates that it may carry bacteria. To avoid problems, begin with boiled water and packaged tea bags. Refrigerate the tea within 4 to 6 hours. If you are still concerned, the safest method is to allow tea to "brew" in the refrigerator overnight. But then I guess it won't be Sun Tea, it will be Refrigerator Tea.

Fill a clean, empty plastic juice jug with water. Add 2 teaspoons of sugar. Stuff 4 tea bags into the mixture, leaving the tab ends of the strings hanging outside the jug. Screw the cap onto the bottle and set it in a sunny spot on your back porch for several hours, until the tea turns amber. Refrigerate. Serve over ice with a squeeze of lime.

MAKES 48 OUNCES

RECIPE FOR TRANQUILITY

Savor the quiet you've prayed for

Meditate for inner peace

Take pleasure in the sights and smells around you

Unplug the phone and take an afternoon nap

Think happy thoughts

Soup for the Soul

I associate soup with home and comfort. My mom always had a pot of water laced with meat bones and vegetables bubbling on the stove. It wasn't lunch unless bowls of soup were set out with our sandwiches. I'd like to say I've carried on the soup tradition with my kids, but between the demand of a full-time job and managing my household and family, I was seldom home long enough to tend a pot. Still, I remember the feeling of warmth, of love; the safety I felt, ensconced at my mother's kitchen table bathed in the aroma of soup in the making. I find myself hoarding scraps for soup, as my mom did, now that I have more time at home. On days when the hole in my being gaps so wide it hurts, I set a pot to simmer, sit down at the kitchen table, close my eyes, and inhale its goodness until I'm smiling again.

Beautiful noise . . .

Today is the kind of day I dream about all winter. When I slide back the patio door, I feel a rush of "no-coat" warm air perfumed with the scent of lush pink peonies. I venture outside and stroll through the yard, plucking an occasional weed and survey-ing my domain. Only the rustle of new leaves and the twitter of crickets break the tranquility of this late afternoon. I feel instant peace.

Silence. How I've come to treasure it. The "sounds of silence" are wonderfully golden, especially to someone like me, who has raised a gang of noisy children. There's no such thing as "quiet" in an active family, with all its nitpicking, arguing, laughter, whining, bargaining, and thunderous chases through the house. By the time the two of us expanded to five, our life had escalated to a consistent roar. Something was always dropping, clanking, thumping, or slamming. Although I miss having the kids at home, I can't say I pine for that ruckus.

I have the whole house to myself now. I can hear a dust ball flutter. I can sit for hours in my living room perusing a magazine, snuggled in my blanket of serenity. Many people who have never raised children turn on music or the television set for companionship as soon as they walk into their home, but I can stay home all day with only the hum of the natural sounds around me—my windows rattling on a blustery day, my furnace charging full steam when I raise the heat. I can almost hear my home heave with relief now that it has a voice of its own—the drone of my clothes dryer, the swish of my dishwasher and the occasional clink of the refrigerator making ice cubes. I never knew my home made so many beautiful noises, the music I've awaited all these years.

I'll admit that at first the dead quiet was oppressive. I longed for the customary commotion until I realized I was alone, truly alone (no offense to my husband)—and it wasn't so bad. In fact, I'd found heaven. The house was mine! With no one to tell me to be quiet or snicker, I could sing at the top of my lungs, blast my Elvis songs, or turn up the volume on the TV, so I could hear it in the kitchen.

Now I can plan. I can think. Everything I do takes less effort. I absolutely love being able to sit at the kitchen table to make up my grocery list, rather than seeking peace and quiet on the "mother's throne" in the bathroom. When the phone rings, I know it's for my husband or me—no more stumbling over lord-knows-what to take a call for a teenager who is not home. A few of our kids' friends had a nasty habit of hanging up whenever my husband or I answered the phone, which always made me hopping mad.

Even our doorbell has forgotten how to chime; at least not like it used to when the children were young. In our old neighborhood, one child used to sneak out early each morning and lean on our bell, and our dog, Gordie, learned to bang our doorbell with his paw when he was ready to come inside. It's amazing how everyone in the household, except me, could sleep through that persistent chiming. One day I cut the wires and gained peace, at last. The only folks that ring our bell now are people we don't know—salespeople, pairs of evangelists, repair people, and an occasional kid selling chocolate bars. Our kids walk in as if they still live here, and our friends just come around back and rap on the kitchen door.

The happy noises of family and friends still thrill me. I love nothing more than to have my home bursting with loved ones. But these are welcome sounds, familiar and nurturing; beautiful noise I can truly enjoy. Especially since I know that as soon as they all leave, my home will be my haven once again, and I can jump into my favorite chair and get back into that novel.

SOUPS & STEWS

Making soups and stews

The secret to rich, strong stock is to use barely enough water to cover the soup bones. The most common mistake is adding too much water. A good stock will be the consistency of gelatin when thoroughly chilled. Some people mix different types of bones together, such as lamb and beef, but our family never did. Make sure to use enough bones, about five pounds or so, or you'll end up with a meager amount of stock for your trouble. Carrots sweeten the stock; add more if this is what you wish. For a heartier flavored stock, I like to add garlic and a can of stewed tomatoes. A soup will be more substantial if you use larger chunks of vegetables and meats and add a bit more of each.

Experiment with different vegetables and greens. There are two types of Swiss chard, red and green. Red is sweeter. Escarole tends to be bitter. Look for organic or baby spinach, as the leaves are usually tenderer. Prepare greens by heaping leaves in a pile and then grabbing the bunch with your left hand and slicing off two-inch chunks. Greens shrink when cooked, so don't be put off by the quantity.

It's okay if you haven't the time to make homemade stock for these recipes; canned stock works interchangeably. Ham stock may not be available canned, so pop a leftover hambone in the freezer until you have time to make the stock. Also, turkey neck bones, wings, and the leftover bones from a rib or lamb roast may be frozen for future stocks. It's easier to add seasoning than to remove it, so hold the salt and pepper from the stock until you are preparing your final soup recipe. If you wish to thicken the broth, add about a fourth cup more of a starchy food, such as potatoes, pasta, or beans. Before adding canned beans, I always dump them into a colander and rinse off the thick juice, as it contains all the gases from the beans.

SOUPS

Homemade Stock

This is the basic recipe for making stock that I inherited from my mom. Use as a base for soups and stews.

1   collection of meat bones and leftover tidbits, including any reserved parts, such as turkey necks, wings, etc. (at least 5 pounds)
    Just enough water to cover the bones
1   clove garlic (optional)
1   onion, cut into chunks
1   or 2 carrots, cut into chunks
2   or 3 stalks celery or celery leaves
1   14½-ounce can stewed tomatoes (optional)
1   or 2 sprigs fresh parsley (or 2 tablespoons dried)

Place the bones in a large stockpot, cracking the carcass or breaking up the bones into smaller pieces so they will fit as near to the bottom of the pan as possible. Add just enough water to cover the bones, keeping in mind that about ½ to 1 cup will evaporate in the cooking process (9 cups of water will make about 8 cups of stock). Add the vegetables and parsley and bring to a boil. Reduce to a simmer and cover the pot. Continue to simmer, covered, for several hours, until meat falls off the bones and the bones appear "white." Remove any large bones and vegetable chunks to a separate bowl and pour the stock through a strainer into a clean pot or large bowl. Refrigerate stock overnight or until well chilled.

Meanwhile, sort through the bones and vegetable remains you've removed from the stock and remove, package, and refrigerate any bits of meat or vegetables you may want to include in your final soup. Discard bones, gristle, and anything else undesirable. The leftover meat and vegetable scraps can be placed back into the de-fatted stock for Simple Soup, or reused for another recipe.

When the stock is chilled, carefully remove and discard the layer of fat that has formed on top. (If you're in a hurry, you can put the stock in the freezer for an hour). Use the stock to make the soup recipe of your choice, or freeze it in quart containers until ready to use.

MAKES ABOUT 2 QUARTS

Simple Soup

Make this soup with fresh, frozen, or canned stock using bits of meat and vegetable that are handy.

½ cup uncooked rice (or small pasta such as orzo, tubettini, or pastina)

4 to 5 cups stock

2 cups meat and vegetable bits reserved from stock base

1 14½-ounce can stewed tomatoes (optional)

1 to 2 tablespoons dried parsley
  Salt and pepper to taste

Precook the rice or pasta in salted water. Drain well. Reheat stock in a covered pan. Add meat and vegetable bits, and stewed tomatoes if desired. Season with salt and pepper. Add the cooked rice or pasta to the soup. Cover and cook on low for 10 to 15 minutes. Serve at once.

SERVES 6

Swiss Chard & Bean Soup with Ham

Swiss chard looks and tastes like a delicate form of spinach with celery-flavored stems. I learned to love it as a child, when we cooked it fresh from the garden. Use ham or chicken stock. It is substantial enough for a light supper.

6 cups ham or chicken stock

1 head fresh Swiss chard, cleaned and sliced crosswise

1 cup chopped ham

1 can cannelloni beans, drained and rinsed

¼ teaspoon black pepper
  Salt to taste
  Parmesan cheese for garnish

In large saucepan bring the stock to a gentle boil. Stir in Swiss chard. Cover and simmer 5 to 10 minutes, until chard softens. Stir in ham and beans and continue to simmer covered until heated through. Add pepper and salt to taste and serve at once with a sprinkle of Parmesan cheese.

Refrigerate any leftover for up to 5 days, or freeze.

MAKES 2 QUARTS

Basic Minestrone

Minestrone is Italian vegetable soup, usually with beans. Experiment with vegetables you have on hand.

2 tablespoons olive oil
1 clove garlic, minced
1½ quarts chicken stock
4 scallions, sliced
2 carrots, cut into ½-inch chunks
2 stalks celery, sliced thin
¼ cup chopped fresh basil (or 1 tablespoon dried)
1 can cannelloni beans, drained and rinsed
1 cup elbow macaroni, uncooked
½ pound yellow squash or zucchini
1 package frozen peas
1 14-ounce can stewed tomatoes
Salt and pepper to taste
Parmesan cheese

In a large stockpot heat the olive oil over medium-high heat. Add garlic and sauté briefly.

Add the stock, scallions, carrots, celery, and basil and bring to a boil. Cover and simmer about 10 minutes. Add the beans, macaroni, squash, peas, and tomatoes. Bring to a boil, and then reduce heat. Cover and simmer until macaroni is just tender. Serve immediately topped with Parmesan cheese.

MAKES 1 QUART

Turkey Sausage Minestrone

The hot sausage gives kick to this dinner soup, but sweet sausage will work if you're not into spicy.

1 teaspoon olive oil
1 pound hot Italian turkey sausage, cut into 1-inch slices
1 medium onion, chopped
2 medium zucchini, chopped
4 cups chicken or turkey stock
1 cup dry vermouth
½ teaspoon fennel seed
1 14½-ounce can stewed tomatoes
1 cup small elbow macaroni, uncooked
¾ teaspoon salt or to taste
⅛ teaspoon black pepper
1 16-ounce can black beans, drained and rinsed

In a 4-quart or larger cooking pot heat the olive oil over medium-high heat. Add the sausage and sauté until browned. Reduce heat to medium. Cover the pot and continue to cook the sausage for 5 more minutes. Drain any excess fat from pan. Add the onion and zucchini. Cover the pot and cook, stirring occasionally, until vegetables begin to soften. Add stock, vermouth, fennel seed, tomatoes, macaroni, salt, and pepper. Bring to a boil, then cover and cook until pasta is done. Stir occasionally and reduce heat if needed. Stir in the beans and bring to a boil, uncovered. Serve at once. Leftovers may be frozen.

MAKES 2½ QUARTS

STEWS

Winter Vegetable Stew

Try this as a cold winter night's supper. Sometimes I add some cooked ground beef or bits of leftover cooked steak, chicken, or turkey during the last 15 minutes of cooking. Zucchini, peppers, or any other vegetables you have on hand will make it more interesting. I use red wine with beef stock and white with chicken stock.

1	tablespoon olive oil
2	large onions, sliced
2	cloves garlic, minced
2	stalks celery, sliced
2	carrots, sliced
1	large potato, chopped
6	cups chicken or beef stock
1	pound sliced mushrooms
1	16-ounce can whole tomatoes or stewed tomatoes, coarsely chopped, undrained
1	cup dry red or white wine
2	teaspoons dried parsley
$1/2$	teaspoon dried rosemary
$1/2$	teaspoon dried thyme
$1/2$	teaspoon salt (or to taste)
$1/4$	teaspoon black pepper

In a large saucepan or stockpot heat the olive oil over medium heat. Add the onions, garlic, celery, carrots, and potato and cook covered until vegetables are tender, about 25 minutes. Stir occasionally. Add the stock, mushrooms, tomatoes and their juice, wine, parsley, rosemary, thyme, salt, and pepper. Simmer for 2 hours uncovered. Serve warm.

SERVES 8 TO 10

Not-Too-Hot Chili

I like hot food, but not when it makes me breathe fire. This recipe will appease your palate for chili without burning your insides.

2	tablespoons olive oil or oil spray
1	clove garlic, minced
1	medium onion, chopped
1	pound lean ground beef or turkey
1	$14^{1}/2$-ounce can stewed tomatoes with juice
1	12-ounce can beer
1	tablespoon chili powder
1	teaspoon ground cumin
	Salt and pepper to taste
1	$15^{1}/2$-ounce can black beans, drained and rinsed
$1/2$	teaspoon molasses (optional)
1	tablespoon cornmeal (optional)

In a 10- or 12-inch skillet or Dutch oven heat 1 tablespoon of the olive oil over medium-high heat. Add the garlic and onion and sauté briefly. Cover and cook for 3 to 5 minutes, until the onion has softened. If the pan is dry add the remaining oil, and then add the ground beef or turkey. Sauté the meat until browned and cooked. Drain off excess fat and then add the remaining ingredients, except for the cornmeal. Cook uncovered on medium-low heat for about 45 minutes. About 5 minutes before cooking is complete, stir in the cornmeal to thicken the chili. Serve with cornbread if desired. Freezes well.

MAKES ABOUT 6 CUPS

Beef Pinot Noir

A great taste. Try this recipe using a variety of red wines, such as Merlots and Cabernet Sauvignons, for subtle flavor changes. Freeze or reheat leftovers.

1½ pounds beef stew meat
¼ cup flour
1 teaspoon salt
½ teaspoon pepper
½ teaspoon dried thyme
3 tablespoons olive oil
1 medium onion, sliced
1 pound sliced mushrooms
1 10½-ounce can beef broth
½ to ¾ cup Pinot Noir (or other red wine)
¼ cup chopped fresh parsley (or 3 tablespoons dried)
   Additional salt and pepper to taste

Place the stew meat, flour, salt, pepper, and thyme in a mixing bowl or plastic bag and mix well to coat the meat. Set aside. Heat 1 tablespoon of the olive oil in a 12-inch skillet over medium-high heat. Add the onion and sauté a few minutes. Add the mushrooms and continue to sauté until the vegetables just begin to soften. Remove them from the pan with a slotted spatula and set aside.

Add the remaining olive oil to the pan. Pour the floured beef mixture into the hot frying pan and spread to make one layer.

Sauté, turning as needed, until the beef is browned on all sides. Add the beef broth to deglaze the pan. Stir with a spatula and scrape any hardened bits from the bottom of the pan. Add the reserved mushroom and onion mixture, wine, and parsley to the frying pan. Stir well and bring to just boiling. Reduce heat. Cover and simmer for about an hour, until the meat is tender. Serve with crusty French bread for dipping.

SERVES 3 TO 4

Classic Beef Stew

¼ cup flour
½ teaspoon salt
¼ teaspoon black pepper
1½ pounds cubed stew meat
3 tablespoons olive oil
1 clove garlic, crushed and minced
1 large onion, sliced into wedges
½ pound sliced mushrooms
1¾ cups beef broth (or bouillon cubes or
granules and water)
4 medium potatoes, scrubbed and sliced
into 1-inch chunks
4 carrots, scrubbed and sliced into 1-inch
chunks (or use a half bag of baby
carrots)
¼ cup chopped fresh Italian parsley (or
3 tablespoons dried)
1 teaspoon dried basil
1 teaspoon thyme
½ cup red wine (or water)

Place the flour, salt, and pepper in a mixing bowl or in a large plastic bag. Add the beef cubes and stir or shake the bag until thoroughly coated with the flour mixture. Set aside. In a 12-inch skillet or Dutch oven heat 2 tablespoons of the olive oil on medium-high heat. Add the garlic and onion and sauté for a few minutes, and then stir in the mushrooms and cook until all the vegetables soften. Remove the vegetables to a small bowl and set aside. Add the remaining oil to the pan, and then add the beef, including any excess flour mix, and brown meat on all sides. Stir in the beef broth to deglaze the pan, scraping browned bits from the bottom of the pan. Add the cooked mushroom and onion mixture, potatoes, carrots, parsley, basil, thyme, and wine. Bring to a simmer and cook covered, stirring occasionally, until beef is tender and potatoes and carrots are cooked (about an hour). Add additional salt and pepper to taste, and more wine or water if sauce is too thick. Serve at once with crusty bread and a green salad.

SERVES 4

Triple-Bean Chicken Stew

I like to make a pot of this when the kids are expected, as it adapts well to a variety of arrival times. Leave the chicken breasts whole for an "entrée" look, or cut up the chicken, stew fashion, and return it to the pan. When served with dumplings, this stew makes a complete meal.

2 chicken breast halves, skinned (boneless
or bone-in)
3 cups chicken broth
1 28-ounce can chopped tomatoes,
undrained
1 medium yellow onion, chopped
1 teaspoon ground cumin
1½ teaspoons dried cilantro
1½ teaspoons medium-hot chili powder
1 teaspoon ground coriander

1   teaspoon Worcestershire sauce
1½ teaspoons salt
¼   teaspoon black pepper
1   10-ounce package frozen green beans
1   15-ounce can black beans, drained
    and rinsed
1   15-ounce can cannelloni beans or other
    white beans, drained and rinsed

Place all the ingredients except the black beans and cannelloni beans in a large stockpot or Dutch oven. Bring to a boil over medium heat. Reduce heat to low and simmer covered for about 40 minutes, until the chicken is almost cooked. Add the black beans and cannelloni beans. If desired, remove chicken from soup, and using a pot holder and fork, remove the meat from the bones. Discard the bones and return chicken to soup. If you wish to make dumplings, do this now; otherwise bring to a boil, then simmer covered for 20 minutes more. Ladle into soup bowls and serve with crusty bread and a crisp green salad.

To make dumplings: Use your own "from scratch" dumpling recipe or mix 1⅔ cups buttermilk baking mix with ⅔ cup milk. Drop by spoonfuls onto the boiling chicken stew. Cook uncovered for 10 minutes, then cover and continue cooking another 10 minutes. Makes 8 dumplings.

MAKES 2½ QUARTS

Tuscan Chicken Stew

Bon Appetit *magazine liked my recipe well enough to publish it, so maybe your crowd will enjoy it, too.*

2   pounds chicken breasts, skinned
    (boneless or bone-in)
4   cups chicken broth
1   14½-ounce can stewed tomatoes
1   large yellow onion, chopped
1   clove garlic, minced
1   10-ounce package frozen green beans
    or spinach
2   teaspoons salt
1   tablespoon dried oregano
2   tablespoons dried parsley
1   tablespoon dried basil
1   15-ounce can cannelloni beans
½   cup red wine

Place all ingredients except the cannelloni beans and wine in a large stockpot or Dutch oven. Bring to a boil over medium heat. Drain and rinse the cannelloni beans and set aside to add to the stock later. Reduce heat to low, and then cover and simmer for about 40 minutes or until chicken is cooked and falls away from the bone. Remove the chicken breasts from the broth and break the meat up into large chunks, de-boning breasts if necessary, then return the chicken to the broth and add the cannelloni beans and the wine. Continue cooking another 10 minutes. Serve hot.

SERVES 8

Veal Stew Marsala

Try this also with stew-sized pork cubes.

2	tablespoons flour
1	pound veal stew meat
2	tablespoons butter or olive oil
1	large clove garlic, minced and crushed
2	medium yellow onions, sliced
8	ounces sliced mushrooms
1	teaspoon salt
1/8	teaspoon black pepper
2	cups beef broth (one 13½-ounce can)
1	cup Marsala wine
1/2	teaspoon dried thyme
1/3	cup chopped fresh parsley leaves

Place the flour in a medium mixing bowl or plastic zip-lock bag. Add the veal cubes and stir or shake to coat. Set aside. In a 10- or 12-inch skillet or Dutch oven heat 1 tablespoon of butter on medium-high heat. Add the garlic and sauté for 1 minute. Add the onions and continue to sauté. Add the mushrooms, salt, and pepper. Cover the pan and cook about 5 minutes, stirring frequently, until the vegetables are slightly browned and begin to soften. Remove to a bowl and set aside.

Add the remaining tablespoon of the butter to the skillet. Pour the veal-flour mixture into the hot skillet and sauté the veal until browned on all sides. Add the beef broth, wine, and thyme to the pan and stir, scrapping browned bits from the bottom of the pan to deglaze the pan. Return the onion mixture to the skillet. Stir in the fresh parsley, and bring to a simmer. Cover and continue to simmer for 1 hour, until veal is tender. Stir occasionally. Serve with biscuits or bread for sopping up the juices and a crisp green salad.

SERVES 3

RECIPE FOR SPOILING YOUR PET

Let him sleep on your bed

Call your home and talk to him on the answering machine

Take photographs of him and show them to your friends

Sneak him food from the dinner table

Hold him like a baby and tell him he's beautiful

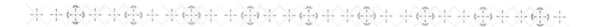

SOLACE FROM THE SEA

I'm sorry, but I can't think about seafood without being reminded of our cats. How they run when I open a can of tuna! I guess I can't blame them. It smells, and I'm sure it tastes, better than their canned cat food. I once snickered at people who treated their pets like their children. Now that I understand, I'm embarrassed. I never realized having a pet could offer so much comfort until the kids moved out.

A *day in the life of a cat*

Sleep Eat, Sleep Play Eat, Sleep Play Eat Sleep, Eat Sleep

Feeding Schedule:
- Two self-feeders: one full of dry cat food and the other with water, both available twenty-four hours a day so they'll never be hungry and won't be tempted to drink out of the toilet bowl.
- Cat treat snacks to be doled out anytime they look particularly cute (which is always).
- Canned cat food for dinner served promptly at five PM—or else they'll stalk you like hungry tigers.
- One pinch catnip to be dealt out sparingly because it makes them act goofy.

You're your pet's mom, now . . .

The days the kids move out of the house are the worst of times. First, there's the hubbub, and then there's the dull emptiness. With a bustle and a hustle, the furniture in their room starts to go. They need a bed, so do you care if they take theirs from home? Of course you do, but you let them anyway. It's not giving up the bed that you mind, but you wonder if it means they don't ever plan to sleep at home again. Then, with a final slam of the door, they're gone. It's quiet. So quiet. You're not sure whether to kick up your heels with glee or to break down and sob. Somehow, they both seem appropriate.

Your home looks different. It seems strange to see the kids' rooms cleared of posters and books. You notice there are stains on the rug, now that it's not covered with piles of clothes. Their room needs painting, and the holes where pictures once hung should be plastered. How did that dent get in the wall? Maybe this would make a good guestroom when it's redone. You cringe at the thought.

There's an obvious gap in the family room where the stereo used to be—and where is the spare TV? You obsess about things that are missing until you go down to the basement to shut off the light and discover that the kids didn't take the stuff you'd been saving for them. Your storage areas are an obstacle course strewed with schoolbooks they'll never look at again, abandoned photos of former beaus, and a washer and dryer that one of them owns and might need one day. Here, there remain enough tables, chairs, lamps, pictures, and small appliances to furnish a couple of apartments. Maybe the Salvation Army will come pick the stuff up.

Not only that, when you poke around, you discover their winter clothes left in cartons and "Goodwill bags" stuffed in corners. Old prom gowns poke fun at you each time you pull back the closet door, and worn-thin Raggedy Ann sheets bring you near tears when you come across them in the linen closet. The kids took the good stuff and left you the memories.

And, because their new place has a no-pets rule, you now have their cat! You find him curled on top of the dryer with his paws over his ears looking for some quiet. Rummaging through your supplies, you locate a treat to lure him. He jumps down and looks cautiously around as if he's just survived an avalanche. He's smart enough to know something is different. You walk away and know you're being watched, and there he is looking up at you with adoring, brown cow eyes. You give him a pat and he trails after you like a little lost lamb.

It used to be the family pet only hung around at mealtimes, like a typical teenager; but since the kids moved out, you've become his sole form of entertainment. Wherever you are, he is. At this point you're weak, and this kind of encouragement is dangerous. You spoil the little guy like a grandchild. After all, he loves you. *He* hasn't moved out.

*   *   *

When our last pet died several years ago, we swore we were through with animals. We bought white rugs and new couches. Our house, the same one that spent years tolerating dog poop on the carpets, claw scratches on doors, and messy pet food bowls on the kitchen floor, finally looked the way I had dreamed. But our home felt cold, like a ghost town. So we did it again. We went to the humane society and picked out Smokey, a beautiful longhaired gray and white cat with a long fluffy tail that looks like a curl of smoke; and soon afterwards we inherited our daughter's cat, Poogaloo, a pedigree Blue Point Himalayan who follows me around like a puppy dog. Who wouldn't love them? Our life was full, and our home again reverberated with the shuffle of tiny feet.

Our cats provide us with better entertainment than a TV sitcom, and the best part is they don't talk back. Scratch them under their chins, and they're in paradise. We pamper them with catnip and scented litter and then trail after them with our camera, taking rolls and rolls of photos. It's so easy to slip back into that familiar role of parenting, isn't it? When we're out, our cats sit and watch for us from the window like new wives, then greet us at the door with a purr and a leg rub. If we arrive home past their self-appointed dinner hour, we suffer their cold shoulders and accusing looks. The old parental guilt takes over, and we're euphoric. It feels so good to be needed.

Like new parents, we seek out fellow pet owners and swap pictures and share stories. When we get together with friends we may spend only a few moments updating them on our kids, and half an hour cooing over our pets. There would be less conversation in our home if we didn't have our pets. "Oh look, Poogs is playing with his toys; see how his tail goes up as every time he struts to his food bowl. Smokey looked real cute all stretched out on the bed." It goes on and on . . . "the kitties should be brushed; one of them just sneezed, should I call the vet?" See? Nothing's changed. We squander more money in the pet store than we've ever spent on birthday presents for our kids—special travel cases, top-of-the-line pet foods. Nothing's too good for our "babies."

We pet owners clip the wings of our freedom, and we do it joyously. We worry about the little guy when we leave him alone too long, so we hire a pet sitter at twenty dollars a visit (more than we used to pay our baby sitter). We put him in a kennel as a last resort because we fret he won't eat. When we're traveling, we call home and sing to him on our answering machines. We're sure he misses us. All this for a lick and a promise of unconditional love. As I write this, I look over my shoulder, and there are our two cats, Smokey and Poogaloo. Their backs are turned toward me so I'll think they don't care. But they do. I reach over and give them a little pat.

Nevertheless, Smokey and Poogaloo are not getting any of this leftover salmon! Experience has taught me that giving people food to pets can turn them into real pests. Case in point is my son's cat, little Emma, who won family fame with her Thanksgiving Day dive bomb onto the turkey carcass. She attacked a hot dog just the other day and has been caught licking food scraps off dirty dishes in the sink. I know many of you won't agree with me. Your pet probably has his own chair at your dinner table.

Seafood Entrées

Seafood is not only delicious, but it's the food of choice for dieters and cholesterol watchers—and *The Wrinkle Cure* author, Dr. Nicholas Perricone, swears it will improve your skin.

Selecting seafood

When purchasing or accepting some of this miracle food, be extra cautious to avoid fish that may be contaminated in any way. Buy it from a reputable source. Be wary of buying shellfish sold off the backs of pick-up trucks in shore areas. Although it may seem fresh, verify that it has not been harvested from contaminated waters by asking to see either the shipping tag or shipping number of the shellfish. (All shellfish caught in approved waters must carry such a number.) The quality and safety of seafood deteriorates if it isn't kept cold, so make fresh fish and shellfish your last market stop, and then get it on ice as quickly as possible. Before cooking, rinse seafood under cold water to remove surface bacteria.

Fish having a strong fishy odor are past their prime. Poke the flesh. It should feel firm and spring back. If whole fresh fish are looking back at you with bright, clear, and shiny eyes, they're fresh. Scales should be shiny and cling like a slinky, sequined ball gown to the skin, and the gills should be bright pink or red. Choose steaks and fillets that are glistening and moist, with no drying or browning around the edges.

When buying packaged fresh fish from the supermarket case, check the sell-by or use-by date and if it has expired, leave it there. Seafood that has been flash frozen and kept that way is usually top quality as this process quickly transforms fresh-caught fish or shellfish to a rock-solid zero degrees Fahrenheit and locks in color, moisture, and flavor. Frozen, prepared seafood items, like crab cakes, should be solid and odorless. Avoid buying packages that are above the frost line in a store display freezer, and choose those that are clean, tightly sealed, and contain fish that is free of ice crystals, freezer burn, and signs of thawed juices. At the deli, avoid cooked seafood products that have been touching raw fish in the display case as the fish may have become contaminated. Smoked seafood should have a pleasant, smoky odor. Keep smoked seafood products refrigerated and use them within ten days.

All shellfish—mussels, clams, oysters, shrimp, crab, and lobster—must be sold alive, and can live for weeks out of water if you tend to them properly. Keep fresh-caught lobsters and crabs alive by placing them in a bucket of saltwater until you are ready to cook them. If you have bought them at a market, keep them chilled and cook them the same day. Look for feisty lobsters and crabs that move their legs and snap their tails when picked up. Sluggish ones will lack flavor and be mushy when cooked.

Make certain clams, mussels, and oysters are still living before committing them to the pot. Tap the shell of slightly open mollusks and ditch those that don't clam up, because they are goners. Healthy freshly shucked oysters and scallops will have a clean, salty odor and be surrounded by clear, slightly milky, or light gray liquid. Cook shucked oysters within a week, and check the sell-by date when purchasing containers of them from the market.

FISH STEAKS & FILETS

Chilean Sea Bass

This fish appears on menus in the finest restaurants for a good reason. It's delicious. Try it with this not-too-spicy Cajun sauce.

- 1¼ pounds Chilean Sea bass steaks, 1- to 1¼-inch thick
- 3 tablespoons olive oil
- 1 tablespoon lime juice
- 2 tablespoons Cajun seasoning

Place all ingredients, including the fish, in a zip-lock plastic bag and mush around until the fish is coated. Allow the fish to marinate while the broiler or grill heats up. Place the fish on a broiler rack and broil it 4 inches from the heat for about 6 minutes per side or until cooked to desired doneness.

SERVES 2

Fiesta-crusted Salmon

For raves, try this easy, exotic entrée. It's good with or without the Orange Salsa.

- 1 tablespoon olive oil
- 2 tablespoons lime juice
- 2 pounds fresh salmon fillet, cut into 4 equal serving sizes if desired
- 1 teaspoon ground coriander
- ½ teaspoon ground cumin
- ½ teaspoon dried cilantro leaves
- ½ teaspoon ground black pepper
- ½ teaspoon salt

Preheat grill or broiler. In a small bowl combine the olive oil and lime juice. Brush the fish lightly on both sides with oil-lime mixture. Combine the coriander, cumin, cilantro, pepper, and salt. Sprinkle mixture lightly and evenly over both sides of the fish. Grill or broil fish for about 7 to 10 minutes on each side or to desired doneness. Serve at once topped with Orange Salsa.

SERVES 4

Orange Salsa

2 navel oranges, peeled and sliced into
$\frac{1}{2}$-inch pieces
2 scallions, sliced thin (or 1 tablespoon
minced onion)
$\frac{1}{4}$ cup fresh lime juice
2 teaspoons dried cilantro (or 2 tablespoons chopped fresh)

Mix the oranges, scallions, lime juice, and cilantro. Refrigerate until ready to serve.

Lemon Salmon

Swordfish or tuna steaks—any firm, mild fish will work equally well. The fish may be grilled, broiled, or baked. Serve with a dollop of Strawberry Salsa from the Appetizer section.

2 pounds swordfish
2 tablespoons olive oil
2 tablespoons lemon juice
$\frac{1}{2}$ teaspoon cilantro
$\frac{1}{2}$ cup Strawberry Salsa for garnish, p. 22

Preheat barbecue grill. Rinse the swordfish and pat dry with paper towels. Mix the olive oil and lemon juice. Using a pastry brush, baste the oil-lemon mixture over both sides of the fish and sprinkle with the cilantro. Place the fish on a hot grill and cook 7 to 10 minutes per side, depending on thickness. Baste as needed with remain-

ing oil-lemon mixture. Fish is done when juice no longer runs clear. Remove the cooked fish to a serving platter, divide into 4 portions, and top each with a spoonful of Strawberry Salsa.

To bake fish: Baste with oil mixture and place fish skin side down on a shallow baking sheet. Bake in a preheated 450° oven for 15 to 20 minutes or until cooked.

SERVES 4

Lime-grilled Swordfish

Low-cal and s-o-o-o simple. The lime rind will burn, leaving the flavor cooked deliciously into the fish. For best results use a grill top designed for fish.

$1\frac{1}{2}$ to 2 pounds swordfish
1 fresh lime
1 tablespoon olive oil or cooking spray

Rinse swordfish and pat dry. Cut the lime into thin rounds. Baste the underside of the fish with a thin coat of olive oil. Evenly distribute the lime slices over the top side of the fish. Baste the remaining oil over the lime slices. Grill, underside first, for 5 to 7 minutes. Turn the steaks by lifting and flipping over carefully using a large spatula. Keep the lime slices under the fish. Grill another 5 to 7 minutes or until fish is cooked as desired. Flip lime slices up onto a serving platter and enjoy.

SERVES 2 OR 3

Basil Swordfish

Use fresh basil leaves for the best flavor and appearance of this dish. Enjoy this entrée in the winter using your oven broiler. Tuna steaks are good, too, with these seasonings.

MARINADE:

¼	cup olive oil
2	tablespoons Dijon mustard
2	tablespoons fresh lemon juice
½	cup chopped fresh basil leaves (or 1½ tablespoons dried)
4	6-ounce swordfish steaks, cut 1-inch thick
	Lemon wedges and/or fresh basil sprigs for garnish

To make the marinade: In a small bowl whisk together the olive oil, Dijon mustard, and lemon juice. Stir in the basil. Pour marinade into a zip-lock plastic bag or large dish. Add the swordfish pieces, and then move them around to coat all sides. Refrigerate swordfish for at least 30 minutes, turning occasionally.

Preheat barbecue grill. Remove the fish from marinade and put it on the grill. Cook to desired doneness, about 7 minutes per side, basting with remaining marinade. Transfer the fish to plates, garnish with lemon wedges and basil sprigs if desired, and serve at once.

SERVES 4

Tequila Tuna

This marinade works well with any whitefish. Try it with swordfish, halibut, cod, or sole.

TEQUILA MARINADE:

1	lime
¼	cup tequila gold
2	tablespoons catsup
1	tablespoon olive oil
1	teaspoon chili powder
1	teaspoon sugar
2	scallions, thinly sliced
½	teaspoon dried cilantro
1½	pounds tuna steak

To make the marinade: Grate the zest from the lime and place it in a small bowl. Cut the remaining lime into quarters and squeeze out all the juice into the bowl. Add the tequila, catsup, oil, chili powder, sugar, scallions, and dried cilantro. Mix well. Marinate the fish for about 20 minutes, then grill or broil the fish for about 10 minutes per inch of thickness per side.

MARINADE MAKES ABOUT ½ CUP

SERVES 2

Grilled Rosemary Tuna Steaks

These steaks are best when barbecued, but what isn't? You can broil off-season. The Rosemary Marinade works equally well with swordfish or any firm, white fish. The most work you'll do is getting out all the ingredients to make the marinade. As fish flavors quickly, do not marinate for more than an hour or two.

ROSEMARY MARINADE:

1/4	cup wine vinegar
3	tablespoons soy sauce
1	tablespoon Dijon mustard
1	tablespoon catsup
1	clove garlic, minced
1	tablespoon lemon juice
1/4	teaspoon black pepper
1	teaspoon dried rosemary leaves
1/2	teaspoon dried basil
1/3	cup olive oil
2	pounds fresh tuna steaks

In a small, lidded container combine all the marinade ingredients; cover and shake until ingredients are blended. Place the steaks in a marinating container or a zip-lock plastic bag. Turn to coat with marinade and chill at least 1 hour. Grill 7 to 10 minutes per side on a hot grill or under a preheated oven broiler until steaks are cooked. Do not overcook.

SERVES 4

Skillet Mustard Sole

2	tablespoons butter or margarine
2	scallions, sliced
1/4	cup milk
2	tablespoons Dijon mustard
1	teaspoon mayonnaise
1	pound filet of sole
	Lemon wedges for garnish

In a 10-inch skillet melt 1 tablespoon of the butter on high or medium-high heat. Add the scallions and sauté briefly. In a medium bowl mix the milk, mustard, and mayonnaise. Dip the fish pieces in the mixture and add one at a time to the sizzling skillet, making a single layer. Leave at least 1 inch between filets or the pan will become watery. Add remaining butter as necessary. Brown filets on each side, turning once. Handle filets gently, as they will break up easily when turned or removed from the pan. As the fish is cooked, move it to a serving platter and cover to keep it warm. Garnish with lemon wedges.

SERVES 2

Dijon Halibut

Great on the grill or broiled. Use the Lemon Dijon basting sauce on any white fish.

LEMON DIJON BASTING SAUCE:
2 tablespoons Dijon mustard
1 teaspoon mayonnaise
1 teaspoon dried parsley
   Juice of half a lemon

1 to 2 pounds halibut steak, 1-inch thick, bone-in

Preheat grill or broiler. In a small bowl mix the basting sauce. Brush on both sides of the steak. Grill or broil for 8 to 10 minutes, turning once. Baste both sides once more with sauce before cooking is complete. Serve with rice pilaf and broccoli.

SERVES 2 TO 3

Old Wives' Cod Loins

In the islands, they cook fresh fish topped with a combination of tomatoes, onions, green peppers, and seasonings. This is my version.

½ yellow onion, sliced
1 tomato, sliced
1 zucchini, sliced
½ teaspoon salt
½ teaspoon allspice
   Pinch dried red pepper flakes (or a few drops of hot sauce)
2 tablespoons fresh chopped basil (or 1½ teaspoons dried)
1 teaspoon dried oregano leaves
2 teaspoons olive oil (or melted butter or margarine)
1 pound fresh captain's cut cod loins, 1-inch thick, boneless

Preheat oven to 450°. Place the onion, tomato, zucchini, and seasonings in a plastic bag or mixing bowl and mix with either 2 teaspoons melted butter or 2 teaspoons olive oil. Lay the cod loins in the center of a 9 x 13 x 2-inch baking pan. Pour the vegetable mixture over the top and spread it around the cod. Bake covered for 10 minutes. Remove cover and stir vegetables and baste fish. Cook uncovered for an additional 10 or 12 minutes until fish is done and vegetables are soft. Serve atop white rice.

SERVES 2

SHELLFISH DISHES

Steamed Mussels

There's little finer than fresh plucked mussels cooked in a large pot over a fire on the beach. Remove the "beard," that hairy portion near the opening of the mussel, by pulling gently toward the hinge. If you pull toward the opening, you risk killing the mussel before its time. To remove excess sand and salt, allow mussels to soak in fresh water for about 20 minutes before lifting them out of their fresh water bath and into a steaming pot. Use this same recipe for steamed clams.

3 to 5 pounds fresh mussels in shells
1/4 cup chopped fresh basil
2 tablespoons chopped fresh oregano
    leaves
1 large clove garlic, chopped
1/2 Vidalia onion, chopped
2 tablespoons butter or margarine
1/2 teaspoon hot sauce
1/2 fresh lemon, sliced with peel

Place clams in a large covered pot with 2 inches of water. Add the remaining ingredients and stir to mix. Bring to a boil. Cover the pot, and then reduce the heat to medium and cook until the clams open. Scoop clams into bowls with broth and serve as a first-course appetizer.

SERVES 4

Oven-barbecued Shrimp

These spicy treats will give you year-round pleasure as they can be either baked in the oven or grilled outdoors.

ZESTY BASTING SAUCE:
1/4 cup (1/2 stick) melted butter or margarine
1 tablespoon hot sauce
2 garlic cloves, minced
1/4 teaspoon salt
1/2 teaspoon black pepper
1/2 teaspoon chopped fresh parsley (or pinch
    of dried)
    Lemon wedges

6 colossal uncooked shrimp, shelled
    and deveined

To grill: Preheat grill. In a small bowl combine all Zesty Basting Sauce ingredients. Add the shrimp and stir until coated. Grill the shrimp for a few minutes on each side, basting in between with remaining sauce. Shrimp are done when they curl and turn pink, and juice is white. Remove the cooked shrimp to a serving platter and squeeze the lemon over all. Serve at once.

To oven-barbecue: Preheat oven to 400°. Select a baking dish large enough to hold the shrimp when placed in a single layer. Stir the butter, hot sauce, garlic, and parsley in the bottom of the dish. Arrange the shrimp on top, and baste with the sauce. Bake for 6 to 8 minutes, and then broil the shrimp for an additional 2 to 4 minutes or until done. Squeeze lemon juice over the shrimp and serve hot.

SERVES 2

Garlic Shrimp over Angel Hair Pasta

4 tablespoons butter or margarine
2 cloves garlic
1/2 cup chopped onion
1 pound fresh shrimp, cleaned
1/2 cup white wine
2 tablespoons lemon juice
1/4 teaspoon crushed red pepper
2 tablespoons dried parsley
1 tablespoon capers
Salt and pepper to taste

Melt the butter in a 10-inch skillet on medium-high heat. Add the garlic and onion and sauté until soft. Cover pan. Add the shrimp, wine, lemon juice, red pepper, parsley, and capers. Sprinkle with salt and black pepper and sauté until shrimp are pink. Serve over buttered angel hair pasta.

SERVES 2 TO 3

Shrimp & Rice Provençal

4 cups cooked rice
1 tablespoon butter or margarine
1/2 onion, sliced
1 cup frozen French-cut green beans, defrosted
1/2 pound frozen cocktail shrimp, precooked, shelled and deveined
1 14 1/2-ounce can stewed tomatoes
1/2 cup white wine
1/2 teaspoon dried basil
Salt and pepper to taste

Cook the rice and set aside. Melt the butter in a 10- or 12-inch skillet on medium-high heat. Add the onion and sauté until it begins to soften. Stir in the green beans and the shrimp, and sauté a few minutes. Add the stewed tomatoes, rice, wine, basil, salt, and pepper. Mix well. Reduce heat to low. Cover and cook an additional 5 minutes.

SERVES 4

TO REMOVE GARLIC SMELL

There are several ways to remove garlic odor (and fishy smells, too) from your hands. Simple soap and water washing doesn't always do the trick. Rubbing lemon juice on the smelly areas is a common solution, but caressing a stainless steel sink faucet works just as well and is more convenient. Wet your hands with cold water and then rub them against back and forth along the stainless steel a few times. A chemical reaction occurs which will neutralize the odor. Give your hands the sniff test. It really works! Garlic breath? Chew on fresh parsley or basil, fennel seeds, coffee beans, or eat lime sherbet.

Shrimp in Jackets

Cooking the shrimp shell-on will intensify the flavor of this well-loved treat. If you prefer to serve the shrimp ready to eat, peel and devein the shrimp, leaving the tail on for flavor. Serve the shrimp as an appetizer, or put it over pasta for a main entrée. Treat yourself to fresh basil for garnish.

2 pounds extra large, easy-peel shrimp, shells left on
1/4 pound (1 stick) butter
2 tablespoons olive oil
4 large cloves garlic, minced
1 cup dry sherry
1/2 cup chopped fresh basil

Rinse shrimp and pat dry. Melt butter with olive oil in a large skillet over medium high heat. Add garlic and brown on both sides. Pour in the sherry. Cook for 1 minute, stirring continuously. Mixture will become light brown, smooth, and bubbling. Add the shrimp and the basil, and sauté until shrimp are bright pink. Serve over cooked thin linguini or alone, with sourdough bread for dipping.

SERVES 4 TO 6

Mussel Linguini

1 pound linguini, cooked in salted water and lightly drained (do not rinse)
4 tablespoons (1/2 stick) butter or margarine
2 tablespoons olive oil
4 cloves garlic, minced
24 fresh mussels, scrubbed clean (about 2 pounds)
1 cup dry white wine
1 1/2 teaspoons dried oregano
1/2 large lemon, sliced thin (do not remove peel)
Salt and pepper to taste

Start the water boiling for the linguini in a large pasta pan and cook the pasta until just tender. Remove from heat. Drain lightly and return to pan. Add 2 tablespoons of the butter and mix well. Cover pot to keep linguini warm until mussels are done. Meanwhile, heat the olive oil in a Dutch oven or 12-inch skillet. Add the garlic and sauté briefly. Add the mussels and sauté for a few minutes. Stir in the wine and the oregano and cook covered on medium heat for about 5 minutes. Remove cover and stir in 2 tablespoons of the butter and the sliced lemon. Add salt and pepper to taste. Cover and continue cooking on medium heat until mussel shells open (about 5 more minutes). Stir occasionally. Remove from heat and set aside, covered, until pasta is ready. Pour pasta in a large pasta-serving bowl. Top with mussels, mix lightly, and serve.

SERVES 4 TO 5

George's Bank Scallops over Rice

2 tablespoons butter or margarine
1 onion
1 tablespoon fresh jalapeño, sliced in thin half circles
1 cup sliced zucchini
1 pound sea scallops
1 14½-ounce can stewed tomatoes
¼ cup red wine
1 tablespoon chopped fresh basil (or 1 teaspoon dried)
¾ teaspoon salt
⅛ teaspoon ground black pepper
4 cups hot cooked rice

In a 10- or 12-inch skillet melt 1 tablespoon of the butter over medium-high heat. Add the onion and jalapeño pepper. Cover and cook a few minutes, and then add the zucchini and sauté. Continue to cook covered, stirring occasionally, until all vegetables begin to soften. Remove the vegetables from the pan and set aside. Add the remaining butter to the pan, and then toss in the scallops. Sauté gently for a few minutes, until the scallops are browned on all sides and cooked. Do not overcook, or scallops will be tough. Reduce heat to medium, and then stir in the cooked vegetables, stewed tomatoes, wine, basil, salt, and pepper. Bring to a boil, stirring continuously, and then remove from heat. Cover to keep warm until ready to serve over the hot rice.

SERVES 2 TO 3

Cajun Scallops

No time to cook? Throw scallops in a hot pan and have dinner ready in minutes, or grill them using a seafood grill cover or foil.

1 tablespoon butter or olive oil (if grilling)
1 pound bay scallops, rinsed and patted dry
1½ tablespoons Cajun seasoning
½ wedge fresh lime
½ teaspoon dried parsley (or 1 tablespoon chopped fresh)

In a frying pan melt the butter on medium heat. Stir in the Cajun seasoning. Add the scallops. Squeeze the wedge of lime over the scallops. Sauté a few minutes, until scallops are cooked. Stir in the parsley and serve at once over rice.

SERVES 2 TO 3

Coquille Saint Joy

One evening I was looking for something different to do with scallops and pulled out an old recipe for Coquille St. Jacques. It sounded so heavy with all that butter and cream that I got full just reading the recipe! I did remember, though, that it had a wonderful flavor. I put my old recipe on a diet and simplified the preparation process. Here it is. If you're careful, you can make this gourmet treat using just a frying pan and a serving dish.

1	tablespoon olive oil
1	clove garlic, minced
1	pound bay scallops, rinsed and patted dry
1/4	cup dry white wine
1/2	pound sliced white mushrooms, washed and patted dry
1/2	cup chicken broth
1	tablespoon flour
1	tablespoon butter
1 1/2	tablespoons chopped fresh parsley (or 1 teaspoon dried)
1	tablespoon Jack Daniel's or other whiskey
1	tablespoon grated Parmesan cheese

In a large frying pan or wok heat 2 teaspoons of the olive oil over medium-high heat. Add the garlic and sauté briefly. Add the scallops and continue to sauté until scallops are just cooked. (Scallops will be tough if overdone, so easy does it.) Using a slotted spatula, lift the scallops out of the pan and set them into a 1 1/2-quart casserole/serving dish. Cover to keep warm. Add the remaining oil to the pan and then the mushrooms. Sauté for a few minutes, until they soften and begin to brown. Add the wine and parsley and stir briefly. Lift the mushrooms from the pan with a slotted spatula and add to the reserved scallops. Recover to keep warm. Leaving juices intact in the pan, remove the pan from the heat.

Preheat broiler. Meanwhile, mix the flour and unheated chicken broth in a small cup until well blended. Return the frying pan to medium heat and add the butter to the pan. When the butter is melted, stir in the chicken broth mixture. Cook, stirring continuously, until the mixture begins to thicken. Combine the thickened sauce with the reserved scallops and mushrooms in the casserole/serving dish. Sprinkle the Jack Daniel's and the cheese evenly over the top. Place casserole in preheated oven and broil 6 inches from the heat until the top is brown and bubbly. Serve at once over angel hair pasta.

SERVES 3 TO 4

Broccoli & Scallop Linguini

1   bunch fresh broccoli florets (or 1 package
     frozen broccoli), cut into 1-inch chunks
1   pound linguini
1/4 cup coarsely chopped fresh basil (or
     1 tablespoon dried)
4   tablespoons butter or margarine
3   tablespoons olive oil
1   large clove garlic, sliced
1   pound bay scallops, rinsed and drained
1   fresh, ripe tomato, diced
1/4 teaspoon dried red pepper
     Salt and pepper to taste
2   teaspoons Parmesan cheese for garnish

Cook the broccoli florets covered in the
microwave for 1 minute or blanch them in
boiling water for 2 minutes. Set aside.
Cook linguini in boiling, salted water until
desired doneness. Drain briefly, but do not
rinse. Pour linguini into a large pasta-
serving bowl. Toss with 2 tablespoons of
the butter and the basil. Salt and pepper to
taste. Cover to keep warm. Meanwhile, in a
10- or 12-inch skillet heat the olive oil and
2 tablespoons of butter on medium high.
Add the garlic and sauté until brown.
Remove from the pan and discard. Reduce
heat to medium. Add the broccoli and
sauté briefly. Add the scallops and continue
to sauté a few more minutes until scallops

are almost done. Season with the red pepper, salt, and pepper. Add the diced tomato
and cover for a minute or two. Pour the
mixture in the skillet over the prepared
linguini. Top with Parmesan cheese. Toss
lightly and serve with a salad and rolls.

SERVES 4

Flaming Choppino

*We often serve this marvelous entrée on Christmas Eve.
It's impressive when flaming. Add an extra half pound
of shrimp in lieu of the squid, if desired.*

1   pound spaghetti
1/4 cup olive oil
1   medium clove garlic, chopped
1/4 teaspoon crushed red peppers
12   Little Neck clams
12   mussels
1/2 pound shrimp, shells left on
1/2 pound cleaned squid, cut in rings
     (optional)
1/2 pound bay scallops
1/2 teaspoon curry powder
2   teaspoons chopped fresh Italian parsley
     (or 3/4 teaspoon dried)
1   tablespoon chopped fresh basil (or
     1 teaspoon dried)
     Salt to taste
1/2 cup white wine
1   cup tomato sauce
1/2 cup 80 percent or higher proof brandy
     or vodka

Cook the spaghetti in boiling salted water until firm to the bite. Meanwhile, in a 12-inch skillet heat the olive oil over medium-high heat. Add the garlic and red peppers. Sauté until garlic is golden. Add the clams and mussels in shells. Cover and steam a few minutes, until clams begin to open. Add the shrimp, squid, and scallops. Sprinkle with the curry, parsley, basil, and salt to taste. Sauté 3 to 5 minutes, tossing shellfish. Add the white wine and cook 2 to 3 minutes. Stir in the tomato sauce. Cover and simmer 10 minutes on medium heat. When the spaghetti is done, drain it (do not rinse it) and then add it to the skillet. Toss ingredients to coat the spaghetti with sauce.

Preheat oven to 500°. Place several large rectangles (long enough to wrap around the casserole dish 1½ times) of medium-weight aluminum foil on a cookie sheet. Place a 3-quart heatproof casserole dish on top of foil. Pour spaghetti mixture into the serving dish. Bring up the sides of the foil around the casserole to make a loose pouch. Seal the edges well to prevent steam from escaping. Bake at 500° for 5 to 10 minutes or until foil pouch begins to puff. Remove from the oven and place on a heatproof pad. Open the pouch, being careful not to burn yourself with the escaping steam. Pour vodka or brandy over top of pasta and ignite. Serve flaming.

SERVES 6

SEAFOOD STEWS

Cuttyhunk Mussel Stew

I created this aboard our boat when faced with making dinner from many pounds of mussels culled from the shores of Cuttyhunk Island.

2	slices bacon, cut into 1-inch pieces
1	clove garlic, minced
1	medium onion, sliced
1	bell pepper, sliced
3	pounds mussels, shells on and scrubbed
1	cup dry white wine
1	14½-ounce can stewed tomatoes
2	teaspoons dried thyme
½	cup water
½	teaspoon salt
⅛	teaspoon black pepper
1	large potato, chopped and cooked in salted water (optional)

In a Dutch oven or stockpot sauté the bacon over medium-high heat until it begins to cook. Add the garlic, onion, and bell pepper and continue to sauté until the bacon is cooked. Add the mussels to the pan, and then pour in the white wine. Sauté for a minute. Add the tomatoes, thyme, water, salt, and pepper. Bring to a boil, and then reduce heat to low and cook covered until clams open, about 5 to 10 minutes. Stir in the cooked potato, if desired. Ladle into bowls and serve with crusty bread.

SERVES 4

Bouillabaisse

Elegant for any special occasion, and well worth the expense and the long wait at the fish market during the holidays. If the market will cut up the lobsters for you, the rest is easy.

3	pounds mixed, firm-fleshed fish, such as swordfish, haddock, or tuna
3	pounds mixed, tender-fleshed fish, such as sole, snapper, or salmon
2	live lobsters, cut into 2-inch pieces (omit bodies)
1	pound fresh shrimp (do not peel and devein)
10	Little Neck clams, scrubbed clean
½	cup olive oil
3½	cups chopped onions (4 medium)
4	cloves garlic, minced
2	cups dry white wine
1	28½-ounce can chopped tomatoes
1	bottle clam juice
½	teaspoon orange peel
½	teaspoon dried thyme
1	teaspoon fennel seed
2	bay leaves
1	tablespoon salt
½	teaspoon pepper
⅓	cup parsley, leaves chopped and stems reserved
	Boiling water

Cut the fish into 2-inch pieces. Keep firm- and tender-fleshed fish separate, as they will be added at different times. Heat oil in a large stockpot over medium heat. Add onion. Cook 5 minutes, stirring frequently.

Add the garlic. Cook 1 minute more. Add the wine, tomatoes, clam juice, orange peel, herbs, seasonings, and parsley stems. Bring to boiling and cook 5 minutes. Place clams and lobster pieces in the pot. Top with firm-fleshed fish. Bring to boiling and cook 5 minutes. Add tender-fleshed fish and shrimp. Add just enough boiling water to barely cover ingredients. Bring to boiling and cook 10 minutes or until clams open. Remove to serving dishes, discarding bay leaves and parsley stems. Sprinkle with chopped parsley and serve. Allow equal amounts of lobster, clams, and shrimp for each serving. Serve with crusty bread and a green salad.

SERVES 10

RECIPE FOR COOKING LESS

Think quality, not quantity

Splurge on sinfully expensive foods you never could afford

Order take-out without guilt

Dine out

Step on a scale

A SKILLET BUILT FOR TWO

Habits are hard to break. For a long time I cooked on the edge, making extras in case one of the kids stopped by. I continued to haul home a ton of groceries until I noticed the fruit was rotting in its bowl, my refrigerator and freezer looked pregnant, and the door to the cookie cupboard wouldn't shut. I was throwing away too much uneaten food, yet it felt like cheating to cook half of a package of pasta instead of the whole thing. And I was always afraid I wouldn't make enough rice. But the sad truth was that three perpetually ravenous teenagers no longer lived at our house.

It was time to rethink my cooking style. We were getting fat, my husband's cholesterol was skyrocketing, and I needed to watch my salt intake. I found cooking from scratch gave me control over the ingredients and calories, and, certainly, I had to scale down quantity. (Dieticians suggest allowing only ¼ pound of meat and ½ cup vegetables per person.)

A roast or casserole produced more leftovers than we could eat in a week, and it hardly seemed worth it to light my oven for two puny chicken breasts. In a spurt of inspiration one fine summer evening, I grabbed my skillet, doused it with salt and pepper and a dab of oil, and rediscovered my stovetop. I could produce a meal in no time—no preheating—and my large skillet was a perfect fit for the portions of food I now needed to prepare.

I made a game of trying to cook an entire meal using that one pan. Cooking was almost fun. I found new uses for old seasonings and brought home bunches of fresh herbs and vegetables from the supermarket. Each evening I dashed joyously into the kitchen, anticipating the new dish I might create that night. It was scary. Was I really that same individual who once avoided the kitchen as if it had the Asian Flu?

Grocery shopping is almost fun . . .

Here I am, strolling through this huge, wonderful supermarket with a nearly empty cart. I chuckle when I think about how my feelings about grocery shopping have changed. Thinking back, I've been chain-linked to a supermarket for almost twenty-five years. As my husband used to joke, there was no need to bother with a door on our refrigerator. The food flew out of it so fast there was hardly anything in it to keep cold. Obviously, he wasn't referring to the Brussels sprouts.

I used to dread going shopping. It was such a hassle when the kids were small. I was forced to buy in dribbles because all the groceries I needed wouldn't fit into the supermarket cart along with a baby, a toddler, or both. The children made a game of helping me shop. While one of them grabbed stuff off the shelf and dumped it into my cart, the other flung out what didn't appeal to him. The child on foot just took off on me. To bribe them into behaving, I fed them Cheerios, animal crackers, and lollipops— leaving a trail of mush in our wake. I seldom knew what I would end up paying for until I got to the checkout.

As the kids got older, shopping with mom lost its fascination. It wasn't "cool" to be seen with one's mother, especially if she was wearing outdated clothing. My kids scrutinized my appearance each time I left the house. They hid my favorite jeans, so their buddies wouldn't see their mom wearing "high waters." I suppose they did me a favor. I have come to value their brutally frank opinions of my attire, and I miss it. Lord knows if today's outfit would pass muster.

Shopping for teens was easier in the respect that I could do it alone, but the quantities of food I bought were staggering. I perfected the art of stacking and balancing two carts' worth of groceries into one cart. I swear my family (my husband was no saint, either) watched for my car to pull up the driveway and then hid until after I had lugged all our groceries upstairs. Finally, they'd descend like locusts to check out the goodies—and it was time to go shopping again.

Now, I sigh with delight, pausing to select a bouquet of bright pink tulips—these will look wonderful on my dinner table. In the gourmet section, the portabella mushrooms are fresh, and I will need gingerroot. I buzz the butcher to order two thick-cut Black Angus filet mignons; and then, sidestepping the Twinkie aisle, splurge on sinful, frosted brownies at the bakery. The only time we make sandwiches now is on weekends when the kids stop over, so I smugly push by the long line at the deli and, instead, opt for a pound of plump cocktail shrimp from the seafood counter.

I've been in this store less than 20 minutes, and that's because I dawdled. I zip through the express line and I'm out, cartless, swinging three plastic bags. No need to rush home and start dinner; we don't eat now until seven. I think I'll pop into Marshalls for a few minutes and check out the clearance rack. I'm on my own schedule now, not everyone else's.

Skillet cooking

A 10- or 12-inch pan will give you the space to cook a piece of meat or fish without overcrowding it. Each type of pan material heats and cooks food differently. Start at a high temperature but reduce it to medium high if the pan seems too hot. Use a small amount of oil, then sprinkle salt and pepper (or my Easy Seasoning Mix) in the pan to help keep food from sticking.

Even though some brands of nonstick pans allow you to cook fat-free, add a bit of oil or butter, anyway. Fat carries flavor and your dish will taste better. If you are faced with a choice of oil, butter, or margarine, know that each has its own properties that affect how it cooks. Olive oil and margarine will not burn as quickly as butter, and light butters and diet margarines contain air, which can affect the end result of a dish when substituted for 100 percent butter or margarine. Olive oil is the healthiest of these fats. Margarine was once thought better for you than butter, but nutritionists now say there is little difference. As a result, I now cook with either butter or olive oil, but you may prefer the taste of margarine.

Many of the meats or fish in these recipes are seared so they will brown and cook quickly. Surrounding the pieces of meat or fish with a few vegetables while searing helps prevent the meat from steam cooking. The vegetables will absorb the excess pan juices, while they continue to add flavor to your dish.

Any of the following recipes can be expanded by cooking in batches. Layer the pieces of food in a casserole dish as they are cooked, and then top with the pan juices. Cover and reheat gently in the oven or microwave. Most of the pork, turkey, chicken, and veal recipes are interchangeable. I find wines and liquors add a sophisticated flavor, so I use them in many of my recipes. However, if this is not your tea bag, substitute beef or chicken broth, water, or fruit juices.

BEEF ENTRÉES

Peppered Jack Daniel's Steak

Men love the flavor of this dish, and you can prepare it in less than 15 minutes. Serve with baked or mashed potatoes using some of the gravy instead of butter. I've found sirloin tip strips or any tender piece of steak that is small enough to sear in a skillet will work as well as rib steaks.

JACK DANIEL'S SAUCE:

1	cup canned beef broth at room temperature
1	teaspoon black pepper
¼	teaspoon dried thyme
¼	teaspoon dried rosemary
¼	teaspoon ground marjoram
1½	teaspoons flour
1	tablespoon chopped fresh parsley (or 1 teaspoon dried)
2	tablespoons Jack Daniel's or other whiskey

4	thin-cut rib eye steaks
¼	teaspoon salt
1½	tablespoons butter or margarine
1	onion, sliced

Place the ingredients for the Jack Daniel's Sauce in a covered container and shake to mix. Set aside. Sprinkle the steaks with the salt. Heat butter on high temperature in a large skillet. Add the onions and sauté briefly. Cook only one or two steaks at a time, arranging onions in between and around steaks. Cook the steaks about one minute per side or until seared to medium-rare. Stir the onion occasionally. Remove the steaks from pan as they are done, and cover them to keep warm. When all of the steaks are done, reduce the pan heat to medium high, and pour the beef broth mixture into the pan. Stir to deglaze pan. The sauce is done when it begins to thicken. Place the steaks on a serving platter and top with the Jack Daniel's Sauce.

SERVES 2 TO 3

Vermouth Pepper Steak

1	tablespoon olive oil
1	clove garlic, crushed
4	sandwich or cubed steaks
¼	teaspoon salt
⅛	teaspoon black pepper
1	onion, sliced
2	frying peppers, seeded and sliced
¼	teaspoon black whole peppercorns
2	tablespoons butter
⅓	cup sweet vermouth

In a 12-inch skillet heat the olive oil over high heat. Add the garlic and sauté for 1 minute. Prepare the steaks by sprinkling with the salt and black pepper. Add the onion and peppers to the skillet and sauté 1 to 2 minutes, until they begin to soften. Stir in the black peppercorns. If you don't have peppercorns, use ¼ teaspoon additional black pepper. Push the vegetables aside, then melt 1 tablespoon of the butter in the pan. Add 2 of the steaks, and cook about 1 minute on each side or as desired. As the steaks are done, remove them to a serving platter and keep warm. Repeat this procedure for the remaining steaks, adding the last tablespoon of butter if the pan is dry. Once all the steaks are cooked, continue sautéing the vegetables for another minute or two until they are soft and browned. Quickly stir in the vermouth, scraping any bits off the bottom of the pan. Remove the pan from heat. Pour the vermouth-vegetable mixture over the steaks and serve. Mashed potatoes make a nice accompaniment.

SERVES 2

Ground Beef Zucchini Bake

This has become a family favorite. I often prepare this dish without the potatoes and serve it with either rice or rolls and a salad for a complete meal.

1   pound ground beef
1   tablespoon butter
1   onion, sliced
1   large Idaho potato, sliced (optional)
1   or 2 zucchini, sliced
2   tomatoes, sliced

½   teaspoon oregano
1   teaspoon dried parsley
    Salt and pepper to taste
4   slices deli cheese

Sprinkle the pan with salt and pepper, and crumble the ground beef into a large 12-inch skillet on medium-high heat. Sauté until cooked and remove from the pan and set aside. Drain off excess fat. Melt the butter in the same pan, and then add the onion and potatoes and sauté until they begin to brown. Reduce the heat to low and then evenly distribute the cooked ground beef on top of the potatoes. Top with a single layer of the zucchini rounds. Follow with a layer of tomato rounds. Sprinkle additional salt and pepper in between layers. Sprinkle the oregano over the zucchini layer and the parsley over the tomatoes. Place the cheese slices over the top, and cover pan tightly. Simmer for about 20 minutes, until the zucchini is cooked.

SERVES 4

PORK CHOPS & CUTLETS

10-minute Pork Chops

1   tablespoon olive oil
2   scallions, sliced
1   pound 1/2-inch-thick, boneless,
      center-cut pork chops
    Salt and pepper
1/4   teaspoon allspice
1   apple, cored and cut into wedges

In a 10-inch skillet heat the olive oil on medium-high heat. Add scallions and sauté briefly. Season chops with salt and pepper, and then add them to the skillet. Once the cutlets are browned on one side, turn them over. Add the allspice and apple to the pan, and mix with the scallions. Reduce the heat to low and cover the pan. Allow the chops and apple mixture to simmer gently until the chops are cooked. Do not over-cook or the chops will be tough.

SERVES 2

Mustard Pork Chops and Pan-Fried Potatoes

Once the chops are done, use the same pan to brown the potatoes. This great weeknight meal can be ready to serve in less than 30 minutes, if you hustle.

3   or 4 medium baking potatoes, scrubbed
1   pound boneless pork cutlets
    Salt and pepper
1   tablespoon olive oil
1/4   cup dry white wine
1   tablespoon plus 1 teaspoon Dijon mustard
1   or 2 tablespoons butter or margarine
1/2   teaspoon dried chives

Cook the potatoes in the microwave oven on high for 5 to 10 minutes or until done. Set aside. Meanwhile, sprinkle the pork chops liberally with salt and pepper. In a large frying pan heat the olive oil over medium-high heat. Brown the pork chops on both sides. Add the wine and reduce the heat to low. Cover and simmer for 10 to 15 minutes, turning the chops once. Remove the chops to a platter while you make the sauce. Raise the heat to medium high and stir the mustard into the pan juices. Return the chops to the pan, turning to coat with the sauce, and cook them another minute. Remove chops to serving platter, and spoon over sauce or reserve sauce to serve on the side. Cover to keep warm.

To brown the potatoes: Slice the cooked potatoes into 1/2-inch rounds. Raise the pan temperature to high and melt 1 tablespoon of the butter. Arrange the potato slices in a single layer in the pan. Sprinkle with salt, pepper, and chives. Brown the potatoes until crisp on both sides, turning with a spatula and adding a bit more butter if the pan is dry. Serve alongside the chops.

SERVES 3 TO 4

Orange Breaded Pork Chops

This cooking method guarantees the chops will be moist and juicy. Sometimes I substitute apple cider for the orange juice and serve the chops with applesauce.

1½ pounds pork chops (4 to 6 chops)
   Salt and pepper to taste
1   egg
4   tablespoons orange juice
½   cup Italian-style seasoned breadcrumbs
2   tablespoons olive oil

Rinse the pork chops and pat dry. Trim off excess fat and season with salt and pepper to taste. In a shallow soup bowl, whisk together the egg and 2 tablespoons of the orange juice. Pour the breadcrumbs on a separate plate or sheet of waxed paper. In a 10- or 12-inch skillet heat the olive oil on medium-high heat. Dip the chops first in egg mixture, then in the breadcrumbs, coating well. Brown the chops in the skillet for 1 to 2 minutes per side. When both sides are browned, add the remaining orange juice to the skillet. Cover and simmer for about 20 minutes, until chops are cooked through. If desired, garnish chops with fresh orange slices and serve with wild rice and a green vegetable or salad.

SERVES 4

Barbecue Sautéed Pork Chops with Fresh Tomato-Basil Salsa

I developed this recipe one evening when I was anxious to try out a new barbecue sauce. Using a ridged skillet will give a grilled effect.

1½ to 2 pounds pork chops (4 chops)
½   cup spicy bottled barbecue sauce
   Cooking oil spray or 1 tablespoon olive oil

FRESH TOMATO-BASIL SALSA:
¼   cup thinly sliced scallions
½   cup chopped tomato (about 1 medium)
1   teaspoon balsamic vinegar
1   teaspoon dried basil (or 1 tablespoon chopped fresh)
   Salt and pepper to taste

Marinate the pork chops in barbecue sauce for 15 to 20 minutes. Meanwhile, prepare the salsa by combining all the salsa ingredients in a medium bowl.

Spray a large 10- or 12-inch skillet lightly with cooking oil. Set over burner for a few minutes, until the pan is hot. Sear the chops for 1 or 2 minutes on each side to brown. Reduce heat to low. Cover the skillet and continue cooking on low for an additional 10 to 20 minutes, until the chops are cooked. To serve, spoon Salsa over the chops. Cinnamon Brown Rice and peas finish this meal off nicely.

SERVES 3 TO 4

Pork Cutlets with Oranges, Scallions, & Coriander

This recipe won honorable mention in the 1994 National Pork Council's "Lick Your Chops" contest. You too can lick your chops (or cutlets). Also try it with turkey, veal, or chicken cutlets.

1	pound pork cutlets
1/4	teaspoon salt or to taste
	Pinch black pepper
2	to 3 tablespoons butter or margarine
1/4	cup sliced scallions
2	navel oranges, peeled and sliced in circles
1/4	cup chicken broth or water
1/4	cup orange juice
1/2	teaspoon ground coriander

Rinse the cutlets, pat dry, and season with the salt and pepper. In a 12-inch skillet melt 1 tablespoon of the butter on medium-high heat. Add the scallions and sauté lightly. Add the pork cutlets in a single layer in the pan. Cook for 1 to 2 minutes on each side or until no pink remains and cutlets are white and juicy. Add the second tablespoon of the butter as needed to keep cutlets from sticking to pan. Remove to a serving platter and cover to keep warm. Melt the third tablespoon of the butter if needed. Add orange slices and sauté lightly. Remove the orange slices and arrange them over the cutlets on the serving platter.

In a small cup stir together the broth, orange juice, and coriander. Pour the juice mixture into the skillet to deglaze the pan, scraping browned bits from the bottom to form a sauce. Simmer a few minutes, until liquid reduces slightly. Pour the sauce over cutlets or serve on the side. Serve on a bed of white rice with a green vegetable or salad.

SERVES 4

Apple Dijon Pork Cutlets

1	tablespoon olive oil
1	cup sliced Vidalia or other mild onion
1	pound boneless pork cutlets (about 5)
1/8	teaspoon each: salt and black pepper
2	tablespoons flour
1	tablespoon butter or margarine
1	Granny Smith or other tart, crisp apple, peeled and sliced
1/2	cup apple cider or apple juice
1/4	teaspoon ground ginger
2	teaspoons Dijon mustard

In a large skillet heat the olive oil over medium-high heat. Add the onion slices and sauté for a few minutes. Meanwhile, season cutlets with salt and pepper. Dust with flour on both sides. Push aside the onions, and melt the margarine in the center of the pan. Add 2 or 3 of the cutlets to the pan, allowing the onion to cook in between them, and brown the cutlets for about 2 minutes per side. Remove the browned cutlets to a plate. Continue cooking in batches until all the cutlets are cooked. Continue to sauté the onions.

Reduce the heat to medium-low and add the apple slices to the onions in the pan. Sauté briefly. Return the cutlets to the pan, placing them on top of the apple-onion mixture. Cover the pan and continue cooking another 10 to 15 minutes, until the chops are cooked and the apples are soft. Remove the cutlets to a serving plate and top with the apple-onion mixture. Cover to keep warm.

To make the sauce: Mix the apple cider, ginger, and mustard. Turn the heat up to medium under the empty skillet and pour the juice mixture into the pan. Stir well as the mixture heats to deglaze pan. Bring to a boil and cook uncovered for a few minutes, until the mixture bubbles and begins to thicken. Offer sauce on the side with the cutlets.

SERVES 3 TO 4

TURKEY AND CHICKEN

Orange-Spice Turkey Cutlets

It's important not to substitute on this one. The combination of fresh ginger and allspice balances the sweetness. Allspice is aromatic and peppery, like cloves, but with hint of cinnamon and nutmeg. Whole allspice looks like a large, brown peppercorn. You can buy ground allspice in the supermarket, and often you can find the Jamaican variety, which is more intense because Jamaican spices have high oil content. Slice the ginger with a garlic slicer.

1	pound thin-sliced turkey cutlets
1/4	teaspoon salt
1	tablespoon olive oil
1	rounded tablespoon thinly sliced fresh ginger (1-inch chunk)
1/2	cup chicken broth
2	tablespoons orange marmalade
1	teaspoon freshly grated orange peel
1/4	teaspoon Jamaican allspice

Sprinkle the turkey cutlets with salt on both sides. In a 12-inch frying pan heat 1 tablespoon olive oil on high. Add the sliced ginger and sauté a few seconds. Add 2 or 3 of the turkey cutlets and cook for 1 minute on each side or until just done. Remove from the pan and keep warm. Continue cooking the remaining cutlets over high heat in the same manner. If the cutlets start to stick, sprinkle a bit more salt in the bottom of the pan. Reduce the heat to medium and stir in the chicken broth to deglaze the pan. Stir in the marmalade, orange peel, and allspice. Cook for about 5 minutes, until the sauce is smooth and glossy and begins to thicken. Return the cutlets to the pan and stir to coat with sauce. Arrange on a serving platter. Pour the remaining sauce over the cutlets before serving or offer sauce on the side.

SERVES 3

Turkey Piccata

¼ cup flour
¾ teaspoon salt
¼ teaspoon black pepper
1 pound turkey cutlets
1 or 2 tablespoons butter or margarine
4 ounces sliced mushrooms (optional)
¾ cup white wine
1½ tablespoons lemon juice
1 teaspoon dried parsley (or 1 tablespoon fresh)
1 tablespoon capers

On a square of waxed paper mix together the flour, salt, and pepper. Dredge the turkey cutlets in the flour mixture to coat both sides. In a 12-inch skillet heat 1½ tablespoons of the butter on high or medium-high. Cook the cutlets about 1 minute per side or until browned. Remove from the pan and keep warm. If using mushrooms, add the remaining ½ table-spoon of butter to the skillet. Add mush-rooms and sauté until they begin to soften. Then, add the wine, lemon juice, and pars-ley to the skillet and stir well to deglaze the pan and form a thin sauce. Reduce the heat to medium-low and return the turkey cutlets to the skillet, and stir in the capers. Cover and continue cooking for 5 to 10 minutes or until the cutlets are done. Serve at once.

SERVES 2 TO 3

Mango Chutney Chicken & Rice

1 tablespoon butter
1 pound chicken tenders
1 fresh peach, peeled, pitted, and cut into bite-sized chunks
¼ cup chicken broth
¼ cup mango chutney
¼ teaspoon nutmeg or ginger
 Salt and pepper to taste
2 cups cooked rice

In a large skillet melt the butter. Sprinkle chicken pieces liberally with salt and pep-per, and then sauté them along with the peaches on medium heat until chicken is cooked. Remove from pan and set aside. Pour the chicken broth into the same pan, and then stir in the chutney and nutmeg. Bring to a boil, stirring constantly. Return the chicken mixture to the pan and stir. Continue to cook until mixture is syrupy. To serve, pour mango chicken over cooked rice.

SERVES 2

Skillet Chicken & Asparagus

This dish is not only attractive to serve, but it tastes as good as it looks.

3   boneless chicken breast quarters (or
      1 pound chicken tenders)
    Salt and pepper
2   scallions, sliced
1   tablespoon olive oil
¼   cup chicken broth
2   tablespoons orange juice
½   bunch asparagus
½   teaspoon dried marjoram leaves
¼   teaspoon dried sage leaves
    Salt and pepper to taste
1   teaspoon flour
1   small orange, peeled, seeded, and sliced
      (optional)

Sprinkle salt and pepper on both sides of the chicken pieces. In a 12-inch skillet heat the oil on high heat. Add the scallions and sauté for 1 minute. Place the chicken in the pan and brown on both sides. Reduce the heat to medium-low. Add 2 tablespoons of the chicken broth and the orange juice. If using chicken breasts, cover and cook for 10 to 15 minutes or until chicken is almost done. Once the chicken is almost cooked, layer asparagus on top. Sprinkle with the marjoram, sage, salt, and pepper. Cover and continue to cook for an additional 5 to 8 minutes, until asparagus and chicken are done. Remove the chicken and asparagus from pan and place on a serving platter.

If using orange slices, sauté them briefly in the empty pan, and then arrange slices on top of the chicken and asparagus. Cover to keep warm. To make a sauce, stir the flour into the remaining chicken broth (cold or room temperature). Raise the heat under the pan, and then stir the flour mixture into the pan juices. Stir constantly until mixture thickens. Pour sauce over the chicken and asparagus, and then offer the remaining sauce on the side.

SERVES 2 TO 3

Chicken Breast Sauté

Both family and guests will enjoy this easy-to-make, one-dish meal.

1 pound boneless, skinless chicken breasts
   Salt and pepper to taste
1 egg
2 tablespoons milk
½ cup seasoned breadcrumbs (or flour)
2 tablespoons cooking oil
½ cup white wine
1 tablespoon lemon juice
1 tablespoon dried parsley
1 fresh tomato, sliced into wedges
½ head broccoli, cut into spears

Season the chicken breasts with salt and pepper on both sides. In a shallow bowl beat the egg and milk with a fork. Pour the breadcrumbs onto a piece of waxed paper. In a 10-inch skillet heat the oil on high or medium-high heat. Dredge the chicken pieces first in the egg mixture, then in the breadcrumbs, and place in the hot oil. Brown on one side for a minute, then turn and brown for another minute. Reduce the heat to medium-low. Add the wine and lemon juice to the pan. Sprinkle with the parsley. Add the tomatoes. Then lay the broccoli spears over the top of the chicken. Sprinkle again with salt and pepper. Cover pan tightly and continue to cook another 15 minutes or until the chicken is cooked through. If the pan becomes dry, add a bit more wine. Serve with rice or orzo.

SERVES 2

Chicken Chardonnay

A family favorite. Try it with turkey, pork, or veal cutlets, or flattened chicken breasts.

1 pound chicken cutlets
   Salt and pepper to taste
¼ cup flour
3 tablespoons butter or margarine
10 ounces sliced portabella or other mushrooms
½ cup Chardonnay or dry white wine
½ cup chicken broth
1 tablespoon chopped fresh parsley or 1 teaspoon dried

Sprinkle the cutlets on both sides with salt and pepper. Dip the cutlets in the flour to thinly coat each side. In a 10- or 12-inch skillet heat the butter on medium. Add the mushrooms and sauté for 1 minute.

Pushing the mushrooms aside, add the cutlets and brown for 1 to 2 minutes on each side. Remove the cutlets to a warm platter as they are cooked and continue cooking the mushrooms until browned. Remove the mushrooms to the platter. Add the wine, chicken broth, and parsley to the pan and stir to deglaze the pan. Return the chicken and mushrooms to the pan and simmer uncovered for an additional 10 to 15 minutes, until the sauce is reduced and slightly thickened. Serve over white rice.

Note: If using chicken breasts, allow more cooking time. Add the liquids and cover the pan. Continue to heat on medium until chicken is cooked. Then remove cover and cook for another 5 minutes or until sauce cooks down and thickens.

SERVES 2 TO 3

Sage-brushed Cutlets

This dish is quick and easy to make, yet tastes like you've slaved for hours.

1/4   cup flour
1/4   teaspoon each: salt and black pepper
1   teaspoon dried sage leaves (or
          1 tablespoon chopped fresh sage)
4   tablespoons olive oil (or a combination of
          2 tablespoons oil and 2 tablespoons
          butter)
1   cup chopped onions
1 1/2 pounds veal, turkey, chicken, or pork
          cutlets
1 1/4 cups dry white wine
1   tablespoon Dijon mustard

Mix the flour, salt, pepper, and sage on a piece of waxed paper. In a 12-inch skillet heat 2 tablespoons of the olive oil on high. Add the onions and sauté briefly. Lightly dredge the cutlets in the flour mixture and, pushing the onions aside, place cutlets in the skillet 2 or 3 at a time. Cook about 1 minute per side until browned, stirring the onions occasionally. Continue in this fashion until all the cutlets are cooked, keeping cooked cutlets warm. Add the wine and stir to deglaze pan. Stir in the mustard. Cook for about 2 minutes or until the sauce thickens slightly and begins to turn glossy. Return the cooked cutlets to the pan and cook another minute just to heat through. Serve at once with buttered egg noodles and green beans.

SERVES 4

Fruit-Glazed Chicken Breasts

6   boneless chicken breast quarters
       (3 whole breasts cut in half)
1/4 teaspoon salt
1   pinch black pepper
1   tablespoon olive oil
1/2 cup chicken broth
1   tablespoon wine vinegar
1/4 cup dried cranberries
1   Granny Smith or other tart pie apple,
       peeled, cored, and sliced into wedges
3   tablespoons raspberry jam
1/8 teaspoon nutmeg
1   teaspoon butter or margarine

Rinse the chicken in cold water and pat dry. Sprinkle with salt and pepper. In a large frying pan heat the olive oil over medium-high heat. Add the chicken breasts and sauté for a few minutes on each side to brown. Add the chicken broth and vinegar, and bring to a boil. Reduce the heat to low. Turn chicken pieces over to coat with juice. Add the dried cranberries and apple wedges. Cover pan and simmer for 15 to 20 minutes or until chicken is cooked. Remove the chicken from the pan and keep warm. Turn up the heat to medium-high. Stir in the raspberry jam, nutmeg, and butter. Boil for a minute or two, stirring continuously, until the mixture begins to thicken and becomes glossy. Return the chicken to the pan, and coat thoroughly with sauce. To serve, place the chicken pieces on a serving platter. Top with a spoonful of sauce and offer additional sauce on the side.

SERVES 3 TO 4

RECIPE FOR RECLAIMING YOUR KITCHEN

Buy new dishes and glassware

Apply fresh paint or wallpaper you love

Start an herb garden on your windowsill

Fill the room with flowers

Refinish or replace your worn kitchen table and gooey chairs

Clean out the cupboards and store away the Mickey Mouse cake pan (sob)

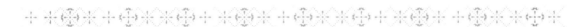

ENTRÉES FOR MORE

When I suspect one or more of the kids may show up around dinnertime, I'll toss a roast or casserole in the oven and dress it up a bit. Now that they are adults and their tastes have matured, my kids appreciate and enjoy gourmet-style fare they wouldn't have touched years ago. I've enjoyed trying out new ideas and, as a result, have created entrées that have served me well for company, holiday meals, and parties.

Home sweet home . . .

I love our house, not so much for its beauty—by normal standards, there's nothing special about it—but because it's our home. It is the place we live, sleep, eat, share joy and sorrow, and solve the problems of the day. So many memories live within these walls that it's almost as if this house and our family have merged.

These days, our home is looking more like a plain old house. Without the clutter and clatter of our family, it's lost its homey feel. Sounds echo and magnify in its stillness, and abandoned rooms cry out for company. When I straighten a room, it stays that way for a long time. Although the lack of activity hasn't deterred the dust balls from collecting. If anything, they're more apparent. It feels odd to live in perpetual neatness; sometimes, when I start to clean the house, I feel almost cheated—cheated out of all my past mutterings about who left what where. I remember finding a dirty cereal bowl stashed in the closet—lord knows how many years it had been there—being appalled when a girlie magazine peeked out from under my son's pillow, and finding still-folded laundry piled in with dirty socks in the hamper.

It's not that I miss the aggravation and extra work, but it seems a sin that a house still gets dirty when there are so few of us to mess it up. Keeping the house clean seemed more vital when the kids lived here. I miss the teamwork—making up those weekly chore lists and then haranguing whoever failed to do their part. It's become a lonely job. I've tried enlisting my husband's help, but The King doesn't respond well to chore lists.

Besides, the house has always been my responsibility, while he's managed the yard duties—such a large yard. That, too, is still. No more feet trampling the grass and my flowerbeds. And our son isn't around to help out, so we are on our own keeping the lawn from growing embarrassingly high. The leaves need raking and the bushes are overgrown. When it snows, my husband and I are out there digging out the cars and clearing the walkways. This whole home maintenance thing has become a burden. Maybe it's time to think about moving into a smaller place, something easier to take care of, perhaps a condo.

Our kids responded to the idea with immediate horror. That we would sell the old homestead was unthinkable. Not that they plan to move back home, but when they come to visit, they want to find things as they remember them. There's always a decision as to whom to please, the kids or ourselves. Despite what your children say, "home" will be wherever you and your husband live, and they will be coming home to you both, not to a house.

We weren't sure we were ready to give up our house, but we needed to investigate the alternatives. There was something wrong with every condo we looked at. It was all too confining, and there were rules. In some, no kids or pets were allowed. What about future grandchildren and our cats? We weren't sure if we wanted neighbors upstairs, downstairs, and on the other side of our home when we'd enjoyed the privacy of a single-family home for so long. I fussed that I had to have enough spare rooms and baths to accommodate the kids when they visited, an office for my work, a large eat-in kitchen for our family dinners, and some sort of yard.

When we considered the bang for the buck, moving to a condo in our area would cost us more than staying put. This may not be true for you if you still carry a hefty mortgage on your house; and some areas of the country, such as Florida, have well-designed, roomy condos that offer more amenities than a private home.

For us, keeping our home turned out to be a wise decision. I found that empty bureau drawers and closets make convenient storage spots for clothes, and I have forsaken the seasonal ritual of packing summer and winter clothes away in cartons and trash bags in the basement. We spread out. I use the second bathroom for my shower now, instead of queuing for the one off our bedroom. The room that held the pullout couch is now my office, and we created a workout area in the basement family room. There always seems to be a reason to walk through each room, each day. The ones we miss, the cats handle, leaving tiny pawprints in the rugs and cat hairs on the furniture.

Our house is truly a home once again, and as my husband and I have managed to fill the spaces, the hollowness of those empty-nest days now seems incredulous. I'm happy we didn't make a sudden move because it wasn't the house that was empty, just our hearts.

Today, our home is full whether it is just the two of us or the entire family comes to spend the Christmas holiday. While we've held their old rooms for them, our children are all married. So, instead of housing three extra people for overnight stays, we must find private space for many more. One day we'll have grandchildren racing through the halls, and the cries of a baby filling our home. I'll keep a crib set up in one of the bedrooms, a highchair in the kitchen, and a laundry basket full of toys in the hall closet. We'll be coming full circle in this home. Maybe we'll need a bigger place.

Roasted & grilled entrées

It's so easy to become spoiled with the speed and ease of skillet cooking that when the opportunity arises to cook larger portions, we're surprised to discover we've lost track of cooking times. I used to be a pro at planning, but now I find myself referring to cooking charts to decide what time I need to tuck a roast in the oven so it will be cooked by dinnertime. As a rule, the tenderer a piece a meat, the more quickly it will cook and the larger a piece of meat, the longer it will take to cook. Beef and lamb are served rare, medium, or well, while pork is now cooked to medium or well.

General Cooking Time Guidelines:

Steaks, 1-inch thick, grilled or broiled

Medium Rare	4–5 minutes per side
Medium	6–7 minutes per side

Beef or Lamb roasts cooked at 325–350 degrees

Rare	20–25 minutes per pound
Medium	27–30 minutes per pound
Well	32–35 minutes per pound

Tenderloin cooked at 400–425 degrees

Rare	15–18 minutes per pound
Medium	20–22 minutes per pound

Tips on selecting and preparing meats

The chewability and palatability of meat depends on the age of the animal, its species, and how it has been fed and raised. Beef, veal, and lamb are graded against standards set in the industry for tenderness, juiciness, and flavor. These desirable qualities have a great deal to do with the amount of fat marbled throughout a piece of meat, as well as the meat's location and function within the animal. Meat is muscle. Less stressed muscle, such as tenderloin, loin, sirloin, and ribs, will have a fine, close-grained texture.

Well-exercised muscles, such as the neck, shoulders, and leg, are leaner, more coarsely grained and generally chewy or grisly—like chuck and shoulder cuts. It's both comforting and distressing to realize that the happy free-range chicken we pay extra for at the market might be a tough bird because it's been allowed to exercise more than its sad sidekicks, who had the misfortune to be raised in confined quarters under controlled conditions.

Meat products are highly regulated and supervised by the United States Department of Agriculture (USDA), who assures buyers that all meat has been inspected for wholesomeness and that its processing and distribution meet sanitation and safety standards. Package labeling can be confusing. Meat labeled as "kosher," for example, certifies cleanliness not quality and that the meat has been processed in accordance with rabbinical law. Although the USDA has set labeling standards, the grading and labeling of meat is not mandatory, even in the United States. Some large meat packers and supermarket chains have developed their own grades, which are used in place of or in addition to USDA grades. Beef, veal, and lamb are usually graded, while pork is not. You might encounter contrived variations such as butcher's choice, top choice, high choice, or star.

USDA Label Guides for Beef, Veal, and Lamb
Highest quality: Prime
Very good: Choice
Good: Good or Select
Mediocre or poor: Standard, Commercial, Utility, Cutter, and Canner

The lowest grades are rarely seen in retail markets. If you encounter nongraded meat, as you might when shopping in a rural area or in a foreign country, this does not necessarily mean it won't be tender or tasty. The best shopping strategy here is to look for well-shaped cuts with clean, pure-looking fat and compact, evenly grained muscle.

Preparing meat

Different cuts from the same grade or same animal will vary as to how they need to be cooked. Cuts that are tough and coarse require special handling to become tender, while those that are buttery and soft can be grilled or roasted as is. As a rule, the larger and leaner a piece of meat, the longer it will keep. Fatty meats, like pork, ground beef, and sausage will spoil quickly. Leave fresh meat in its original packaging when you store it. The plastic wrap used at the supermarket allows meat to breathe. Meat wrapped in butcher paper should be stored with the paper loosened for ventilation.

Always give raw meat the once-over before cooking it. The surface should be moist, not slimy, and it shouldn't have an off odor. Keep meat chilled right up until cooking time.

Poultry

The most common birds we'll feast on are chickens, but poultry includes a variety of foul, such as turkey, duck, quail, and ostrich. Assuming your poultry comes from the supermarket, you'll need to check the sell date on the package and avoid poultry whose hour is nigh. If the package contains an unusual amount of liquid, feels sticky, or has the faintest off odor, the contents are suspect. Most chicken arrives frozen and is left to slowly defrost in a chilled meat case. Store chicken, left in its original packaging, in the refrigerator, as you would other meats, and use it within two days or freeze it. Meat that has been refrozen will still be safe to eat, but it will have diminished in flavor, texture, and overall quality.

BEEF & LAMB: ROASTED & GRILLED

Tenderloin of Beef with Red Wine Marinade

This is special occasion fare. It's so well liked that you'll want to make this entrée repeatedly. The beef can be baked or grilled, depending on the time of year. And don't reserve the Red Wine Marinade just for tenderloin; try it on any cut of beef or with lamb.

RED WINE MARINADE:

1/2	cup dry red wine
2	tablespoons wine vinegar
2	cloves garlic, minced
1	small onion, minced
1	tablespoon Dijon mustard
1	teaspoon ground black pepper
1/4	teaspoon dried thyme
1/4	cup chopped fresh parsley (or 3 tablespoons dried)
1	tablespoon Worcestershire sauce
1/4	cup soy sauce
1/2	cup olive oil
1	whole tenderloin, about 8 to 9 pounds (have butcher cut it in half and clean all fat and skin)

To make the marinade: Combine all but the last three ingredients in a food processor or blender. Process briefly. Add the Worcestershire sauce, soy sauce, and olive oil and process until blended.

To bake tenderloin: Preheat oven to 400°. Baste the meat liberally with half the marinade, then place both pieces side by side in a large roasting pan. Bake the roast for 15 minutes. Reduce oven temperature to 350° and continue to cook, basting occasionally with the remainder of the marinade and pan juices, for an additional 20 to 30 minutes or until meat thermometer registers "Beef Rare." (It will take more time to cook a larger roast.) Remove the roast from the oven. Place the roast on a slicing board or serving platter and slice into 1-inch-thick rounds. Pour off the pan juices and add to any remaining marinade. Bring this mixture to a boil, and then serve on the side with the sliced tenderloin—and take a bow!

SERVES 8 TO 10

Pot Roast in a Bag

No basting or tending, no messy pan to soak, and no gravy to make. This simple and flavorful one-dish meal hits the spot on cold rainy nights when you're looking for comfort food.

1	14 x 20-inch (large) Reynolds Oven Bag
¼	cup flour
1	teaspoon salt
½	teaspoon black pepper
1	teaspoon dried thyme
1	bay leaf
2	tablespoons dried parsley
¼	teaspoon ground marjoram
1	4½-pound bottom round or rump roast
3	yellow onions, peeled and sliced lengthwise into wedges
6	carrots, scrubbed and sliced into 2-inch chunks
6	medium baking potatoes, scrubbed and sliced lengthwise into wedges
½	cup beef broth or red wine

Preheat oven to 325°. Set roasting bag in a 9 x 13 x 2-inch or larger roasting pan. Add the flour, salt, pepper, thyme, bay leaf, parsley, and marjoram to the bag. Gripping the top of the bag shut, shake the flour and seasoning together. This mixture will lightly coat the inside of the roasting bag. Place the roast, onions, carrots, potatoes, and beef broth in the bag. Seal the top of the bag using the tie provided with the bag. Gently turn the bag over a few times to lightly coat the roast and vegetables with the seasoned flour mixture. Reopen the bag and pour in the broth or red wine.

Set the bag in the roasting pan and adjust the contents so that the roast is sitting flat in the pan and surrounded by the vegetables. Pierce the bag once or twice with a fork or sharp knife to allow steam to escape. Place prepared roast in a preheated 325° oven and bake for 2 to 2¾ hours or until the meat is tender. If the roasting bag puffs too much, pierce again it with a fork or knife. To remove food from bag, tip the bag slightly upwards, and undo fastener or snip off the end with scissors. Hot steam will escape, so do this carefully.

To serve: Remove the roast to a carving platter and slice it. I like to pour the vegetables and gravy right out into the roasting pan, then scoop out the vegetables with a slotted spoon and arrange them around the meat on a serving platter. Pour the remaining gravy into a gravy boat and serve it on the side.

SERVES 6

London Broil with Rum Marinade

This marinade works well for lamb, as well. It enhances the meat flavor without overpowering it. For a 1-inch, medium-rare steak, grill about 7 minutes on the first side, then flip over and grill for another 5 minutes. Test for doneness.

RUM MARINADE (makes ¹/₂ cup):

- ¹/₂ cup soy sauce
- 3 tablespoons brown sugar
- 2 tablespoons lemon juice
- 1 tablespoon olive oil
- 2 tablespoons dark rum
- ¹/₄ teaspoon ground black pepper
- 1 clove fresh garlic, minced
- 1 teaspoon dried parsley (or 1 tablespoon of chopped fresh)

1¹/₂ to 2 pounds London broil cut steak

Mix all marinade ingredients and pour over the meat. Allow to marinate for at least half an hour before broiling or grilling. Preheat the grill. Place marinated steak on the grill and cook 5 to 10 minutes on each side until the meat is your desired doneness. Reserve the marinade and baste with additional sauce.

To serve: Place the meat on a flat platter or cutting board with a well and slice thinly, holding the knife on the diagonal. If desired, heat leftover marinade to just boiling in a small saucepan or in the microwave oven to cook any meat juices which the sauce acquired in the marinating process. Offer on the side.

SERVES 3 TO 4

Healthy Meat Loaf

Use a meat loaf pan with drainage holes to eliminate excess fat. Grate the potatoes, onion, and garlic in the food processor to save time.

- 2 medium potatoes, scrubbed and grated
- 1 egg or 2 egg whites
- ¹/₂ small onion, diced
- 1 clove garlic, minced
- 2 tablespoons chopped fresh Italian parsley (or 1 tablespoon dried)
- ¹/₂ teaspoon salt
- ¹/₄ teaspoon black pepper
- 2 dashes hot pepper sauce
- ¹/₃ cup prepared barbecue sauce
- 1 pound lean ground beef or "meat loaf mix"*
- 2 strips bacon (optional)

Preheat oven to 375°. In a large mixing bowl whisk together the potatoes, egg, onion, garlic, parsley, salt, pepper, hot pepper sauce, and all but 2 tablespoons of the barbecue sauce. Mix in the ground beef with a fork or your hands until well blended. Pack into a 9 x 5 x 3-inch meat loaf pan. Top with 2 strips of bacon and brush with the remaining barbecue sauce. Bake for about an hour or until the meat is cooked through. Slice and serve with mashed potatoes and green beans amandine. Offer additional barbecue sauce on the side.

Meat loaf mix is a combination of beef, veal, and pork.

SERVES 4

Osso Buco

Men have been raving over Osso Buco for years. Its hearty meat-imbued flavor that can only come from long-cooking with fine ingredients has made it an Italian delicacy. Traditionally, it's made with veal shanks, but lamb or beef shanks are easier (and cheaper) to come by.

4	cloves garlic, minced
1	carrot, diced
1	medium yellow onion, diced
3	stalks celery, diced
4	lamb, veal, or beef shanks (about 8 pounds)
1	teaspoon salt
$1/8$	teaspoon black pepper
$1/4$	cup flour
4	tablespoons olive oil
1	anchovy
2	cups red wine
$1/2$	cup tomato paste
3	tablespoons chopped parsley (or 1 teaspoon dried)
2	or 3 cups water (or as needed to cover shanks within $1/2$ inch of the tops)

Mince the garlic and dice the carrot, onion, and celery. Set aside. Locate a large roasting pan with a cover (or cover with aluminum foil). I found a Dutch oven too small. This dish requires stovetop browning and oven baking. If your roasting pan cannot be set over a burner, use a large skillet for the first step.

Preheat oven to 350°. Sprinkle shanks liberally with half of the salt and the pepper. Measure flour onto a sheet of waxed paper and set aside. Heat 2 tablespoons of the olive oil in the pan over medium-high heat. Add the garlic and sauté gently, and then lightly flour shanks and add them to the pan. Brown them on both sides. Remove the shanks and crusts of garlic to a plate. Add the remaining oil to the pan and then add the carrot, onion, celery, and the anchovy. Sauté the vegetables until they begin to brown and soften, about 6 or 7 minutes. The process will go more quickly (and you will use less oil) if you cover the pan.

Stir in the red wine and the tomato paste, deglazing the pan by scrapping the brown bits from the bottom. If you are switching pans, do this now. Otherwise, return the shanks to the pan. Cover them with enough water so that about $1/8$ of the shanks are still visible. Cover the pan and place it in the oven. Cook for about $1\frac{1}{2}$ hours or until the meat is fork-tender and begins to fall off the bone. Baste with pan juices every half hour or so, and turn shanks once during the cooking process. Serve with a side of mashed potatoes and a green vegetable or salad.

SERVES 4

Peppercorn-crusted Roast Lamb

Ask the butcher for the lamb bone and make some great stock with it! Use a blender, coffee grinder, or rolling pin to crush the peppercorns.

ROSEMARY PEPPERCORN MARINADE:

3	tablespoons crushed peppercorns
1½	teaspoons dried rosemary leaves
2	tablespoons dried mint leaves
5	garlic cloves, crushed
¼	cup wine vinegar
¼	cup soy sauce
½	cup dry red wine

1	boned 5-pound leg of lamb, untied and with fat removed
2	tablespoons Dijon mustard

To make the marinade: In a shallow bowl or marinating pan combine 1 tablespoon of the crushed peppercorns (set aside the rest), the rosemary, mint, garlic, vinegar, soy sauce, and red wine. Marinate the lamb in this mixture for at least 8 hours, turning occasionally.

Preheat oven to 350°. Remove the meat from the marinade and drain, reserving marinade. Roll and tie the meat with kitchen twine. Spread the mustard over meat, and pat the reserved two tablespoons of crushed peppercorns into the mustard. Set the meat in a shallow roasting pan and pour the reserved marinade carefully around but not over the roast. Bake for 1½ hours or until at desired doneness, basting occasionally. For medium-rare roast cook 18 minutes per pound. Allow the roast to stand for 20 minutes before carving. Serve with pan juices on the side.

SERVES 6 TO 8

Roast Lamb with Potatoes, Carrots, & Onions

1	3-pound lamb roast, boned and rolled
4	baking potatoes, quartered lengthwise
1	onion, cut into wedges
4	carrots, sliced into chunks
1	lemon, sliced thin

OREGANO LEMON BASTING MIX:

2	tablespoons olive oil
2	tablespoons lemon juice
¼	teaspoon paprika
1	teaspoon dried oregano
	Salt and pepper

Preheat oven to 350°. Set roast in the center of a 9 x 13 x 2-inch baking pan. Mix the ingredients for Basting Mix in a large zip-lock bag or mixing bowl. Add the potatoes, onion, and carrots and mix until well coated. Empty the vegetables into the pan over top of the lamb roast, arranging them evenly around the sides of the roast. Layer lemon slices over the top. Bake, basting every 20 minutes and turning the vegetables, until lamb is just pink in the center and meat thermometer registers 170°. Remove the lamb to a platter and keep warm. Raise oven temperature to 425°. Return the vegetables to the oven, and continue to bake for an additional 10 to 15 minutes, until the vegetables are crisp and sizzling. Slice the roast and serve at once with the roasted vegetables and a crisp green salad.

SERVES 3 TO 4

GOURMET BURGERS

These burgers are thick, juicy, and flavorful, as well as quick to toss together. These recipes use vegetables and such as fillers to plump out the burgers. Try this technique with both the beef and turkey burgers. The turkey burgers will surprise you. They're good!

Beef Burgers

1	pound lean ground beef
1	small ripe tomato, cored and diced into 1/4-inch pieces
1/2	cup sliced black olives
1	clove minced garlic
1/2	teaspoon Dijon mustard
1	teaspoon chili powder
1	teaspoon lemon juice
1/4	teaspoon dried basil
1/4	teaspoon dried oregano
2	tablespoons chopped fresh parsley (or 1 teaspoon dried)
	Salt and black pepper to taste
4	slices cheddar cheese (optional)

4	knotted egg buns
	Catsup (optional)

Preheat barbecue grill or broiler. Place beef in a medium mixing bowl, and gently mix together with the tomato, olives, garlic, mustard, chili powder, lemon juice, and other seasonings. If you overmix the ingredients the burgers will be too dense. Gently form mixture into 4 soft, loose patties. Grill over hot barbecue or under broiler for about 5 to 7 minutes per side. Top with a slice of cheese, and serve on toasted buns with catsup, if desired.

MAKES 4

Turkey Burgers

1	pound ground turkey
1/4	chopped Vidalia onion or sliced scallions
1/2	cup sliced black olives
3/4	teaspoon thyme
2	tablespoons chopped fresh cilantro (or 1 teaspoon dried)
1/2	teaspoon ground cumin
1/2	teaspoon paprika
1	teaspoon fresh lemon or lime juice
1/4	teaspoon salt or to taste
1/8	teaspoon black pepper
4	whole-wheat buns
	Ripe tomato slices
	Avocado slices
	A1® Steak Sauce (optional)

Preheat barbecue grill or broiler. In a medium mixing bowl break up the ground turkey and then gently mix in the scallions, olives, thyme, cilantro, cumin, paprika, lime juice, salt, and pepper. If you overmix, the burgers will be too dense. Gently form the mixture into 4 soft, loose patties. Grill over hot barbecue or under broiler (about 3 inches from heat) for 5 to 7 minutes per side. Serve on whole-wheat buns, topped with slices of tomato and avocado and a shake of steak sauce, if desired.

MAKES 4

PORK ROASTS & RIBS

Peachtree Pork Tenderloin

When you unwrap vacuum-packed pork tenderloin, which is normally the way it is sold, you will find two long pieces that fit together as one. These can be cooked separately, which works well for grilling, or tied together as a roast for baking.

1½	pounds pork tenderloin
	Cooking oil spray
½	teaspoon salt
⅛	teaspoon black pepper
½	teaspoon allspice
2	scallions, sliced
¼	cup Peachtree Schnapps (or other fruit-based liqueur or use the ¼ cup of reserved peach juice)
1	16-ounce can sliced peaches, drained

Preheat oven to 400°. Lay the 2 pieces of the tenderloin in a 9 x 13 x 2-inch baking pan, about 2 inches apart. Spray lightly with cooking oil spray. Sprinkle with the salt and pepper. Rub in the allspice with your fingers or a pastry brush. Sprinkle with the scallions. Pour the Peachtree Schnapps over all. Bake for 20 to 30 minutes, basting and checking every 10 minutes, until the pork is almost cooked. (Place a meat thermometer in the center of the largest tenderloin.) About 5 minutes before the roast will be done, pour the sliced peaches over the roasts. Brush with the pan drippings, and allow them to cook alongside the roast until heated through and slightly browned. Remove the meat to a serving platter and slice it into ½-inch rings. Serve topped with a spoonful of the peaches and pan juices.

SERVES 3 TO 4

Pork Loin with Potatoes, Apples, & Onions

This cooks up nicely. The apples mush into the potatoes and onions, adding sweetness. If you have some jelly in the fridge, brush a teaspoonful over the roast for a nice glaze. If you are not using a nonstick roasting pan, I recommend you line it with foil to simplify cleanup.

2	baking potatoes, sliced in wedges
1	sweet potato, sliced in rings
1	large onion, sliced in rings

2 small apples, peeled, cored, and
   quartered
1 to 2 tablespoons olive oil
1/4 teaspoon paprika
1 1/2 teaspoons salt
1/4 teaspoon black pepper
1 tablespoon dried sage leaves
1 2/3 pounds boneless pork loin*

Preheat oven to 400°. Place the potatoes, onion, apples, oil, paprika, 3/4 teaspoon of the salt, and 1/8 teaspoon of the pepper in a plastic bag or mixing bowl and mix to coat them. Sprinkle 1/2 teaspoon of the sage and some of the salt and pepper on the roast. If using a tenderloin, sprinkle the inner portions of the 2 pieces that make up the tenderloin and tie them together with butcher's string. Place the pork loin in a 9 x 13 x 2-inch or larger casserole dish. Pour the potato mixture around the roast, picking out the apples and arranging them on top of the roast. Sprinkle with the remaining sage, salt, and pepper. Cook for 30 to 60 minutes or until pork is 160° in its center and vegetables are crisp and brown. Baste the roast and stir the vegetables every 20 minutes. Serve with cranberry sauce.

Note: This recipe also works well with a pork tenderloin roast.

SERVES 3 TO 4

Fruited Pork Roast

This roast is a nice change from beef for a fancy sit-down dinner. If you don't have the liquors indicated, experiment with fruit liquors or brandies on hand.

FRUIT COMPOTE STUFFING:
2 cups canned pineapple, juice drained
   and reserved
1 large can sliced peaches, juice drained
   and reserved
2 or 3 large apples, peeled and sliced
1 cup dried cranberries or cherries
1/2 cup Peachtree Schnapps
3 tablespoons Kir or blackberry brandy

1 8-pound boneless pork loin or fresh ham
   for stuffing
   Salt and pepper to taste
1/4 cup brown sugar

To make the Fruit Compote Stuffing: In a large mixing bowl combine the pineapple, peaches, apples, and cranberries with the Peachtree Schnapps and Kir. Add 1/4 cup of the reserved fruit juices. Allow the fruit to marinate about 15 minutes.

   Preheat oven to 325°. Stuff roast with one-fourth of the fruit mixture. Place the roast in a large roasting pan and season with salt and pepper. Baste liberally with the fruit marinade liquid. Sprinkle with 2 tablespoons of the brown sugar. Bake at 325° for 2 1/2 to 3 hours or until pork is no longer pink, basting occasionally with the pan juices. Meanwhile, pour the remaining fruit mixture into an 8 x 8 x 2-inch ovenproof casserole dish. Sprinkle with the remaining brown sugar. Bake uncovered in 325° oven (alongside the pork roast) for about 30 minutes, until the fruit is brown and bubbling. Remove from the oven and set aside until the pork is ready. Serve the pork slices topped with warm fruit compote.

SERVES 12

occasionally, until a meat thermometer registers 160° (about 30 minutes). To serve, remove string and slice the roast into rounds. Offer 3 or 4 slices per person. Oven-baked sweet potatoes and a green vegetable make a nice accompaniment.

SERVES 3

Basil Pork Tenderloin with Mango Chutney Glaze

This will become your favorite company meal. It's simple, yet elegant.

- 1½ pounds pork tenderloin
- 6   fresh basil leaves
     Salt and pepper to taste
- ¼   cup prepared mango chutney

❧

Preheat oven to 400°. If using a whole tenderloin, separate the 2 pieces; otherwise, slice 1 of the pieces in half lengthwise. Season both halves with salt and pepper. Lay basil leaves on bottom half of the roast in a single layer. Top with the other half and tie the halves together in several places with butcher's string. Place the tenderloin in a small roasting pan and brush liberally with the mango chutney. Bake, basting

Honey Barbecued Spareribs

The precooking not only makes the ribs a snap to barbecue, but the process keeps them moist and tender, while steaming off excess fat. For a crowd, I've done up a batch early in the day and marinated the ribs in a large plastic bag. For country-style ribs, allow 2 to 3 per person. Baby back ribs have less meat, so you will need half a rack per person, or 4 to 6 ribs. If you get lazy, you can substitute 1 cup purchased barbecue sauce for homemade.

- 1   clove garlic, sliced
- ¼   cup wine vinegar
- 5   pounds country-style spareribs
     (10 ribs)
- ¼   cup honey

HOMEMADE BARBECUE SAUCE:
- 1   medium onion, diced
- 1   large clove garlic, minced
- ¼   cup soy sauce
- 1   tablespoon molasses
- ¾   cup catsup
- ¼   cup water
- ½   teaspoon red pepper sauce

Pour about 2 inches of water into an 8-quart or larger stockpot or Dutch oven. Add the garlic and wine vinegar. Add the ribs, cut into 2- or 3-rib sections. Bring to a boil. Cover and steam for 30 to 40 minutes or until ribs are no longer pink. Stir ribs once or twice during the cooking process.

To make the Homemade Barbecue Sauce: Mix all ingredients in a small microwave-proof bowl. For a quick flavor blend, heat the sauce until bubbly in the microwave or on the stovetop. Once the ribs are cooked, use tongs to remove them from the pan, and drain them in a strainer or colander. Place the ribs in a plastic bag or large pan along with the marinade, and toss them to coat thoroughly. Chill the ribs until you are ready to barbecue, turning them occasionally.

To grill: Preheat barbecue grill. Remove ribs from marinade and drizzle both sides with the honey. Grill for about 10 minutes, turning once or twice to brown ribs on all sides. Serve immediately with Grilled Vegetable Packets and pasta salad.

BARBECUE SAUCE MAKES 1¼ CUPS

SERVES 4 TO 6

TURKEY & CHICKEN: ROASTED & GRILLED

Apple-stuffed Cornish Hens with Marsala Sauce

One year, when I was looking for something nice to make for our anniversary, I devised this gourmet-style dinner. Allow one hen per person. The apple remains whole and tastes like a baked apple.

MARSALA SAUCE:
¾	cup Marsala wine
2	tablespoons molasses
1	large clove garlic, minced
2	teaspoons thyme

6	Cornish hens
6	teaspoons butter
	Salt and pepper
6	small apples, cored

To make the Marsala Sauce: In a small bowl mix the wine, molasses, garlic, and thyme. Set aside.

Prepare the hens: Remove giblets, etc. from the cavities of the hens and immerse hens in a pan of cold, salted water for a few minutes. Remove and drain on paper towels, stuffing some towels in cavities of hens to absorb excess water. Pat hens dry. Preheat oven to 350°. Remove and discard all paper toweling from hens. Stuff an apple into the cavity of each hen.

To roast the hens: Arrange hens to fit in a large roasting pan, and rub each hen with 1 teaspoon of the butter. Sprinkle liberally with salt and pepper. Pour the Marsala Sauce over the hens and bake at 350° for 1 hour, basting every 10 minutes. Serve with wild rice and a green vegetable or salad.

SERVES 6

bony side down until they are almost done, about 35 to 40 minutes. As gas grill temperatures vary, depending on the type of grill you are using, monitor the fire and test for doneness periodically. Chicken is cooked when you can wiggle the leg. Turn the chicken to top side and brown it for 5 to 10 minutes. Serve with potato salad and corn on the cob.

SERVES 8

Grill-roasted Chicken Halves

Few who tasted it could ever forget my dad's grilled chicken, slowly roasted to golden brown perfection on a handmade backyard grill constructed of cinder blocks—the "piece d' resistance" of my childhood summer outings. Cinder block charcoal grills have been replaced by modern propane grills with controlled heat. Here's today's version of Dad's simply delicious chicken halves.

4   frying chickens, split
4   teaspoons butter or margarine
     Garlic salt to taste
     Paprika

Wash the chicken in salted water and pat dry with paper towels. Rub each half with about one teaspoon of the butter. Sprinkle liberally with garlic salt and paprika. Layer in a roasting pan, using waxed paper to separate layers, and chill until ready to roast.

To roast chickens on a propane grill: Preheat grill for 10 minutes on high to get it started, and then reduce temperature to low for 5 minutes before putting the chickens on to roast. Cook the chickens

How to Roast a Turkey

Like most of us, I've prepared turkeys for years. While my recipe is basic, cooking times and stuffing information bear updating. Here's the latest scoop from the USDA. These days, it's considered unsafe to stuff a turkey. Make your favorite stuffing recipe, whether it be from scratch or out of the box, place it in a heatproof serving dish, and cook or brown it in the oven alongside the turkey. If you've added giblets, sausage, or any sort of meat, be certain the stuffing has reached an internal temperature of 165° before pronouncing it "done."

Cooking instructions are often plastered somewhere on prepackaged turkeys or turkey breasts, and many have a pop-out doneness sensor. Double-check that your bird is cooked by using a food thermometer to test it in several places, including the fattest part of the breast and the innermost part of the thigh. Dark meat is denser, and thus takes longer to cook than white meat. If you can wiggle the leg, it's a visible sign that the turkey is done.

The USDA recommends cooking a whole turkey to 185° at center, and a turkey breast to 170° at center. Bear in mind that large roasts continue to cook a bit once they are removed from the oven. Thus, I typically take my turkey from the oven when it reads 175° to ensure it won't overcook. Allow the bird to "stand" for about 20 minutes before carving it.

Estimated roasting times for turkey breasts and whole, unstuffed birds:

Weight	Cook Time at 325° F.	Internal Temperature
4–6 pound breast	1½ to 2¼ hours	170° F.
6–8 pound breast	2¼ to 3¼ hours	170° F.
6–8 pound turkey	3 to 3½ hours	185° F.
8–12 pound turkey	3½ to 4½ hours	185° F.
12–16 pound turkey	4½ to 5½ hours	185° F.
16–20 pound turkey	5½ to 6½ hours	185° F.
20–24 pound turkey	6½ to 7 hours	185° F.

On average, figure 15 minutes per pound for unstuffed birds. If your turkey is cooked long before these estimated times or seems to take forever, understand that several factors can affect cooking time. A turkey will cook more quickly if placed in a deep dark-colored roasting pan, rather than a shallow, light-colored one, or in a cooking bag. Using a lid on the pan will speed things up, while using a foil tent will slow down cooking. A frozen turkey will take at least 50 percent longer to cook than a completely thawed turkey. If you've jammed other items in the oven with the turkey, as we often do around the holidays, this may decrease heat circulation and slow down cooking. Always check that there is space on the sides of casseroles and pans in the oven to allow the heat to surround them.

Basic Roast Turkey

1   turkey breast or whole turkey
½   stick softened butter or margarine
     Salt and pepper
     Paprika
     Thyme

To prepare turkey, remove wrappings and take the giblets out of the neck or body cavities. Place the turkey in a bath of cold, salted water for a few minutes to clean it. Remove the carcass from the water and allow it to drain on paper towels. Pat dry. Stuff the cavity with paper towels to absorb extra moisture, remove and discard the soggy paper towels before baking.

Preheat oven to 325°. Select a roasting pan that is at least 2 inches wider and longer than the bird. If you have a V-shaped rack, place this at the bottom of the baking pan to keep the turkey off the floor of the pan. Place the bird in the pan

and sprinkle liberally with salt and pepper. Take a clean paper towel and grease the turkey with softened butter or margarine. Sprinkle with paprika and thyme and place in the oven to bake.

Baste the turkey frequently, using a turkey baster. Add a bit more butter or margarine if the turkey looks dry. If the turkey is getting too brown, place a foil tent over it lightly and continue cooking. When turkey is done to 10° below recommended temperature (i.e., for breasts, 160°; for whole, unstuffed birds, 175°), remove it from the oven and allow it to rest on a separate platter for about 20 minutes, lightly covered with foil. Make the Pan Gravy as instructed on page 93. Now, invite your favorite gentleman into the kitchen to do the carving honors, or perform this feat at the dinner table. Serve with hot gravy.

MEATLESS AND BRUNCH FARE

Grilled Vegetable Medley with Garlic Linguini

This three-step entrée is nice on a hot summer evening. Add a piece of grilled meat or fish for heartier fare or serve the vegetables alone as a side dish. Leftovers re-heat nicely in the microwave.

LINGUINI:

½ pound linguini, cooked al dente in boiling salted water and drained

2 tablespoons olive oil

2 small cloves garlic, minced

1 teaspoon Parmesan cheese (optional)

MARINADE:

2 tablespoons olive oil

1 teaspoon oregano

½ teaspoon salt

1 small clove garlic, minced

Pinch black pepper

VEGETABLES:

½ yellow pepper, cut in half

2 large plum tomatoes, cut in half

2 small zucchini squash, cut in half

2 portabella mushroom caps

½ Vidalia onion sliced horizontally into 1-inch rounds

Preheat grill and cook the linguini. Mix all ingredients for the marinade in a large bowl or a plastic bag. Add the vegetables and mix well to coat. If desired, this may be done 30 minutes ahead to allow vegetables to marinate. Using tongs, lift vegetable pieces from the marinade and place on the hot grill. Turn when brown on underside. Baste with reserved marinade and continue to cook until tender when pierced. Remove vegetables to a covered platter as they are cooked (tomatoes and mushrooms will be done first). This will take about 10 minutes. When the vegetables are cooked, cover to keep warm and set aside.

To prepare the pasta: In a 10-inch skillet heat the olive oil over medium heat. Add the garlic and sauté for a few minutes. Add the drained, cooked pasta and sauté a few minutes, until pasta is coated with the garlic oil mixture.

To serve: Place the pasta in a shallow pasta bowl or platter and toss the grilled vegetables over the top. Sprinkle with Parmesan cheese, if desired.

SERVES 2

Regatta Ham & Cheese Strata

This dish won first prize as the best-tasting potluck dish at the Ericson Regatta. Make it ahead and pop it in the freezer for an upcoming luncheon or brunch. It travels well, even on a boat.

5	tablespoons butter or margarine, softened
2	tablespoons diced onion
1	tablespoon Dijon mustard
10	slices whole wheat (or multi-grain) bread, crusts removed
½	cup chopped ham
1	8-ounce package shredded, sharp cheddar cheese (2 cups)
2	tablespoons chopped dried tomato in olive oil, drained
½	cup cooked broccoli florets
1	teaspoon salt
⅛	teaspoon black pepper
	Dash red pepper
½	teaspoon Worcestershire sauce
1	teaspoon dried parsley (or 2 tablespoons chopped fresh)
4	eggs
2¼	cups milk
⅔	cup dry white wine

Mix the butter, onion, and mustard. Spread about 1 teaspoon of the butter mixture over one side of each slice of bread. Cut each slice of bread into thirds, and line the bottom and sides of an ungreased 8 x 8 x 2-inch baking pan, with every other slice placed buttered side down. Set aside remaining bread. In a medium bowl combine the ham, cheese, tomato, broccoli, salt, black and red ground peppers, Worcestershire sauce, and parsley. Pour into center of bread-lined casserole, and spread to evenly distribute. Top with reserved bread slices, placed buttered side up (there will not be enough to completely cover filling). In a separate bowl beat together the eggs, milk, and wine with a wire whisk or fork. Pour the egg mixture over top of the bread in the prepared casserole dish. Cover and refrigerate for at least 2 hours before cooking or place casserole in the freezer if you plan to cook it several days later.

To cook: Preheat oven to 325°. Place uncovered, defrosted (if applicable) casserole in the oven and bake for 1 hour and 15 minutes or until a knife inserted in the center comes out clean. Slice into portions, and serve warm.

MAKES AN 8 x 8-INCH CASSEROLE

Praline French Toast

Butter
1   loaf French bread, 13 to 16 ounces
8   large eggs
2   cups half and half
1   cup milk
2   tablespoons granulated sugar
1   teaspoon vanilla extract
¼   teaspoon ground cinnamon
¼   teaspoon ground nutmeg
     Pinch salt

PRALINE TOPPING:
2   sticks or ½ pound butter, cut into
        small pieces
1   cup packed light brown sugar
1   cup chopped pecans
2   tablespoons light corn syrup
½   teaspoon ground cinnamon
½   teaspoon nutmeg

Grease a 9 x 13 x 2-inch baking dish with butter. Slice bread into 20 1-inch-wide slices and arrange the bread in rows in the bottom of the pan, overlapping slices. In a large mixing bowl combine the eggs, half and half, milk, sugar, vanilla, ¼ teaspoon cinnamon, ¼ teaspoon nutmeg, and salt. Beat with an electric mixer or a wire whisk until blended thoroughly. Pour egg mixture evenly over the bread slices, spooning some between slices. Cover with foil and refrigerate overnight.

Just before baking, place all Praline Topping ingredients into a small bowl.

Blend by stirring and mashing the butter with a fork. Preheat oven to 350°. Spread topping evenly over the bread and bake uncovered for 40 minutes, until puffed and lightly golden. Serve with maple syrup.

SERVES 6 TO 8

GRAVIES, MARINADES, & SEASONINGS

Pan Gravy

1   cup cold water
2   tablespoons flour
¼   teaspoon salt
     Dash black pepper
     Dash garlic powder
1   dash molasses or Gravy Master for color
     Pan drippings from a turkey, chicken,
        or roast

Place all ingredients except the pan drippings in a jar. Cover tightly and shake well to blend the flour.

For stovetop gravy: Pour water mixture into the bottom of the roasting pan containing the pan drippings and cook on medium heat on stovetop, stirring constantly until gravy thickens.

For microwave gravy: Pour water mixture in bottom of pan and stir to loosen pan drippings. Pour all into a microwave-safe bowl or glass measuring cup and cook on high, stirring every 2 minutes, until gravy thickens.

MAKES 1¼ CUP

Mushroom Gravy

Too many times I've had a leftover roast that begs for gravy to moisten it. Use this recipe when your pan gravy is gone to extend the life of your leftovers.

5	ounces (½ package) sliced mushrooms
1	tablespoon flour
½	cup water
1	teaspoon granulated chicken or beef bouillon
⅓	teaspoon salt
⅛	teaspoon black pepper
1	tablespoon milk
¼	teaspoon molasses or Gravy Master for color

Combine all ingredients in a zip-lock plastic bag and shake to blend in the flour. Pour into a microwave-safe bowl and cover. Microwave on high for 3 to 5 minutes, stirring every minute or two, or until mushrooms are cooked and gravy has thickened. Stir in the milk and the molasses. Serve over any kind of meat.

MAKES ABOUT ¾ CUP

Orange-Ginger Sauce

Use as a basting sauce for grilled chicken, pork, shrimp, or any firm fish, such as tuna steak or swordfish steaks.

1	clove garlic, minced
1	tablespoon chopped fresh ginger

½	cup orange juice
¼	cup catsup
¼	cup soy sauce
1½	to 2 tablespoons sesame seeds (optional)

Mix all ingredients in a small glass cup or microwave-proof bowl. Microwave 30 seconds on high. If using on chicken or pork, brush on during the last 5 minutes of cooking to prevent burning.

MAKES 1 CUP

Snappy Pineapple Sauce

Easy and terrific on seafood, pork, or chicken. Also makes a great dipping sauce with appetizers. Make cocktail-size meatballs and steep them in this snappy sauce.

1	cup prepared barbecue sauce
1	14-ounce can pineapple chunks, drained, juice reserved
1	tablespoon fresh ginger, chopped

Drain off pineapple juice into a small bowl, reserving chunks. Add the barbecue sauce and the ginger to the pineapple juice and mix well. Use as a marinade or basting sauce. Boil any leftover sauce, and serve on the side with the pineapple chunks.

MAKES 1 CUP

Glazed Barbecue Sauce

Good with chicken or pork.

1/4   cup Worcestershire sauce
2   tablespoons soy sauce
2   tablespoons catsup
2   tablespoons orange marmalade
1   teaspoon dried chives
1/4   teaspoon hot sauce

Mix all ingredients in a small bowl, and use as a basting sauce for grilled chicken. Put on the chicken during the last 5 minutes of cooking to prevent burning.

MAKES 1/2 CUP

Cajun Seasoning Mix

1   tablespoon paprika
2 1/2   teaspoons salt
1   teaspoon onion powder
1   teaspoon garlic powder
1   teaspoon cayenne pepper
1 1/2   teaspoons black pepper
1   teaspoon dried oregano

Mix all ingredients in a small jar. Close tightly to store.

Easy Seasoning Mix

Years ago I fell in love with Morton's seasoning salt, but not all stores still carry it. I developed my own alternative so I would never again be without. Keep this seasoned salt in a shaker near your oven and use it in lieu of salt and pepper in all recipes. It will add a bit more flavor to your cooking without overwhelming the other flavorings in your dish.

1/2   teaspoon minced dried garlic*
1   tablespoon minced onion*
2   teaspoons dried parsley flakes
1   teaspoon dried basil
1/2   teaspoon dried oregano or thyme
1/4   cup salt
1   teaspoon ground black pepper

Measure out the garlic, onion, parsley, basil, and oregano into a blender or coffee grinder and whirl until fine. Pour into a small jar, brushing the excess spice dust from the blender with a pastry brush. Add the salt and pepper. Cover jar and shake. Pour some into a seasoning shaker using a funnel and store the rest. Keeps indefinitely.

* Substitute 1/4 teaspoon garlic powder and 1 1/2 teaspoons onion powder for the dried minced and omit from the grinding process.

MAKES ABOUT 1/2 CUP

THE HERB STORY

Fresh garden herbs are wonderful, and easy to grow if you've a sunny spot and the patience and time to care for them. However, fresh herbs are readily available at the supermarket, either fresh picked or potted. Their flavor and appearance in a dish is not only far superior to dried herbs, but a spark of green adds visual interest to monotone foods. When I am vacationing aboard our boat, I take along a potted herb—basil, oregano, sage, or whatever suits my fancy—and experiment by adding snips of it to my creation in progress.

To preserve fresh herbs, put them in the refrigerator, unwashed. Store bunches with their stems in water and keep loose leaves in a ventilated plastic bag. It's also possible to dry herbs that have been fresh picked by hanging them by their stems in bunches in a cool, dry place. Crumble dried herbs into lidded containers and store at room temperature.

Rinse fresh herbs before using them by placing a handful briefly under cool water and patting dry with paper towels. You can freeze the leaves of fresh herbs, whole or chopped. Once they are washed and dried, pack them into bags or airtight containers.

Fresh herbs are less concentrated because they contain water, so you will need approximately three times the quantity of fresh herbs when substituting them for dried; ground herbs are three times stronger than dried herbs. By chopping fresh herbs finely, you will expose maximum surface areas and reap the best flavor. Heat releases aroma and flavor but extended cooking will diminish it, so add fresh herbs to stews, sauces, or soup no more than one hour before the dish will be cooked. Crush dried herbs to release the aromatic oils before using them, and add them at the onset of the cooking cycle.

Italian Seasoning

2   tablespoons dried parsley
1   tablespoon dried basil
1   teaspoon oregano

Mix all ingredients and store in a shaker jar.

MAKES ABOUT ¼ CUP

RECIPE FOR A GREAT WEDDING

Be flexible

Respect your child's wishes

Dote on your "new" son or daughter

Keep your husband calm

Plan well and double-check everything

Light lavender candles to reduce prewedding tensions

Relax and enjoy the party

ITALIAN RECIPES TO PASS DOWN

Every Italian family has its own methods of making sauce and cooking pasta. When my first daughter planned to be married, she asked for the recipes for our traditional dishes. Italian food has always been part of our lives, so I consider myself somewhat of an expert in its preparation. After figuring out how to recreate my mother's recipes, which were never written down, I went on to produce my own versions.

There goes the bride . . .

The problem with being a parent is that we lose our kids repeatedly. Once would be plenty, thank you. First they are off to college and then to their own apartments. Even though they are "gone," the apron string is still tied tight—until they decide to get married. It seems like a great idea until you start to get selfish about it. They want it their way, and you want it yours. I've married off two brides and a groom over the past years and it was more stressful than childbirth, yet almost as joyous.

Who would have guessed that the sparkle of a tiny diamond would be powerful enough to consume our lives for more than a year and wreak such havoc on our bank account? The estimates that rolled in for the caterer, photographer, and florist were appalling. We started out building something small and simple and ended up with a palace. Planning a wedding was hard work fraught with stressful situations, such as what do we do with their father, my ex-husband, and how much is too much to pay for the reception?

Yet, it was a special, wonderful time for my to-be-wed daughter or son and me. We shopped for the perfect wedding gown, and deliberated over the bridesmaids. Should the tux jackets be black with tails, or white? I obsessed over finding a dress to wear that wasn't lacy or glitzy and that didn't make me look like a refrigerator from the rear. We lunched out and talked, and talked, and talked. I held a shower for forty people in my living room and then scheduled having the carpet cleaned the next day to get rid of the punch spills. The closeness I developed with my children during the prewedding planning will, I hope, endure for as long as it takes us to pay off the loans.

All this for one glorious wedding day—a short walk down the aisle on the arm of my husband and a thirty-minute ceremony that was so moving I ruined my eye makeup and sniffed through a whole packet of tissues. It's not fair that such happiness should bring tears. We gave our kids wedding days they'll remember each time they relocate living quarters and have to drag along an eternally preserved couturier gown complete with headpiece and shoes, a bulky leather-bound photo album, a delicately dried bridal bouquet, and the video of us all dancing the YMCA (by the third wedding, I still couldn't get it right).

A wedding's a lot like Christmas. The real meaning can get buried in all the froth. At Christmas, amid the presents and parties, a baby is born. A wedding works in reverse; we give our baby away. As parents, once the wedding balloon pops, it leaves us feeling worse than we did when the kids left home for school or for their first apartment. This time they're leaving for keeps. Talk about postpartum blues! When the wedded couple was away on their honeymoon, this reality hit me hard. At first, I was glad for the respite, and then I spiraled into a tulle funk.

Once our newlyweds returned, I realized they were deliriously happy and that they didn't forget about me. They can't wait to entertain us, and when they invite my husband and me to dinner, they say the magic words, "Don't bring anything but yourselves." So, I buy them a huge plant. We are nervous when we ring their doorbell; we don't quite know what to expect. I enter plant first, and my handsome new son-in-law enfolds me in a bear hug and calls me "Mom."

Their apartment is darling, so comfortable—and so familiar. Our old kitchen table, refinished and spiffed up with a pretty cloth, peeks out at me from their tiny kitchen. It's set for dinner with their new china, flatware—and crystal wineglasses, yet. The two candles atop it and smaller candles scattered throughout the house are glowing in our honor. I plop myself on the sofa, our old one recovered. My son-in-law hands me a glass of my favorite Chardonnay and my husband, a Jack Daniel's. To their happiness, we toast. But I feel guilty just sitting there making small talk while there's a dinner in the making. My daughter must need my help in the kitchen.

So, I pick up my wineglass and follow my nose toward a familiar aroma—my chicken recipe. I offer to make the salad, but she's already done it. She's even remembered to buy Coffee Mate for our coffee and is grinding the beans and setting up the pot for dessert. A luscious coconut cake garnishes the countertop. Everything is perfect. I take a sip of my wine to hide the tears of pride glistening in my eyes, and I can't stop myself from smiling. She's just like me.

Italian Favorites

When I was going through the trauma of lost motherhood, I treated myself to some new kitchen toys, one of which was a pasta maker. Here was my chance to recreate the homemade pasta my mom often made by hand as a Sunday dinner specialty. And then there was the sauce. When the kids were little, I spent a day making huge batches, enough to last for several months, and then divided it into one-meal portions for the freezer. Once I took on a full-time job, I no longer had time to fuss, and for a while I walked the bottled-sauce trail. When my husband's cholesterol soared, and I began to read labels, I found it was just as easy to produce a quick-cooking, healthy sauce as it was to doctor up bottled sauce that was already laced with too much salt, fat, and additives.

On cooking pasta

Work with pasta when it's hot to avoid stickiness. Unless you are using the pasta in a dish that might benefit from a starchy, slightly sticky texture, such as the Broccoli Scallop Linguini in the Seafood Section, it's not necessary to add oil to the cooking water. While it's true that adding oil will keep pasta from clinging together after it's cooked, I found that running water over the pasta while it's being drained removes the excess starch that congeals and makes the pasta gummy. Doing this also saves calories. After rinsing, return the pasta to the cooking pan or serving bowl and stir in a few spoonfuls of sauce to seal the pasta and prevent it from becoming watery.

TRADITIONAL ITALIAN DISHES

Homemade Pasta

Homemade pasta cooks in just a few minutes, so sample it often to prevent mushiness.

3$\frac{1}{2}$ cups all-purpose or Seminole pasta flour
$\frac{1}{2}$ teaspoon salt
2   large eggs
1$\frac{1}{4}$ cups water

Electric Pasta Maker: Measure out flour and pour into electric pasta maker per manufacturer's directions.

Mix remaining ingredients, and add them to the flour in the mixer. Mix until blended, and then extrude per manufacturer's directions. Cook, or freeze pasta in a plastic bag until ready to use.

Food Processor: Use $\frac{1}{4}$ cup additional flour. Place flour and salt in processor bowl and whirl to mix. Mix eggs and water. With processor running, pour in egg/water mixture and process just until dough begins to congeal and form course balls. Gather dough in a ball and place it in a covered bowl to rest for about 30 minutes. Knead, and then roll out to desired shapes.

SERVES 4

Mint Ricotta Filling

Our family has always used mint in lieu of parsley when making fillings for ravioli or lasagna.

2   eggs
2   tablespoons dried mint leaves (or 1 sprig chopped fresh)
      Salt and pepper to taste
1   pound ricotta cheese, drained

In a large bowl whisk together eggs, mint, salt, and pepper. Add the ricotta cheese and stir until well blended. Use at once or refrigerate until ready to use.

MAKES 1 POUND OF FILLING

Italian Meat Sauce

We used to call this "gravy" instead of sauce, because the flavor comes from the meat; the more kinds used the better. It is especially important to include pork of some type—sausage, chops, or spareribs—to get that "sweet" flavor that counteracts the acid in the tomato sauce. Some folks like to add molasses or sugar. I've found I don't like the taste of chicken or turkey in this sauce. Also, while meatballs taste great, don't rely on them for adding flavor. Freeze leftover scraps of meat or a bone from an especially delicious steak to add to this sauce when the time comes.

As in soup making, a meat sauce needs to cook long enough for the entire flavor to leech from the meat and bones, about 4 to 5 hours. When the meat falls away from the bones and the sauce gets a velvety dark color, the sauce is done. Leave the cover on the pot for the first hour or so to be sure all meat is cooked through, and then remove it for the remainder of the cooking time. If the sauce gets too thick, just add a little water. When the sauce is done, divide it into meal-sized portions and ladle into freezer containers. Allow about one scoop of sauce and one or more pieces of meat per portion. Freeze any sauce you will not use within the next 4 or 5 days.

You'll need a 10- or 12-quart stockpot. If you don't have one, divide this recipe into two smaller pans. If you plan to add Braciola, prepare it now per the directions on the opposite page, and set aside.

Heat 2 tablespoons olive oil in the bottom of the pot. Add the garlic, and sauté a minute and then add the braciola and brown it in the garlic oil. Leaving the braciola in the pan, add the tomatoes, salt, pepper, parsley, basil, oregano, and any cooked, leftover meat or bones, if you wish. Stir well, and heat sauce to simmering.

Prepare meatballs per the directions on opposite page, and add them to the sauce as they are cooked. Simmer the sauce covered for about 1 hour. Remove the cover, add the red wine, and continue to simmer for an additional 3 to 4 hours or until "done," as described above. Stir occasionally. Add water if the sauce gets too thick. Correct seasoning to taste.

MAKES ABOUT 8 QUARTS

2	tablespoons olive oil
5	to 6 cloves garlic, minced
4	pounds any combination of meats
8	28-ounce cans crushed tomatoes in tomato puree (or 4 cans crushed, 4 cans puree)
3	tablespoons salt
1	teaspoon black pepper
$^1/_2$	cup dried parsley
$^1/_4$	cup dried basil
3	tablespoons dried oregano
$^1/_4$	cup red wine (optional)

Soft Meatballs

The secret of soft meatballs is to use lots of eggs; one-egg recipes are liable to produce golf balls. If cholesterol is a concern, use the equivalent in egg substitute or replace some of the eggs with egg whites (2 egg whites equal 1 whole egg). A combination of beef, veal, and pork (meat loaf mix) will be more flavorful than plain ground beef. When adjusting this recipe, allow 4 eggs per pound of meat and 2 tablespoons of breadcrumbs per each egg added.

6	eggs
1	clove garlic, crushed and minced
3/4	cup Italian seasoned breadcrumbs
1 1/2	pounds ground meat
3	teaspoons salt
3/4	teaspoon black pepper
1 1/2	tablespoons dried parsley,
1	tablespoon dried basil
3/4	teaspoon dried oregano
	Cooking oil spray

Preheat oven to 400°. In a large mixing bowl whisk together the eggs and garlic. Add the breadcrumbs and beat with a fork until thoroughly mixed. Let mixture sit a few minutes until it thickens. Add the ground meat and remainder of seasonings. Mix well using hands or fork until completely blended. Form into balls by rolling between hands. Wet hands if meat is sticky. For uniform size, try an ice cream scoop. Use a melon scoop if making cocktail size meatballs. Lightly spray a broiler pan with cooking oil and place the meatballs on it about 1 inch apart. Bake at 400° for about 15 minutes or until cooked. Turn once halfway through. Serve plain or steep in pasta sauce or one of the marinades in the Gravies, Marinades, & Seasonings section.

MAKES 25 1 1/2-INCH MEATBALLS

Braciola

This highly seasoned beef roll is a specialty everyone will vie for. Use thin-sliced sandwich steaks in lieu of expensive cuts, as meat will tenderize as it cooks in the sauce. Be sure to cut away the string before serving.

4	sandwich steaks (about 1 pound)
1/2	teaspoon salt
1/4	teaspoon pepper
2	teaspoons dried oregano,
4	teaspoons dried parsley
2	teaspoons dried basil
	Butcher twine
1	tablespoon olive oil
1	clove garlic, crushed and minced

Lay steaks out in a single layer and sprinkle with seasonings, dividing evenly among steaks. Starting at smallest side, roll tightly and secure with string. Brown braciola in garlic and olive oil. Braise in the Italian Meat Sauce for several hours, until meat is tender.

MAKES 4 ROLLS

Baked Ziti

Make it for a crowd and freeze the leftovers. This meal tastes better each time you reheat it. Substitute home-made sauce for a real treat.

1   quart ricotta cheese, drained
1   egg, beaten
1/4 cup Parmesan cheese
1/2 teaspoon salt
     Dash black pepper
1 1/2 pounds ziti, uncooked
2   26-ounce jars prepared spaghetti sauce
     or the equivalent in a homemade or
     speed sauce
1   8-ounce package mozzarella cheese
1   8-ounce package shredded mozzarella

In a medium mixing bowl combine the ricotta cheese, egg, Parmesan cheese, salt, and pepper and set aside. Cook the ziti al dente in a large pot of boiling, salted water. Drain, rinse, and return to cooking pan for mixing. Preheat oven to 350°. Cut up the package of whole mozzarella into 1/2-inch cubes. Stir the mozzarella cubes and the ricotta mixture into the ziti with 1/2 cup of the spaghetti sauce until well combined. Pour ziti mixture into a 9 x 13 x 2-inch or larger casserole dish. Spread remaining sauce over the top, being sure to get the sides. Sprinkle shredded mozzarella over all. Bake for about 30 minutes in a 350° oven until cheese is melted and ziti is heated through. Serve with a green salad and Garlic Bread.

SERVES 8 TO 10

Stovetop Chicken Cacciatore

1   tablespoon olive oil
1   clove garlic
1/2 Vidalia or other mild onion, sliced
2   frying peppers
1   pound chicken tenders or boneless
     chicken breasts cut in two
5   ounces (1/2 package) sliced mushrooms
1   14-ounce can stewed tomatoes
1   teaspoon salt
1/8 teaspoon black pepper
1   teaspoon oregano
1   teaspoon dried basil or parsley
1/2 14-ounce can pitted black olives
1/4 to 1/2 cup red wine, chicken broth,
     or water

In a 12-inch skillet heat the olive oil over medium-high heat. Add the garlic, onion, and green pepper and sauté briefly. Add the chicken and mushrooms to the pan. Continue sautéing until chicken is browned on both sides and onions are cooked. Stir in the tomatoes, salt, pepper, oregano, basil, olives, and wine. When mixture is bubbling, cover pan and reduce heat. Cook for 20 to 30 minutes, stirring occasionally until chicken is done. Serve over rice or pasta.

To make the oven version of this popu-lar dish: Brown the chicken and vegeta-bles, stir in the remaining ingredients, and then remove them to an 8 x 8 x 2-inch square casserole dish. Cover with foil. Bake in a 350° oven for about 40 minutes, stirring once or twice. Remove cover and move chicken pieces to the top of the mixture. Continue baking uncovered another 10 minutes, until mixture is bubbly and chicken is slightly browned.

SERVES 3 TO 4

Sausage and Peppers

Everyone always enjoys this Italian favorite. Bring it to a party or make it into sandwiches. Cook the sausage and peppers separately, and then mix them afterwards to avoid a "greasy" taste.

2   1-pound packages of sweet sausages
2   1-pound packages of hot sausages
2   tablespoons olive oil
3   onions, sliced
20 frying peppers, seeded and cut into
       bite-sized pieces
2   hot Italian peppers, seeded and diced
       (optional)

Preheat oven to 400°. Cut sausages into bite-sized pieces. Place on a broiler pan and broil for 10 to 15 minutes, until cooked through. Remove from oven and set aside.

Meanwhile, in a 12-inch skillet heat the olive oil. Add the onions and sauté for a minute. Add the peppers and sauté for about 5 more minutes. Cover pan, and continue to cook on medium low until the

peppers and onions soften. Combine the cooked sausage and cooked peppers in a heatproof 2-quart casserole serving dish. Heat to serve by covering sausage and peppers casserole and placing in a 350° oven for 10 to 15 minutes. Easily reheats in the microwave.

MAKES AN 8 x 8 CASSEROLE

SPEED SAUCES

These sauces can be completed in under an hour. They are fairly healthy and fun to make. Keep your shelves stocked with canned tomatoes—stewed, pasta-ready, whole, or chopped, as well as tomato puree and/or tomato sauce (not prepared sauces, such as Ragu)—and you'll always be able to toss together a pasta topping. Use ingredients on hand and your imagination.

Fresh Herb Turkey Sauce

It might interest you to know this recipe was healthy enough to be considered for the Bon Appetit: Light, Fresh, & Easy *cookbook. For best results stick to fresh herbs. Grow them or buy them at the market, but don't give in to the temptation to substitute them with the dried ones sitting on your shelf. Cook the sauce long enough to allow the flavors to permeate this delicate sauce.*

2   tablespoons olive oil
2   cloves garlic, sliced
1   pound ground turkey
2   28-ounce cans crushed tomatoes in
       tomato puree
3/4 cup chopped fresh parsley
1/2 cup chopped fresh basil

¼ cup chopped fresh oregano

2½ teaspoons salt

¾ teaspoon black pepper

¾ cup dry white wine

2 tablespoons dried oregano

3 tablespoons dried sweet basil

½ teaspoon dried crushed red pepper

⅛ cup water or red wine

Heat the olive oil in a large 12-inch skillet or Dutch oven on medium-high heat. Sauté the garlic until browned. Sauté the turkey until it turns white. Drain excess juices from skillet, and then add the tomatoes, parsley, basil, oregano, salt, pepper, and ½ cup of the wine. Reduce the heat and simmer about 30 minutes, adding additional wine if sauce is too thick. Serve immediately over linguini or penne. Sauce may be made ahead. Store chilled or freeze until ready to use again.

MAKES ABOUT 1½ QUARTS

Ground Beef Pasta Sauce

1 tablespoon olive oil

1 large clove garlic, crushed and minced

1 small yellow onion, sliced

8 ounces mushrooms, sliced

½ teaspoon salt or to taste

½ teaspoon black pepper

1 pound meat loaf mix* or lean ground beef

1 28-ounce can crushed tomatoes in tomato purée

1 15-ounce can tomato sauce

¼ cup red wine

½ cup chopped fresh Italian parsley (or 3 to 4 tablespoons dried)

In a 12-inch skillet or heavy saucepan heat the olive oil. Add the garlic and sauté briefly. Add the onion and sauté for a few minutes, and then add the mushrooms and continue to sauté until all vegetables are softened. Remove vegetables from the pan and set aside. Sprinkle the skillet with salt and pepper. Put the ground meat in the skillet, breaking it up. Sauté until cooked. Remove the cooked meat from the pan and drain in a colander or strainer. If desired, rinse it briefly to remove surface fat. Return meat and reserved vegetables to the skillet. Add the remaining ingredients. Simmer for 30 to 45 minutes or until ready to serve. Freeze any leftover sauce.

*Meat loaf mix is a combination of beef, veal, and pork.

MAKES 1½ QUARTS

Two-Meat Sauce

This recipe calls for the sausages to be microwaved. However you can also bake, broil, or fry them.

- ½ pound sweet sausage
- ½ pound hot sausage
- 2 tablespoons olive oil
- 2 large cloves garlic, minced
- 1 large Vidalia onion or other mild onion, chopped (1½ cups)
- 8 ounces thinly sliced mushrooms
- 1½ pounds ground beef, veal, and pork mix, or lean ground beef
- 4 28-ounce cans diced seasoned tomatoes with tomato purée
- ½ cup chopped fresh Italian parsley (or 4 tablespoons dried)
- 2 tablespoons dried basil
- 1 tablespoon dried oregano
- ½ cup sliced, pitted black olives
- ¾ cup red wine
- 1 tablespoon salt or to taste
- 1½ teaspoons black pepper

Slice sausages into 1-inch pieces. Place on paper towels in a 2-quart, covered, microwave-safe container and microwave on high for 5 to 7 minutes, until cooked. (You can also bake sausage bits on a broiler pan at 400° for about 5 minutes, or fry them.) Be sure the sausage pieces are cooked through before adding them to the sauce.

In a large 12-inch skillet or Dutch oven heat the olive oil. Add the garlic and sauté briefly. Add the onion and sauté until it begins to soften. Add the ground meat and sauté until cooked. Drain the cooked sausage and ground meat in a colander or strainer to remove excess fat. Return both meats to the pan. Stir in the remaining ingredients and reheat to a simmer. Cook uncovered for 30 to 40 minutes. Serve over pasta. Freeze any remaining sauce in meal-sized containers.

MAKES ABOUT 4 QUARTS

Sausage Anise Sauce

Especially nice in the fall when fresh fennel (anise) is in season.

- 1 tablespoon olive oil
- 1 large clove garlic, crushed and minced
- 1 medium onion, chopped
- ½ head chopped fresh anise (fennel), tops removed and sliced
- ½ pound mushrooms, sliced
- 1 pound sweet Italian sausage, cut into 1-inch slices
- 2 28-ounce cans crushed tomatoes in tomato purée
- ¾ cup red wine
- ½ cup chopped fresh Italian parsley (or 4 tablespoons dried)
- 1 tablespoon oregano
- ½ teaspoon fennel seed
- ¾ teaspoon salt or to taste
- ¼ teaspoon black pepper

In a 12-inch skillet heat the olive oil. Add the garlic and sauté briefly. Add the onion and fresh anise and continue to sauté. Add the mushrooms and sauté until all the vegetables begin to soften. Meanwhile, cook the sausage in the microwave on high for about 5 minutes. Drain the sausage in a colander or strainer, and then add it to the vegetables in the skillet. (You can also cook sausage by browning in a frying pan and then covering the pan and continuing to cook on low for about 10 minutes.) Add the tomatoes, red wine, parsley, oregano, fennel seed, salt, and pepper to the pan and bring the mixture to a low boil. Cook uncovered for 30 to 45 minutes, stirring occasionally. Serve over pasta topped with Parmesan cheese.

MAKES ABOUT 1 QUART

Veggie Pasta Sauce

This sauce is so flavorful that meat lovers will swear it contains meat. Serve over hot pasta and top with shredded, soft cheese, such as mozzarella or Havarti. The cheese will melt deliciously.

1   to 2 tablespoons olive oil
2   cloves garlic, crushed and minced
1   large onion, sliced
1   small green bell pepper, seeded and sliced
1   small hot Italian or jalapeño pepper, minced (or ½ teaspoon crushed red pepper)
1   zucchini, cut in quarters and sliced
10   ounces sliced mushrooms
1   14½-ounce can stewed or diced tomatoes
1   28-ounce can crushed tomatoes with added purée
¼   cup chopped fresh Italian parsley (or 3 tablespoons dried)
1   tablespoon dried basil
2   teaspoons salt or to taste
¾   teaspoon black pepper or to taste
¼   to ½ cup red wine
½   cup sliced, pitted black olives
8   tablespoons shredded Havarti or mozzarella cheese

In a 12-inch skillet or Dutch oven sauté the garlic in olive oil on medium-high heat. Add the onion and bell pepper. Cover the pan and stir occasionally until they begin to soften. Stir in the zucchini and mushrooms. Continue cooking in the covered pan until all the vegetables are browned. Add the tomatoes, parsley, basil, salt, and pepper, and bring to a low boil. Reduce heat to low, and add the wine and olives. Simmer for 45 minutes to 1 hour. Serve over linguini or ziti, topping each portion with 2 tablespoons of the shredded cheese.

MAKES ABOUT 2 QUARTS

Mushroom-Onion Pasta Sauce

2   tablespoons olive oil
2   large cloves garlic, minced
2   medium yellow onions, sliced into rings
       (about 3 cups)
1   pound mushrooms, sliced (about 6 cups)
2   28-ounce cans tomatoes in tomato purée
½   cup red wine
1   teaspoon dried oregano
2   tablespoons dried basil
¼   teaspoon crushed red pepper
½   cup chopped fresh Italian parsley (or
       ¼ cup dried)
¾   teaspoon salt or to taste
    Shredded Havarti or mozzarella cheese
       for garnish (allow 2 tablespoons per
       person)

Heat the olive oil on medium-high in a
12-inch skillet or Dutch oven. Add the
garlic and sauté briefly. Stir in the onions,
breaking up rings. Reduce heat to medium
and cook, covered, for 5 minutes, stirring
occasionally. Stir in the mushrooms.
Continue to cook, covered, for another 10
to 15 minutes, until vegetables soften. Add
remaining ingredients except the cheese
and bring to a low boil. Continue to cook
uncovered for 30 to 40 minutes. Stir occasionally. Sauce will begin to thicken and
become glossy. Serve over ziti topped with
2 tablespoons shredded cheese per portion.

MAKES ABOUT 1¾ QUARTS

Part 2: Specialty Menus

RECIPE FOR SEDUCTION

Kiss in public

Remind him that he has a cute butt

Plan a surprise getaway vacation

Remember that the way to a man's heart is through his stomach

Ditch the sweat clothes

Smile and act interested in everything he says, no matter how boring

Wear thong underwear

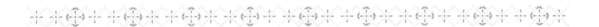

ROMANTIC MENUS FOR TWO

Oh, why not? What else are you and your hubby doing tonight besides fighting over the TV remote?—and you have the whole house to yourselves!

No need to shut the bedroom door . . .

I would have sold my soul for an iota of privacy when the kids were growing up. I love them—but. It's not long after the honeymoon that babies come along. You and your husband are so thrilled to have them that you don't miss your privacy at first. You're much too busy doting over your children to notice that life as a "couple" has drastically changed. You can barely sit down to dinner and have an intelligent conversation, let alone go out for a spontaneous dinner by yourselves. So you adapt and learn the art of compromise. You take the kids out with you or you hire a sitter. Those heart-to-heart talks about your feelings and aspirations that once formed the foundation for your relationship now take low priority as conversations twist toward school-work, sports, dancing lessons, and clean bedrooms.

Your kids' lives have become so integrated with yours that it's a supreme effort to preserve your love life. This happens so gradually that you don't realize it until the first time you cast your arm over the side of the bed whilst in the throes of passion and it lands atop a curly little head. So you start closing your bedroom door and training the kids to knock. When they're little, it's easy to invent excuses to explain these situations. But they get smarter with age. After all, they're your kids. When they start mimicking the moans they've heard emanating from your room at the dinner table, you know they're on to your little trysts. So, when you decide you want to make love, you not only shut the door, but you lock it and turn up the clock radio. Noisy, not necessarily romantic, but it gets the job done.

Well, you can forget all that now that it's just the two of you. Your privacy is back if you want it. At first you feel nervous doing something as simple as walking around the house in your underwear. You half expect to run into some pimply teenager hanging out with your son. After the first few times, you become comfortable with the freedom. You dash down to the laundry area in your bra and panties to touch up your blouse or pull something to wear out of the dryer and get dressed on the spot.

Finally, you and your husband can languish in bed with the door open, enjoying an early morning quickie or an afternoon delight. Granted, we aren't as agile and inventive as we used to be, and everything is hanging a bit lower, but we shouldn't allow this to spoil our fun. Approach the situation with practicality. Showering together will save water. Sexual exercise will reduce stress and keep you fit. Your time and life are yours once again. You no longer need to close your bedroom door to get dressed or to munch down that candy bar you don't want the kids to know you have.

MENUS FOR ROMANCE

You'll probably notice there is no dessert included in these menus. Use your imagination. If the meal falls flat, keep some candy around as a default dessert. You can never go wrong with chocolate kisses.

*   *   *

It's a beautiful evening. The sun has just set and the sky is a riot of orange and lavender streaks. I fluff my hair, repair my lipstick, and fight the urge to change into my favorite sweats tonight. It's our anniversary, and I want to cook a special meal. Something sumptuous but easy. We'll eat in the dining room, and I'll use our good china, the sterling silver flatware that was my mother's, and the crystal wineglasses. He won't even notice he's only eating beef stew with this setup. I keep preparation simple and rely on an exotic ingredient or special liquor to give my stew a gourmet twist. I select a bottle of Pinot Noir wine from our pitiful supply of reds and uncork it to "breathe." Haven't you always wondered why wine has to breathe? Does it suffocate in the bottle? I pour myself a taster and start cooking. . . .

Beef Pinot Noir, p. 37

SOURDOUGH FRENCH BREAD
STRAWBERRY GINGER TOSSED SALAD, P. 185
THE REMAINDER OF THE BOTTLE OF PINOT NOIR WINE

Buy some fresh, crusty bread for dipping into the stew. Start the stew cooking, and then make the vinaigrette. Prepare the ingredients for the salad and place in them in a salad bowl. Chill the salad ingredients and the vinaigrette separately while the stew is cooking. When you are ready to dine, toss the salad with the dressing and serve the stew in soup bowls.

Pour the Pinot Noir wine and drop an extra strawberry in each glass. Heat the bread, so it will be hot, but don't slice it. Look deep into each other's eyes and, à la Tom Jones style, rip hunks of bread from the loaf and dunk them into the stew. If this doesn't get your old geezer going, open a second bottle of wine, or try again with the next dinner.

Peppered Jack Daniel's Steak, p.62

MICROWAVE BAKED POTATOES
RED LETTUCE WITH APPLES AND FENNEL, P. 182
CABERNET SAUVIGNON RED WINE

Cook two large baking potatoes either in the microwave oven or the old-fashioned way. Once the potatoes are cooked, wrap them in aluminum foil to keep them hot. Prepare the salad dressing and cut up the vegetables you will need to make the salad and the steak recipe. The steaks are prepared last, so go ahead and put the salad together; dress it at the last minute.

When the last batch of steaks is cooking, toss the salad and set out the potatoes. Ask your husband to uncork the wine and pour it (if you haven't already dipped into it). Serve the steaks on a platter with the sauce on top or on the side. Use the sauce on your baked potato instead of butter. Men love this meal. This will work as long as he doesn't eat too much and fall asleep on you.

Basil Pork Tenderloin with Mango Chutney Glaze, p.86

OVEN-BAKED SWEET POTATOES
MINTED PEAS, P. 172
BASIC GARDEN SALAD WITH "WING IT" VINAIGRETTE, PGS. 180–181
MERLOT RED WINE

Preheat oven to 400° about an hour before dinner. Start two well-scrubbed sweet potatoes baking while you prepare the tenderloin. Place the tenderloin in the oven to bake about half an hour before serving time. While food is cooking, prepare and cook the peas and set the table. Ask your husband to listen for the oven timer while you run into your dressing room and put on something daring. If the buzzer goes off before you're ready, keep him occupied by asking him to slice the meat, light the candles, and pour you another glass of Merlot.

Chicken Chardonnay, p.70

MICROWAVE GLAZED CARROTS, P. 172
WHITE RICE
CAESAR SALAD, P. 183
THE REMAINDER OF THE CHARDONNAY

This meal takes only 30 minutes to make, so start by making the salad dressing and setting the table. Open the wine and pour yourself a dollop while you work. Prepare the carrots and microwave them just before you begin cooking the cutlets. While the last cutlets are cooking, complete the salad and put the carrots on the table. Call your honey and finish making the sauce while he's pouring the wine. Prospects for romance are good with this dinner.

PASSIONATE MIMOSAS, P. 24

Apple-stuffed Cornish Hens, p.87

RICE PILAF WITH LIME, PINE NUTS, AND GOLDEN RAISINS, P. 160
BABY GREENS WITH MUSTARD VINAIGRETTE, P. 184
THE REST OF THE CHAMPAGNE

Preheat the oven and prepare the hens. While the hens are baking, prepare the Rice Pilaf and set the table. Ask your man to open the champagne bottle and make up the mimosas. Prepare the salad 10 minutes before the hens are done. Your husband will feast like a king, and you'll be Queen for the night.

Coquille Saint Joy, p.55

RECYCLED CHINESE RICE, P. 162
BROCCOLI-ORANGE SALAD, P. 189
PINOT GRIGIO WINE

Start preparation about 40 minutes before you and your honey will be ready to dig in. Prepare the salad, dress, and chill it. Then, prepare the scallops up to the point of baking them. Mix the rice and heat. Run a comb through your hair and smear on some dark red lipstick (men love red). Bake the scallops and assemble the salad. Good luck.

Garlic Shrimp, p.52

BUTTERED ANGEL HAIR PASTA, P. 52
SOURDOUGH ROLLS
MULTI-COLORED TOMATO SALAD, P. 189
LIME SHERBET
PARSLEY LEAVES
WHITE ZINFANDEL WINE

Make the salad, dress it, and refrigerate it. If you wish to shell the shrimp, do this in advance. Although the shrimp and pasta won't take more than 20 minutes to prepare, they need to be cooked last minute, so beautify yourself and set up the table. Garlic is okay if both of you are eating it, so chow down without guilt. My recommendation is to serve the shrimp with shells on. This may keep your sweetie at the dinner table long enough to develop a bit of romance—maybe he'll even forgo that game on TV. I've read lime sherbet counteracts garlic breath, and it will go well with this meal. The parsley? Oh that's to chew on to get rid of the garlic smell if the sherbet fails you.

Bon appetit—and good luck!

RECIPE FOR LURING THE KIDS HOME

Listen to them without judgment

Know when to keep your mouth shut and your eyes closed

Ditch the guilt trip

Appreciate everything they do for you

Display photos of them throughout your home

Never send them home empty-handed

Offer to do their laundry

FAMILY VISITS

Good, basic stick-to-the-ribs foods that have always been favorites at our house fit the bill on those Sunday evenings or weeknights when our gang is together for a good "new-fashioned" family dinner. I make stuff ahead and freeze it so I don't have to spend precious hours in the kitchen, when I could be helping to select a wedding gown for my bride-to-be or looking at cars with my son.

The kids are coming . . .

This weekend all the kids will be coming home—with their families. I can't stand the excitement. I've been running around changing beds and sprucing up their old rooms. My grocery list fills the backs of two #10 envelopes. The phone lines have been buzzing all week. They'll all arrive at different times on Friday night, so a large pot of soup or stew will do for dinner. Saturday, the girls and I will go shopping, and I'll find something outrageous to buy each one of them. The guys will play golf. Our boat's not in the water yet, otherwise we would all spend the weekend at the shore. No matter what our activities, we'll squeeze in a family dinner. I've been scouring through the magazines and all my cookbooks for ideas.

They're here, and it feels just like old times again! It's early Saturday morning. I sit at the kitchen table, sipping my coffee long before the kids straggle downstairs, and putting together a "chore list" for our dinner. Dinner preparation at our house is a family affair. Even the men chop and peel, except The King. He's in the family room plugged into the TV, blatantly refusing to do "women's work." We've come to enjoy dining in our dining room, using our good china and linen tablecloths. Why not? They are expendable; my family isn't. Most times we sit at the table for hours, laughing and rehashing old stories. Friends stop over and join us. It's a wild time. And, the best part is that the dishes are magically disappearing from the table and into the dishwasher without me having to leave my roost on the chair closest to the kitchen.

What a change from those old mealtimes that were fraught with pea fights and complaints. There was always someone who didn't like something or someone. It's amazing. Now that my children have grown, they'll eat almost anything—even raw clams. When they were little, the only pork that would pass their lips was a hot dog. They thought beef was a burger, and veggies were fries. None of them are fussy eaters anymore, except for the Brussels sprouts, and they've even acquired "gourmet" appetites.

"All this togetherness is bliss," you tell yourself. It's wonderful to be in the midst of their familiar commotion again. You work out the sleeping arrangements so only the married ones share the same beds; then you shut your bedroom door when you go to sleep. In the morning, you hustle to the kitchen without looking up, down, or sideways. Some things parents are better off not knowing. You get back into the groove, hoping the smell of those cinnamon buns you're baking will get your gang up sooner, so you can sit in your robes and gab over pots and pots of coffee.

It's noisy. It's messy. Your countertops are littered with half-full glasses and plates with crumbs, none of which you can put into your dishwasher because it's full of last night's dinner dishes. The sinks in your bathrooms are speckled with wisps of hair, and the toilet paper roll needs to be changed. Wet towels droop from doorknobs and puddle to the floor. Someone left the bathroom fan on. They're home. Your babies. And, despite all this clutter, you're loving it because you know by this time tomorrow, as much as you'll miss them, they'll be gone. And you'll have all the time in the world to restore your house to order.

FAMILY DINNERS

When making any kind of meal where the kitchen will be busy with people traffic, I find it helps to write down the list of items to be served and a cooking and preparation timetable. Having a written reference can prevent finding the cranberry salad intact in the fridge the next day, or committing the unforgivable sin of neglecting to put the roast in the oven.

You'll notice that many of these menus call for homemade bread. I had to find some way to use up all the loaves stored in my freezer! You'll read about my new toy, the electric bread maker, later. But suffice it to say that I make up several loaves whenever I have time and am in the mood and keep them frozen until an opportunity arises to serve bread. Everyone thinks I've been slaving all day. If you don't want to spend the time making bread, buy it. For before-dinner munchies I usually put out some cheese and crackers, and maybe some mixed nuts.

Pot Roast in a Bag, p.79

MIXED GREENS, GRAPES, & ALMONDS WITH LIME VINAIGRETTE, P. 186
SEEDED ONION BREAD, P. 199
CLASSIC APPLE PIE, P. 216
FRENCH VANILLA ICE CREAM

Make the onion bread ahead and freeze it, or place the ingredients in your electric bread maker and turn it on. (This is guaranteed to wake the kids up.) Once the kids are sitting around the kitchen table gabbing over morning coffee, put out the apples and peelers and set them to work. (Fruit pies can also be made ahead and frozen for baking another time.) Bake the pie and let it cool in a place where it will be safe from sampling. Remove bread from the freezer and allow it to defrost completely.

About 3 hours before dinner: Prepare the pot roast and place it into the oven. Have the kids help you prepare the vegetables for the roast and the salad, and mix up the salad dressing. Once the roast is done, crisp up the bread, toss the salad and dinner is served. I usually place the pie into the turned-off oven to warm while we are eating dinner. Scoop the ice cream over the pie.

Roast Lamb with Potatoes, Carrots, and Onions, p.82

TOSSED GREENS WITH ORANGE-OREGANO VINAIGRETTE, P. 182
SUNFLOWER BREAD, P. 202
MILE-HIGH LEMON MERINGUE PIE, P. 218

Make the pie and the Sunflower Bread in advance. Wrap the sunflower bread tightly in foil and freeze it as soon as it is cool. Chill the pie in the basement refrigerator to guarantee it will be intact by dinnertime. Remove the bread from the freezer sometime before noon and let it defrost. About 2 hours before dinnertime, gather your children around you in the kitchen and prepare the lamb for the oven. Snack on cheese and crackers and gab while you prepare the salad and lamb chops and set the table for dinner. When the roast is ready, put the bread in the oven to crisp the crust. While the dinner dishes are being cleared, start the coffee and send your son-in-law down to retrieve the pie.

London Broil with Rum Marinade, p. 80

GRILLED GARDEN VEGETABLE PACKETS, P. 170
HOME-FRIED POTATOES, P. 154
FRENCH BAGUETTE
PINEAPPLE TOSSED GREENS, P. 186
VANILLA ICE CREAM WITH FRESH BLUEBERRIES

Wash blueberries and prepare salad greens and vegetables in advance. About an hour before dinner, invite the kids into the kitchen and assign chores. Make the meat marinade and the salad dressing. (Set aside the pineapple chunks.) Place the meat in a marinating dish (or a zip-lock plastic bag) and chill. Turn once or twice. Prepare home fries for cooking and set the table.

30 minutes before dinner: Start the home fries cooking and preheat the grill or broiler.

20 minutes before serving: Begin cooking steaks; make and dress salad.

When steaks and home fries are done, dinner is ready!

Gourmet Turkey Burgers, p.83

PERFECT POTATO SALAD, P. 159
BROCCOLI-VIDALIA SALAD, P. 190
HAZELNUT BROWNIES, P. 222

Make the potato salad, broccoli salad, and brownies in advance. About ½ hour before dinner, have your son or husband fire up the grill and ask your daughters to mix up the burgers while you fuss with the paper plates, rolls, and garnishes. Once the burgers are on the grill, you have 10 or 15 minutes to set up the condiments and prepare the table ready for dining. If it's not grilling weather, I'm afraid you'll be broiling indoors, but you'll enjoy the meal just the same because you'll be together.

Healthy Meat Loaf, p.80

SMASHED PARSLEY POTATOES, P. 157
OREGANO GREEN BEANS, P. 172
GARDEN SALAD WITH "WING IT" VINAIGRETTE, PGS. 180–181
ORANGE CHOCOLATE-CHIP COOKIES, P. 224

Make the cookies ahead and store them in a plastic container. About 1½ hours before dinner prepare the meat loaf and put it into the oven. (If I have 8 people, I make two meat loaves.) Thirty minutes before dinner, cook and prepare the potatoes and make the salad. Cook the beans. When the meat loaf is done, serve dinner. Hopefully, there will still be cookies left for dessert.

Triple-Bean Chicken Stew with Dumplings, p. 38

FRESH ORANGE SALAD, P. 191
SPICED BANANA-NUT CAKE, P. 213

This is a good dinner for days when you are not certain who and how many will arrive for dinner, just like old times. One day ahead, make the Carrot Pineapple Mold and the cake. Prepare the stew at least one hour before you plan to serve your first dinner shift and allow it to simmer until the last kid is fed.

Baked Ziti with Two-Meat Pasta Sauce, pgs. 103 & 106

ORANGE-FENNEL SALAD, P. 190
GARLIC BREAD, P. 206
ITALIAN PASTRIES

Stop at a good Italian bakery and buy the pastries. Get extra cannolies and eat them in the car on the way home. Make ziti and sauce one day or more ahead (both freeze well) and reheat about 1½ hours before dinner. Make salad and chill. Prepare Garlic Bread and heat 5 minutes before dinner. Now, go ahead, gorge yourselves!

RECIPE FOR BEING MERRY

Lead a Congo line through the dance floor to the tune of "Jingle Bells"

Do a good deed for someone in need

Smile and say hello to people you don't know

Sing along with your car radio with the windows open

Surround yourself with happy people

Give the gift of love

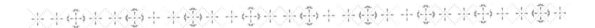

HOLIDAY FEASTS

Enjoy special occasions by doing as much in advance as possible. Set the table with the good china, silverware, crystal, and linens. Some simple decorations— a floral centerpiece and a festive item, such as a candy cane or a tiny basket filled with Easter candy at each place setting—will make your table look appealing. If you have animals, close off the dining room once the table is set or you may find your pet snacking on your centerpiece.

Joy to the world?

It's wonderful to share holiday meals with family and good friends. I'd gotten so accustomed to cooking celebratory meals many times a year that, when I no longer had the occasion to cook these dinners, I felt hollow inside. Of all the holidays, Christmas is the most special to me, not only because it's my birthday, and I get double presents, but because it has always been a time of joy and celebration in our home. I've been dreading the first Christmas without the kids since diamond rings started sparkling on their fingers. It was coming. I just didn't know when. It was after one of our most splendid holidays, which now included fiancés, that our kids dropped the bomb. They would spend the next Christmas with their in-laws. That way it would work out that we'd be together every other year. It made sense. Fair is fair. But, what do my husband and I do with ourselves on our "off" years?

I had almost a year to obsess about Christmas without the kids. The closer Christmas came, the more depressed I became. Being bombarded with all the "merriness" was like a slap in the face, underscoring what we wouldn't have. I took to writing morose little poems, which I've cleverly hidden away. My husband and I toyed with the idea of spending Christmas on a sunny beach drinking Piña Coladas. But it's Christmas everywhere! So, I resorted to whining about our situation to our friends and relatives, until holiday invitations started to roll in. All the time I'd been reassuring the kids, who were becoming increasingly concerned about us, that we would be "just fine." And we were.

My husband and I put on a brave front and went through the customary motions. We struck out one miserable, sleety day in search of the family Christmas tree and slopped through the tree farm in slushy muck to get it and bring it home. The two of us managed to erect this 12-foot monster, but left it stark naked for weeks until we could lure some of the kids to the house to help trim it. The only thing more depressing than decorating the tree alone is wrapping packages and listening to Christmas music by oneself. I usually manage to soak a few packages with tears reminiscing about loved ones to whom I can no longer give gifts. I experience many emotions at Christmas time, even on a normal year.

For the most part, Christmas alone wasn't so bad. We had enough invites out to be embarrassing. I decorated the house with "boughs of holly" and made some sorry attempts at "fa-la-la-la-la-ing." Yet, I couldn't shake the depression. So, I planned a large party to entice the kids into coming for New Year's. And then it hit me. There was no need to miss Christmas with the kids. We would merely delay it one week. We saved our presents until then—which gave me time to buy more stuff. While other folks were out exchanging gifts after Christmas, I was still shopping. I enjoyed lolling around on those hectic pre-Christmas days, when everyone else was caught up in the crush. I stayed out of the supermarket, ate sumptuous meals out, and didn't bake one damn Christmas cookie. But it was odd leaving the packages I'd wrapped sitting under the tree after December 25—the cats got bored chewing on the ribbons and batting the Christmas balls.

That year, when the kids arrived on December 30th, we mentally set back the clock and pretended it was Christmas Eve. We hung stockings and shook packages, and then feasted on traditional fare. We stayed up well past midnight singing carols, unwrapping presents, and swigging eggnog, and then woke up the next morning and raced around cleaning up the mess and making hors d'oeuvres for our New Year's party that evening.

It was exhausting, but I can honestly say we had a "merry" Christmas, two of them. Our friends came through for us on Christmas Eve, our niece spoiled us with dinner and presents on Christmas Day, and we celebrated Christmas with the kids after all. I realized that it might not work out as well on our next "off" year. But, I learned that it doesn't matter when we celebrate, as long as we can spend time together sometime during the Christmas season.

A few years have past since that first Christmas alone, and my husband and I have mellowed. The years the kids can make it home are the most joyous, but some years we travel to their homes or share the holiday with good friends. Friends—what would we do without them? On the "off" years, we choose a smaller tree and decorate it ourselves. We plan a party, and sometimes I even bake cookies.

HOLIDAY MENUS

To simplify last-minute kitchen chores and leave more time for merriment, prepare and freeze long-cooking or complex dishes, such as soups, pies, cookies, and homemade breads. I draw on this cache of meal accompaniments and desserts throughout the holidays. If you aren't into devoting time to homemade treats, buy desserts and breads from a reputable baker, and doctor up canned soups.

Set up your table early in the day, expand it as needed, and make certain you have enough chairs to seat your guests. Place tags can eliminate last minute scurrying for seats. Rather than deal with the awkwardness of passing large bowls of foods when serving a crowd of 10 or more, I find it easiest either to set out the main course foods on a buffet table or to prepare plates and serve them from the kitchen. Always be sure to offer seconds! To enhance the festiveness of the occasion, serve both red and white wines with dinner, as well as before-dinner cocktails or champagne and after-dinner liqueurs.

Another consideration when producing a roasted meal is oven space. Wouldn't it be nice if we all had double ovens available for company occasions? If you are operating on one oven and a microwave like most of us, think through the size of casserole dishes and roasting pans you use to be certain that two or more will fit on your oven racks at the same time. Having sufficient refrigerator space can also be an issue. One holiday, our refrigerator had the audacity to conk out on us. We functioned out of coolers, and because it was wintertime, we were able to set many things outdoors. Cold weather can be a godsend! Should you set food outdoors, be sure to cover it well to protect it from the neighborhood dogs, cats, and squirrels.

TURKEY SAUSAGE MINESTRONE, P. 35

Tenderloin of Beef with Red Wine Marinade, p. 78

STUFFED POTATOES, P. 155
LEMON SAGE GREEN BEANS, P. 171
HOMEMADE BRIOCHE, P. 201
HOLIDAY TOSSED SALAD, P. 187
APPLE PIE WITH CRANBERRIES & CURRANTS, P. 217
FRENCH VANILLA ICE CREAM
COFFEE WITH BAILEY'S IRISH CREAM

Make the soup, brioche, marinade, and the pie in advance. I usually make several apple pies each fall and freeze them unbaked. Defrost and bake the pie early in the day, and bake the potatoes in the same oven. While potatoes are still warm, scoop out the insides and prepare the stuffing. Stuff the potatoes and set them on a cookie sheet. Chill until just before dinner, when they will be warmed and top-browned. Marinate the meat at least 1 hour before roasting it. Wash and prepare the lettuce and make the salad dressing. (Do not refrigerate the dressing.)

Put the roast in the oven 1 or 2 hours before serving time, depending on its size and the doneness desired. Reheat the soup and allow it to simmer until you are ready to serve it. When the roast is cooked, remove it from oven and cover lightly with foil. Cook the green beans and let stand covered. Heat the rolls and serve them with the soup. Slice the meat and serve the main course. Don't forget to pour lots of wine. Offer coffee with a choice of cream or Bailey's for whitening and serve it with warm pie topped with ice cream. Save the dishes for later.

SHRIMP COCKTAIL WITH LOUIE-STYLE SAUCE, PGS. 16-17

Roast Turkey, p. 90

MAKE-AHEAD MASHED POTATOES, P. 156
SPICED ACORN SQUASH, P. 173
BROCCOLI DIJON, P. 170
DINNER ROLLS
GINGER-PEAR CRANBERRY SAUCE, P. 176
CELERY, ANISE, AND OLIVE PLATTER WITH SEASONED DIPPING OIL, P. 192
MOUNT GAY PUMPKIN PIE WITH WHIPPED CREAM, P. 219
GOURMET HAZELNUT COFFEE

Buy ready-to-eat cocktail shrimp and keep them cold. Make the pie, potatoes, squash, cranberry and Louie sauces up to one day ahead. Clean, cut up, and prepare the celery platter and wash and prepare the broccoli. The day of, set and decorate the table. Arrange the shrimp in serving cups and top with sauce. Cover and chill. Put the turkey in the oven according to the cooking chart, timing it so it will be cooked about 30 minutes before you plan to serve the first course. Whip (and chill) the cream.

1½ hours before serving: Slip the potatoes in with the turkey. Once the turkey is cooked, remove it from the oven and cover it lightly with foil. Make the gravy and allow it to simmer on low, or set it aside and reheat it in the microwave just before serving.

30 minutes before serving: Cook the broccoli and the reheat the acorn squash. (This is also when you'll be making the turkey gravy.) Cover all cooked foods to keep them hot until serving time.

10 minutes before serving: Light the candles, fill wine glasses, set out the shrimp cocktail and rolls, and then ring the dinner bell.

For the main course, ask The King to carve the turkey. Do this at the table or in the kitchen depending on his flair for entertaining. In the meantime, set out all other main course accompaniments. Serve the celery platter as a next course. Mix up the oil dipping sauce in small cups at the table. Start the coffee. For dessert, serve the pie with dollops of whipped cream. If you like liqueurs, Frangelico will give regular coffee a hazelnut kick.

MIXED GREEN SALAD PLATTER WITH WALNUTS AND BLUE CHEESE, P. 184

Peppercorn-Crusted Roast Lamb, p. 82

ROSEMARY ASPARAGUS, P. 171
ORANGE-THYME POTATOES AND ONIONS, P. 158
CINNAMON FRUIT, P. 176
SOFT ROLLS
SPONGE CAKE WITH KIRSCH CREAM, P. 214
FRENCH VANILLA COFFEE

Early in the day, prepare salad platter and dressing. Chill both until ready to serve. Bake sponge cake. Set the table.

2½ hours before serving time: Prepare the roast and place it into the oven to bake. Make Kirsch Cream and chill.

45 minutes before serving time: Cut up the potatoes and onions and place them in the oven with the roast. Prepare the asparagus but do not cook it until ten minutes before serving time. Heat the Cinnamon Fruit either in the oven or in the microwave.

When roast is done, remove it from oven and allow it to rest, lightly covered with foil. Turn oven temperature up and continue cooking potatoes until they are brown and crispy. If you wish, make Pan Gravy. Heat the rolls and serve with the salad. Carve the roast and serve the main course. You may frost the cake with the cream just before serving or serve it in squares with dollops of the Kirsch Cream.

SWISS CHARD AND BEAN SOUP WITH HAM, P. 34

Fruited Pork Roast, p. 85

LEMON ROASTED VEGETABLES, P. 168
PILLSBURY REFRIGERATED BISCUITS
ROASTED CHESTNUTS, P. 176
PRALINE-CRUSTED APPLE PIE, P. 217
CINNAMON TEA

Make the soup and pie ahead and freeze them. Spend some time the morning of your dinner party getting some of the messy work out of the way. Bake the pie, and then start the chestnuts soaking. Prepare the fruit compote and stuff the pork roast. Place the prepared roast in a baking pan and chill it until you are ready to cook it. Place leftover compote stuffing in a small heatproof casserole and set it aside. Set the table.

3 hours before dinner: Put the pork roast and compote casserole into the oven to bake. Remove the compote casserole as soon as it is bubbling and set aside to serve at room temperature with the entrée.

1½ hours before dinner: Prepare vegetable casserole and put it in the oven along with the pork. Start heating the soup.

30 minutes before dinner: When the roast is done, remove it from the oven and cover it lightly. Bake the biscuits, and then serve them with the soup as a first course.

Carve the pork roast and serve it with the roasted vegetables and the compote. Put the chestnuts in to roast, timing them to be cooked by the time you have devoured the main course. Your guests can snack on these while you boil the water for the tea and get some of the dishes cleared. By the time your kitchen is semi-presentable, your diners will be ready for dessert.

Bouillabaisse, p. 58

DRIED TOMATO BRIE WITH CRACKERS, P. 19
PINEAPPLE TOSSED SALAD, P. 186
HOMEMADE FRENCH BREAD, P. 199
STRAWBERRY PIE WITH AMARETTO CRUST, P. 220

This is an elegant, easy to prepare dinner. Make the bread and pie, and prepare (but do not bake) the Brie in advance. Buy only the freshest seafood for the Bouillabaisse. If your pocketbook smarts, you'll find the Flaming Choppino is also very good, at a lower price.

Prepare the fish. Separate each type of seafood into layers in a storage container, placing the quickest cooking seafood on the bottom. Cover and refrigerate until 30 minutes before dinner.

Prepare as much of the salad in advance as you can and refrigerate it in the bowl. Set the table. Bake the brie once your first guest arrives, and set out with crackers as an hors d'oeuvre. If you are in the kitchen working, chances are you won't be alone, so have all your ingredients premeasured and set out in case you get distracted. Heat the bread. Ask someone to assemble the salad and slice the bread while you watch the pot. Serve the Bouillabaisse as soon as it is done. I usually dish it out in the kitchen to make certain each person has an equal amount of shellfish. Relax. The bulk of your work is done. Sit back and enjoy the compliments.

This section wouldn't be complete without a brunch menu. Serving brunch works well when you have houseguests during the holidays or when you are splitting the family with in-laws and you lost the dinner bid.

PASSIONATE MIMOSAS, P. 24

Regatta Strata, p. 92

SPIRAL-CUT BAKED HAM
BLUEBERRY-PEAR COBBLER, P. 208
WINTER FRUIT COMPOTE, P. 191
ORANGE JUICE
COFFEE OR TEA

Make the strata one day in advance, as it needs to be refrigerated overnight. Order a spiral-cut honeybaked ham or cook your own. Serve ham cold or at room temperature. The cobbler and fruit compote will taste freshest if made the same day, but if you haven't the time or assistance to get it done, do it the day before as well. Slip the strata in the oven about an hour before serving. When your company arrives, offer mimosas or orange juice and *mangé*.

RECIPE FOR HAVING FUN

Omit unkind people from your guest list

Take shortcuts

Visit with your guests

Mix age groups and interest groups

Kick off your shoes

Dance 'til you drop

PARTY HEARTY

What better way to lift your spirits than to share time with your favorite people? Once you get started by choosing the date, time, place, and type of party, the rest will fall into place. Send out formal invitations, make a dozen phone calls, or generate emails to share your information, and then have a good time planning the fun.

Happiness is gratitude . . .

If you are feeling lonely and empty because the kids are gone, it means that you've made them your primary source of happiness. What a terrible responsibility to place on those you love. Each new day brings new reasons to be grateful. Look around and see with new eyes that you are blessed. Life is seldom perfect, and if it were, there would be no way for us to appreciate goodness when it comes along.

Contrast helps us understand how much we truly have, and how fortunate we are. If you've a soft bed to sleep on, a full larder, shelter from the elements, and a loving family, you are armed to handle almost anything life can deal out. You have a support network waiting to catch you when you are ill, someone you care about dies, you lose your job, or are simply embarrassed about your bad haircut. The learning part of life is dealing with adversity and coming out on top. To do this, we need to fight with every ounce of internal strength we can muster. We need to fight against depression, shyness—if you don't speak up about a problem, you are cheating yourself—and, also against prejudice and hatred. How we choose to react and handle adversity makes us the person we are.

Years ago I was pretty mellow as a stay-at-home housewife with three children. When my former husband became an abusive alcoholic who took pleasure in making me feel as important as a pea, I blamed myself. The turning point was when I realized that there was nothing wrong with me, only him. I couldn't salvage that relationship, but I did save myself and my children from further destitution by pulling myself together and recreating our lives. I found strength I never thought I had, and traded my doormat ways for independence and self-sufficiency. With three young children to support—my ex was jobless by now—I used a can-do attitude to secure a sitter and a decent job. I gathered my children around me and we were one, a new family, a strong one whose bonds remain today, which is probably why I've been whining so much about them leaving our nest.

I thank God every day for having experienced that crisis, because if my ex-husband hadn't been such a jerk, I might've never tested my personal strength and learned that life is what you make it. I've been married a second time for more than twenty-five years, now, to a wonderful guy who took on three babies as his own. I have so much to be grateful for; if you sit down and think about it, so do you.

General Party Planning

Is this a special occasion? If so, it will be easy to gear decorations and foods to the event. The type of event may also dictate the time of day and the kind of guests you'll invite. For example, few men will want to attend a bridal shower or a baby shower—except when the food is being served. While daytime events may call for tea, coffee, or punch, evening soirées beg for cocktails. Most men go for basic hearty foods while women are more apt to be tempted by tiny sandwiches and fancy hors d'oeuvres.

What to serve

I've found fussing over intricate appetizers breeds leftovers that no one will touch. I learned my lesson at one Christmas cocktail party when all the fancy stuff was barely touched, yet the mini-meatballs in sauce and the shrimp were history. When menu planning, also keep in mind that you will need to please many kinds of palates:

vegans, dieters, and those with food intolerances such as lactose or gluten. Include foods that everyone will or can eat to avoid grumbling stomachs.

Serving both a raw vegetable and a fresh fruit platter at any party helps dieters and vegetarians stick to their guns, supplements the meal or selection of prepared appetizers, and is healthy snack food that can be easily offered to children. Leftovers store easily and can always be enjoyed. I usually pick up fruit and vegetable platters from the supermarket. Depending on how elegant your party will be, the vegetables and fruits can be either left in their original plastic platter or rearranged on your own platter. Buy a selection of cheeses and cut them up, or have a platter made up by the deli. Also, find the olive mixtures, fancy mustards, small rolls, pretzels, and tortilla chips there.

Another versatile food is a spiral-cut ham (or turkey breast), which can be used as a main entrée or stuffed in small rolls for cocktail sandwiches. I find the Honey Baked Ham brand, though expensive, has excellent texture and taste. I have to stop guests from picking at it long after I've removed it from the table.

Location

If your party will be outdoors, you'll need to see that the lawn is mowed and the weeds are hacked down. Hose down plastic or wooden chairs that are exposed, and rearrange lawn furniture. Beg, borrow, or rent additional chairs for large parties. Have a few lawn games handy for daytime parties. Set up a grill and coolers. I've found it pays to be prepared to move a party indoors, as outdoor events—unless you've arranged for cover—occasionally are rained out. Decide where you can relocate the party—a tent, a screened-in porch, the garage, or indoors—to avoid last-minute scampers or provide a rain date along with your invitation.

Set-up for an indoor party

Your home is undoubtedly neater and cleaner since the kids have moved out. Tidy up, vacuum, dust, and tend to any chronic problem areas. I always remind myself to check the upholstery for cat hair, lest someone wearing a dark color sits down and then arises with a furry butt. If you are decorating for an occasion, do this next. Prepare the buffet table. Organize utensils, plates, napkins, and serving pieces. Arrange some sort of centerpiece. Set some candles and flowers around your home, along with small bowls of nuts, candy, or party mix.

Commission a beverage area. For large parties, I use the corner of the kitchen between the table and the sliding glass door. All the glasses and liquor bottles and red wines go on the table, while beer, white wines, and soft drinks are kept chilled in a large cooler set on the floor or on the porch. Depending on the nature of the party, a punch bowl may be situated either on the kitchen table, on a nearby countertop, or on the dining room table.

Food serving precautions

It's not nice to send your guests home with food poisoning, so do exercise food safety precautions when handling foods containing meat, seafood, or dairy products. Bacterial life begins at 40°F and expires at 140°F. During their prime breeding temperatures, known as the "Danger Zone," bacteria can double in number in less than twenty minutes.

Keep hot foods hot by using warming trays or chafing dishes and by keeping food covered whenever possible. To keep salads and deli meat platters safe, serve them on ice. Create a simple ice nest for your bowl or platter by putting some ice cubes in a shallow baking pan or in a zip-lock bag. Pay attention to how long particular dishes are left out and how they are displayed. Avoid leaving hot or cold perishable foods out for more than two hours, one hour in hot weather. At a party, where several dishes are left out buffet-style, set out only amounts you feel will be eaten. Keep extra food ready to go—on ice or hot in the oven or on the stove. Instead of adding more food to a dwindling casserole, remove it from the table and set out a fresh one. Either reheat or chill the leftover food. Toss out questionable leftovers.

Simple Buffet Supper

Buffet serving works well when you are trying to feed a meal to more people than you can seat around your largest table. It allows for more interaction among guests. People will sit anywhere there is a seat, so be sure to have tray tables available. This menu works well for a gathering of 15 to 20 people. As dinner is served readily, appetizers aren't necessary.

BOWLS OF NUTS, PRETZELS, SNACK MIXES

Chicken Cacciatore, p. 103

BASIL LINGUINI, P. 163
ORANGE-FENNEL SALAD, P. 190
GARLIC BREAD, P. 206
SPICED BANANA-NUT CAKE (MAKE 2), P. 213
COFFEE, TEA, HARD CANDY, MINTS, OR CHOCOLATES

Advance Preparation and Serving

Make a double batch of the oven version of the Chicken Cacciatore. Cut the chicken breasts in half so there will be more pieces. This dish can be made ahead and frozen or prepared one day in advance and kept cold. Make the cake. Prepare the garlic bread and wrap it tightly in foil, but do not cook it.

Day of: Defrost chicken dish if necessary. Prepare the orange salad. Fill bowls with snacks and candies to be set around just before guests arrive.

2 hours before party: Shower and fluff.

1½ hours before party: Warm up chicken casserole in oven. A large casserole will take longer to heat than two smaller ones.

Just before guests are expected, set a large pan of water boiling for the pasta. The pasta will take about 10 to 15 minutes to cook. Plan to have it ready by serving time. Put the garlic loaves in the oven, leaving them wrapped in foil to heat through. While the pasta is cooking, set everything out except the chicken dish and pasta. When the chicken is cooked, remove it from the oven and turn on the broiler. Open up the garlic bread and top-brown the open halves until bubbly. Drain and prepare the pasta. Slice the garlic bread and toss it in a waiting basket. Ask everyone to line up and pig out. Set up cake and coffee as people are completing their meals.

COCKTAIL PARTY

A cocktail party can require more fussing than a sit-down dinner. However, you can minimize the work if you plan smart. Go ahead, leaf through all the latest magazines and cut out dozens of new recipes—and then toss them aside, because you'll find many of your efforts will be left clinging to their serving platters. People are attracted to food they can recognize, so it's wiser to stick to time-tested favorites and to appease your culinary side by including only one or two experimental recipes.

Be cautious about the number of hot appetizers you serve. One year I spent most of a good party bent over the oven checking for doneness. Also, because hot appetizers taste best hot, they often need to be passed around. If you've hired some kitchen help for the occasion, this may not present a problem. I've learned to serve no more than two hot appetizers, other than those in heated pots that can be set up once. Cold appetizers can be fully prepared in advance and left out for nibbling, requiring no more tending than occasional replenishment.

Should friends offer to bring food, suggest they bring only dishes that do not require cooking or last-minute preparation. Your kitchen will be hectic enough without unplanned messes and demands on the oven. Also, folks congregate in the kitchen no matter how large a home, which can make navigating in and around the oven and sink an "excuse me" nightmare.

Decide what you will do for beverages. For large parties I find a bowl of punch or a signature drink, wine, beer, and soft drinks is sufficient. Clean up is simple if you can stick to plastic cups and paper plates, too.

When people will be drinking all night, they need hearty nosh food. Plan this party to begin at 8 PM or later, and make it obvious that dinner will not be served. This quantity of food will suffice for 25 to 30 people. If you have fewer, cut down on the number of appetizers.

Cocktail Fare

PARTY AREA
Rosemary Pecans, p. 21
Strawberry Salsa and tortilla chips, p. 22
Cajun Shrimp with Zippy Sauce, p. 16
Raw vegetable platter with Quick Dip, p. 22
Fresh fruit platter with Honey Anise
Dip, p. 22
Pretzels with cranberry mustard

ON DESSERT TABLE
Coffee pot, teapot, sugar, cream, teabags
Orange Chocolate-Chip cookies, p. 224
Sheet cake (if this is an occasion)
Secret Fudge, p. 226, or store-bought
chocolates

ON SERVING TABLE
Small rolls, sliced partway through
Fully cooked, spiral-cut ham
Sliced turkey breast
Assortment of toppings
Cheese platter garnished with grapes
Marinated olives and pepper mix

Advance preparation and serving

If you want to drive yourself nuts, make everything from scratch, but why bother? Begin by ordering the ham or turkey and the cake, if you need one. Bake and freeze the cookies, and either buy good chocolate or make and freeze the fudge.

The day before: Prepare all the dips and sauces and store them in ready-to-put-out containers. Make up a batch of the pecans. These keep well in airtight containers.

The day of: Prepare shrimp. Use precooked shrimp, which you can buy fresh or frozen. Arrange cookies and candies on platters and cover. Fudge needs to be kept cold until served to prevent it from becoming too squishy.

2 hours before party: Take a shower and get spiffed. Ask your husband to light the candles, put on music, and set up the bar. Set around dishes of nuts (I usually leave one in the bar area) and the salsa and chips. If you are serving punch, pour it in the bowl, now, minus the ice.

15 minutes before the party: Set out the vegetable and fruit platters, the shrimp, and lay all the food out on the serving table. Use warming trays and cold packs to keep hot foods hot and cold foods chilled, so they will remain safe to eat. Your work is done, now enjoy the party. Pour yourself a drink and mingle. (We have a rule that we only make the first drink for guests. After that, they get their own.)

Cocktail Buffet

When my daughter was to be married, she didn't want the traditional bridal shower. She wanted a Jack and Jill, a couples' party, at the house. We had 40 to 50 people show up, and some of their friends brought their children, which required some extra planning. The kids picked at the fruits and veggies, the mothers fed the babies the macaroni and cheese and some ham, and helped the older kids dine from the adult table. We left gift opening until after dinner, and it was conducted informally. The start time of this party is 7 PM.

APPETIZERS
Fruit Slush Punch, p. 26
Beer, wine, soft drinks, juice boxes
Cranberry-Pecan Cheese Ball and crackers, p. 20
Fresh fruit platter with Apricot Walnut Dip, p. 22
Raw vegetable platter with Quick Dip, p. 22
Island Guacamole with pita chips, p. 21
Disappearing Crab Bites with Louie Dip, p. 17
Crackers & assorted cheeses

ON STOVE FOR KIDS
Macaroni & Cheese—use a box mix or
buy premade frozen

ON SERVING TABLE
Meatballs (cocktail size), p. 102, cooked in
pasta sauce or Spicy Pineapple Sauce, p. 94
Penne with Mushroom-Onion Pasta Sauce, p. 108
Spiral ham and/or turkey breast (bought)
Baked beans
Assorted mustards
Small rolls
Mixed Greens, Grapes & Almonds
with Lime Vinaigrette, p. 186

ON DESSERT TABLE
Large sheet cake
Cookie platter
Microwave Brittle, p. 227, or hard candy

Advance Preparation and Serving

You're in luck; you'll have bridesmaids fluttering about who would just love to pick out and send invitations and buy matching plate and decorations. And, the day of the party they will be around, as will your other children, to help with preparations. Prepare the meatballs and sauce in advance—these can be frozen. An alternative is to order large containers of these or other dishes from a good Italian restaurant and send one of the boys over to pick them up, hot and ready to serve, at party time. Large quantities of food, especially if solidly frozen, take a long time to heat through, so allow several hours for this; keep in mind that it will tie up your oven. Order the cake, cookie platter, and rolls from a good bakery and make the Microwave Brittle or buy hard candy.

One day ahead: To eliminate last-minute messes, prepare the pasta. Mix cooked and drained pasta with some of the sauce and then pour it in a large heatproof casserole dish. Cover and chill until it's time to rewarm it. When rewarming the pasta, add a little water, cover it with foil, and then heat it in a 350° oven. Prepare the punch. Wash and cut up salad vegetables and cakes on an oiled cookie sheet and freeze them until ready to cook.

Day of: The house will be chaotic because all the kids will be around. Make up a chore list early in the day. Put them to work running errands and hound them to pick up last-minute messes in company areas. Assign someone to make sure that the bathrooms are tidy. Eliminate having candles on low tables if children will be present. Set up serving areas and prepare serving platters, utensils, and dinnerware. You are, I hope, using paper plates. Get out your punch bowl and dust it off. (I've found a large plastic salad bowl purchased from a party goods store is more forgiving than glass.) All the cooking is done so all that is needed is coordination and last-minute set up. Prepare side platters and cold appetizer platters and chill. Put salad ingredients in bowl, with wettest ingredients, such as tomatoes, on the bottom and lettuce on top. Do not add dressing. Cover and chill in bowl.

5:00: Heat up the oven and start cooking any frozen casseroles. Plan to have them done by the start of the party so your oven will be free to cook the crab cakes. Otherwise, remove casseroles briefly, and replace them to continue cooking in the oven. You'd better get dressed because it will be crazy soon. Have the King do his thing setting up the bar, and the boys can assist him in hauling up cases of beer from the basement—and don't forget some nice music. Make macaroni and cheese. Set up a trash bag in the kitchen for used plates, etc.

6:45: Put out non-cold appetizers.

7:00: Put out cold appetizers and start the Crab Cakes heating.

8:00: Put out bread and condiments. Heat beans. Toss salad. Put remainder of food on the table and ask folks to grab a plate and chow down. Whew. The worst is done. Now you can relax.

Ladies Luncheon

This menu works well for all-women bridal and baby showers.

AREA BUFFET TABLE

Strawberry Mint Party Punch, p. 26

White wine, seltzer, or water

Assorted mints, packaged party snacks, and nuts

Curried Chicken Paté with sliced apples and crackers, p. 19

SERVING TABLE

Turkey Picatta, p. 68

Butter Mint Orzo, p. 162

Tossed Mandarin Salad with Glazed Almonds, p. 181

Tiny croissants

Glazed Cranberries and Onions, p. 175

DESSERT TABLE

Sheet Cake

Chocolate Truffles

Tea, coffee

Advance preparation and serving

One day ahead, make up several batches of the Turkey Picatta. Cut turkey cutlets in half and layer meat slices in one or more 9 x 13 x 2-inch casserole dishes. Top with remaining sauce. Cover and chill. Prepare ice block for punch bowl. Wash and prepare salad ingredients and make dressing. Make Chicken Pâté and the cranberry dish. Chill.

Day of: Slice apples for pate and store them in a plastic bag with 1 teaspoon of lemon juice or orange juice to prevent browning.

Just before guests arrive: Mix the punch ingredients and then unmold the ice block into punch bowl. Set around small bowls of mints and snacks. Set up cake table. Perk coffee.

As presents are bring opened: Pass around Chicken Pate appetizers and leave the platter near the punch bowl. Allow yourself 30 to 45 minutes to reheat the Turkey Picatta. Cover it and place it in a 350° oven until bubbly. Remove the cover and cook for a few more minutes to brown the top. Meanwhile, cook the orzo, and keep it hot until serving time. Toss the salad and put the rolls and remaining items on the table.

Backyard Picnic

SUN TEA, P. 27
BEER, WINE, SODA, JUICE BOXES (FOR KIDS)
GRILL-ROASTED CHICKEN HALVES, P. 88
HONEY BARBECUED SPARERIBS, P. 86
HOT DOGS & HAMBURGERS FOR THE KIDS
ROLLS
TWISTER PASTA SALAD, P. 163
ORANGE-OLIVE SALAD, P. 191
CORN ON THE COB
TOASTED MARSHMALLOWS
POPSICLES
WATERMELON
JOY'S JUMBLES COOKIES, P. 225

Advance preparation and serving

Buy the party goods and nonperishables, such as the wine, beer, and soda well in advance. If you have a large cooler or two, these will make dandy ice buckets to keep the soda chilled. It's always nice to have a few games handy, such as bocce (lawn bowling), croquet, badminton, or if you've a field nearby, baseball.

Day ahead: Clean and prepare the chicken for the grill and precook and marinate the spareribs. Make the pasta salad and the Orange-Olive Salad. Chill all.

Day of: Set up tables and paper goods, organize beverages. Buy the corn, and solicit help of guests in shucking ears while the chickens are cooking.

1½ hours before serving: Preheat the grill and cook the chickens. When the chickens are done, remove them from the grill and place them in a covered serving pan.

15 minutes before serving: Put the spareribs on the grill, drizzle them with honey, and cook until sizzling and browned on both sides (10 to 15 minutes). Make grill space to cook enough hot dogs and hamburgers to appease the kids. They're probably ravenous by now. Meanwhile, cook the corn on an indoor stovetop. If you wish to serve the corn after dinner, set the cooking pot on the grill as soon as the meat is done. The best way to offer butter for corn at a picnic is to set a stick on a plate and roll hot corn over it to coat.

Serving time: Set up salads and cooked foods buffet style and chow down. Have the dessert foods—popsicles, marshmallow, cookies, and watermelon—available for snacking afterwards.

Part 3: Side Dishes to Desserts

RECIPE FOR PERSONAL GROWTH

Get out into the world and be part of it

Think positive thoughts and good things will happen

Set goals and work toward them

Tell yourself how wonderful you are until you believe it

Never say, "I can't"

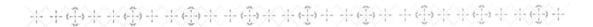

STARCHY ASIDES

Potatoes, rice, pasta, and other carbohydrates have been given a bad rap—supposedly they make us fat. With so much controversy about what defines healthy eating and which foods wreak havoc with cholesterol and metabolism, it's hard to rule out any food. I say eat the foods you enjoy in moderation, and you won't have any problems. So, have a dollop of mashed potatoes with that piece of fish, just leave some for everyone else!

Who are you?

It's not surprising that once our little birds fly the coop, we parents suffer an identity crisis. Those of us who have unselfishly allowed our lives to revolve around the kids feel devastated because we are no longer needed. It's a struggle not to be too clingy. Sometimes you can be a real pest. You call them on the phone to hear their voice, and gain reassurance that you are still part of their lives. "What did you do today?" "Did you eat a good breakfast?" You invite them to dinner with just the right tone of not caring so they won't feel obligated to come. Restraint is hard.

You're restless. You feel like a nobody who's been fired from a job. Perhaps it's time to go back to work, to school, start a business—anything to give life meaning again. If you are already working, you toy with changing to a more challenging career. You have talks with yourself because you just can't seem to get motivated to adapt to the changes in your life. Tackling the real world can be intimidating after spending years in the womb of motherhood. You were secure, needed, and important to so many.

You dye your hair, have a makeover at the department store cosmetic counter, start a fad diet, and join a gym, but all the external help in the world does nothing more than boost your self-confidence. The real changes need to come from within, because you still haven't figured out how to deal with the void in your life. Maybe you're happy with your life as it is because you've already been through this process, and it's working for you. If so, consider yourself one of the lucky ones.

When I went through this period, I brought home heaps of self-help books and tapes. "What are your goals?" they all asked. I realized, then, that I had no goals of my own, only my husband's and my children's. And that I needed to change my thinking from *them* to *me, me, me*. Putting oneself first is difficult for a mother who's always given the best away. It takes practice to take a stand on what you choose to do. Goal setting is easier said than done, because first you must clear away all the shouldn'ts, can'ts, and don'ts that have been holding you back. Next, you need to dig into your past and think about what you've always wanted to do, to be.

This indecisiveness can make you feel like a lump of nothing, but you're not. You are internally readying yourself for the next chapter in your life and, before long your path will be clear. I started by writing down all the things I thought about doing but never did. I drew upon anything; I was desperate. One goal was writing down my recipes for my children. Once I said it out loud and wrote it down, writing a book became real and doable. Creating a family cookbook led me to a career as a writer. A dear friend who had always been a stay-at-home mom went back to school and is now a surgical nurse. My sister-in-law tells me she's always wanted to train seeing eye dogs. What you choose as your goal can be anything as long as it breathes new life into you.

Once you've done the thinking, the hardest part is behind you. The person smiling back at you in the mirror is no longer a discarded mom but a woman exploring her full potential. Your only limits are those you set on yourself. You're free from the velvet ropes of parenthood, free to be the real you.

STARCHY SIDE DISHES

Potato smarts

When perusing the potatoes section, you'll find three basic types of potatoes: boiling potatoes, baking potatoes, and all-purpose potatoes. The amount of moisture and starch in a potato gives it its unique cooking properties. When choosing potatoes, look for those that are firm and heavy for their size with tight skin that is free of blemishes or signs of spoilage. Avoid potatoes with a greenish cast, as they will be bitter and are mildly toxic.

New red, white, and long potatoes are high moisture, low starch. This makes them ideal for boiling, as they hold their shape when cooked. Recognize these by their smooth thin skin—so thin you can almost rub it off. These are normally cooked with the skin left on. Idaho and Russet potatoes have the lowest moisture content and highest starch content that gives them a mealy texture when cooked, dry and fluffy inside. These have a thick, brown skin that almost looks like a layer of dirt, and are oval-shaped and often knobby. These make delicious baking potatoes and their high-starch content helps thicken stews and soups; starch is released into a liquid when heated. All-purpose potatoes, such as Maine and Yukon gold, will work well in most recipes. They cook up with waxy, mealy centers, due to their moderate balance of starch and moisture.

Store unwashed fresh potatoes (for up to six months, if you keep them dry) in a cool, dark, aerated area, such as in an open or lightly covered bin or in or a brown paper bag. Sort through your cache of potatoes periodically, and toss out the wrinkled ones. If eyes have sprouted, cut them off, along with the green portion, before preparing the potatoes for cooking. Avoid refrigerating potatoes, as cold temperatures will turn the potato starches into sugar, resulting in a mealy, dark potato.

Potatoes are a root vegetable grown underground, so they tend to be dirty. When preparing them for cooking, always scrub the skins with a vegetable brush to remove surface bacteria and dirt. Years ago, homemakers peeled potatoes, except for new potatoes, before cooking. Today, few us have the time for that nonsense and, boosted by the findings that potato skins are loaded with healthy nutrients, we may only peel potatoes for specific dishes. (I peel potatoes when making mashed potatoes, but otherwise it's skins-on for me.) When baking skin-on whole potatoes in the oven or microwave, be sure to pierce the skin so that pressure built up within won't cause an offended potato to explode all over your oven.

Once potatoes are peeled, they will darken and turn reddish if exposed to the air for very long. If possible, peel potatoes as closely as possible to cooking time. If you must hold them over for an hour or so, immerse them in cold water to which a few drops of lemon juice or vinegar have been added to prevent discoloration. I've read that peeling potatoes with a stainless blade will also discolor the flesh, and I know that cooking them in aluminum and iron pots will turn them gray.

POTATO DISHES

Home-Fried Potatoes

Start these about 50 minutes before serving dinner. Once the potatoes are cooking, they need very little attention. The secret to crispy home fries is not to cover the pan and to turn the potatoes only once during cooking. Also, once the potatoes are cooked, avoid the temptation to allow them to remain in the skillet on low heat; they will soften and lose their crispness. Timing is important here.

8   baking potatoes, scrubbed with the skin
        left intact
1   medium onion (optional)
4   to 5 tablespoons butter or margarine
     Salt and pepper to taste

Slice the potatoes and onion in thin rounds by hand or with the slicing attachment of a food processor. In a 12-inch skillet melt half of the margarine on medium-high heat (350°). Add the potatoes and onion, one layer at a time, covering the bottom of the pan. Sprinkle salt and pepper between the layers. Cook on medium heat for 20 to 30 minutes, until the tops of the potatoes begin to look dry. Add remaining margarine in small dots around the edges of the pan and then turn the potatoes over carefully, in sections, using a wide spatula. Continue cooking an additional 10 minutes or until potatoes are cooked through. Serve at once.

SERVES 3 TO 4

Stuffed Potatoes

Men love these! To save time, use the microwave oven to bake the potatoes for stuffing. Make these up to one day in advance and refrigerate them until ready to final-bake.

4   medium or large baking potatoes,
        scrubbed
2   egg whites
3   tablespoons butter or margarine
1/2 cup milk
3   tablespoons sour cream
1   teaspoon dried parsley
    Salt and pepper to taste
    Parmesan cheese (optional)

Preheat oven to 350°. Pierce potatoes with a knife to allow steam to escape while baking and place them directly on rack in a preheated oven. Bake approximately 1 hour or until soft when pricked with a knife or toothpick. Remove potatoes from the oven and set aside. In a small bowl beat the egg whites until soft peaks form. Set aside.

To prepare and stuff potatoes: Cut each potato in half lengthwise. Carefully scoop out the cooked potato, leaving the shells intact, and place potato meat in a large mixing bowl. Arrange potato shells cut side up on a cookie sheet. To the cooked potatoes, add the butter or margarine, 1/4 cup of the milk, sour cream, parsley, salt, and pepper. Whip the potatoes with an electric mixer until they are light and

fluffy. Add some of the additional milk if potatoes seem dry. Carefully fold the beaten egg whites into the potato mixture. To stuff, place a scoop of the potato mixture into each of the reserved potato skins. Sprinkle halves with paprika or with Parmesan cheese, if desired.

To final-bake and brown potatoes: Preheat oven to 400° and cook for 5 to 10 minutes, until potatoes puff and begin to brown. If necessary, turn on the broiler to crisp the tops. If you are making these in advance, refrigerate them once they are stuffed and complete cooking just before serving.

SERVES 4

Red & White Herb-Roasted Potatoes

A colorful and fragrant side dish with any roast.

14	new potatoes (7 red, 7 white)
1	teaspoon salt
1/2	teaspoon rosemary
1/4	teaspoon fennel seed
1/2	teaspoon pepper
1/2	teaspoon paprika
4	tablespoons olive oil

Scrub potatoes well. Leaving skin on, cut potatoes into quarters. Mix spices and olive oil in large plastic bag or large bowl. Add prepared potatoes and seal plastic bag. Shake bag or stir in a bowl until potatoes are well coated with the oil mixture. In a shallow roasting pan, arrange the potatoes in single layer. Bake at 425° for 30 to 40 minutes or until potatoes are crispy and brown on the outside and soft in the middle. Turn over with a spatula once or twice during cooking.

To cook potatoes alongside a roast, cook them at 350° for approximately 45 minutes and then turn up the oven temperature to 450° for the last 10 to 15 minutes of baking to crisp them. Serve immediately and enjoy!

SERVES 6 TO 8

Make-ahead Mashed Potatoes

The convenience of getting a major project out of the way ahead of time makes these yummy potatoes winners. They travel well and don't have that steamed taste regular mashed potatoes get when reheated. You won't have any leftovers.

5	pounds baking potatoes, peeled and cut into cubes
1	small onion, minced
1	tablespoon, plus 1 teaspoon salt
1	8-ounce package cream cheese, softened
1/2	cup butter or margarine, softened
1/2	to 1 cup half and half
1/4	teaspoon ground black pepper
1	tablespoon melted butter or margarine
	Paprika for garnish

Cook the potatoes and onion in boiling water to which 1 tablespoon of the salt has been added until they are fork-tender. Drain well. In a large mixing bowl beat the cream cheese and butter together with an electric mixer. Beat in hot drained potatoes, onion, and 1/2 to 1 cup of the half and half until the mixture is slightly lumpy. Season to taste using the remaining salt and pepper. Pour into a 3-quart buttered casserole dish. Brush top with 1 tablespoon of melted butter and sprinkle with the paprika. Refrigerate to bake the next day, or bake casserole immediately in a pre-heated 350° oven for 30 to 40 minutes (if potatoes have been refrigerated, allow about 60 minutes), until heated through. Do not cover casserole. Top will puff when done. Reheat in microwave.

SERVES 8

Smashed Parsley Potatoes

These taste like mashed potatoes but don't require as much work or forethought. New potatoes are nice, but I use whatever I have on hand.

10 red or white new potatoes, scrubbed and cut into 1-inch chunks
1   teaspoon salt
1/4 teaspoon black pepper
1/2 stick or 4 tablespoons butter or margarine
1/3 cup chopped fresh parsley (or 3 tablespoons dried)

In a large pot boil the potatoes along with the salt and pepper until tender when pierced with a fork. Drain excess water from the pan. Add the butter and parsley and stir for a minute with a wooden spoon, until the butter is melted and potatoes are coated. Do not overmix or potatoes will be too mushy. Serve at once.

SERVES 5 TO 6

Caramelized Potatoes

2   tablespoons butter or margarine
1   tablespoon granulated sugar
1/4 teaspoon thyme
1/4 teaspoon red (cayenne)pepper
1/4 teaspoon salt
5   new potatoes, sliced into 1/2-inch rings

In a 12-inch skillet heat all ingredients except the potatoes on medium temperature until the mixture is bubbly. Place the potatoes in the pan, in a single layer if possible. Cook for 3 to 5 minutes on each side or until potatoes are browned and tender. For easy cleanup, put some soapy water in the pan and heat to boiling to loosen burnt-on bits—or cook with a nonstick pan.

SERVES 2 TO 3

Orange-Thyme Potatoes and Onions

3 or 4 medium baking potatoes, scrubbed
  and quartered
1 large Vidalia or mild onion, sliced
1 navel orange, peeled and sliced
1 teaspoon grated orange peel
2 tablespoons fresh orange juice
1 teaspoon thyme
½ teaspoon salt or to taste
⅛ teaspoon black pepper
2 tablespoons butter or margarine, cut into
  small pieces

Preheat oven to 400°. Put potatoes, onion, orange slices, and orange peel in an 8 x 8 x 2-inch pan. Pour in the fresh orange juice and then season with thyme, salt, and pepper. Mix well in pan. Dot with butter. Bake for 40 minutes to 1 hour or until potatoes are soft when pierced with a fork. Stir several times while cooking, basting the potatoes with the pan juices.

SERVES 3 TO 4

Bourbon Sweet Potato Casserole

These easy-to-make potatoes are a coveted staple at our holiday dinners.

3 20-ounce cans vacuum-packed sweet
  potatoes
½ cup butter or margarine
¾ cup sugar
⅓ cup bourbon
½ teaspoon vanilla
  Miniature marshmallows or Streusel
  Topping recipe, p. 159

Drain the canned sweet potatoes, place them in a mixing bowl, and mash them enough to break them up. Melt the butter, and then add it to the potatoes along with the sugar, bourbon, and vanilla. Mix well by hand or use an electric mixer. Pour potatoes into a buttered heatproof 2-quart casserole dish and, if desired, top with Streusel Topping and bake for 30 minutes. If using marshmallows, spread them in a single layer on top of the cooked potatoes and return the casserole to the oven for about 5 minutes, until marshmallows are puffy and golden brown. Serve.

Note: If making ahead, refrigerate without adding topping to bake later.

SERVES 8

Streusel Topping

½ cup flour
⅓ cup brown sugar
¼ cup pecans, chopped and toasted
2 tablespoons butter or margarine, melted
⅛ teaspoon cinnamon
Cooking oil

Combine all ingredients and sprinkle evenly on top of the prepared sweet potato casserole. Spray lightly with cooking oil. Place in the oven and bake for 30 minutes, until potatoes are heated through and topping is lightly browned.

Perfect Potato Salad

Did you ever try to season one of these and get the mix just right? It always seems there's too much or too little of something. Why do you think Hellmann's came out with a special mayonnaise just for potato salad? When I finally got the seasoning the way I liked it, I wrote it down for posterity.

5 medium baking potatoes, scrubbed and cut into 1-inch chunks
1 egg
2 tablespoons chopped fresh parsley (or 1 teaspoon dried)
½ cup chopped Vidalia or other mild onion
1 teaspoon chopped fresh jalapeño pepper (optional)
1 cup chopped celery (3 to 4 stalks)

PERFECT DRESSING:
1 tablespoon Dijon mustard
1 teaspoon wine vinegar
1 tablespoon olive oil
6 tablespoons Hellmann's mayonnaise
½ to 1 teaspoon salt or to taste
⅛ teaspoon black pepper or to taste
¼ teaspoon paprika

Place the potatoes and the egg in a medium saucepan, and cover them with salted water. Bring to a boil. Cover the pan and reduce to medium heat. Continue to cook for 20 to 30 minutes, until potatoes are soft but not mushy. Drain and rinse them in cold water. Peel and chop the egg. Place the cooked potatoes and egg in a large mixing bowl and refrigerate to cool. Once potatoes have cooled to room temperature, mix in the parsley, onion, jalapeño pepper, celery, and all the dressing ingredients until well blended. Cover and refrigerate for at least an hour before serving.

SERVES 4 TO 5

Warm Potato Salad

This potato salad goes together quickly, and because it can be served immediately it can be made along with dinner, rather than beforehand. Chill leftovers and serve again cold.

2 pounds new potatoes, scrubbed and unpeeled
1 teaspoon dried mint leaves (or 1 tablespoon chopped fresh)
  Salted water
1 bunch or 6 scallions, chopped

LEMON VINAIGRETTE:
4 tablespoons lemon juice
4 tablespoons olive oil
1¼ teaspoons Dijon mustard
1 clove garlic, minced
  Salt and pepper

Put the potatoes and mint in a saucepan with salted water and boil the potatoes until they are soft, but not falling apart. Drain and transfer them to a serving bowl. Make the vinaigrette by combining the lemon juice, oil, mustard, garlic, salt, and pepper. Pour the dressing over the potatoes, and then add the scallions. Mix well. Serve hot or lukewarm.

SERVES 4 TO 6

RICE

Rice Pilaf with Lime, Pine Nuts, & Golden Raisins

A good way to improve on plain white rice.

1½ teaspoons olive oil
1 scallion stalk, sliced
3 tablespoons pine nuts or sliced almonds
1 cup uncooked rice
2¼ cups chicken stock
⅓ cup golden raisins
2 teaspoons grated lime zest
½ teaspoon salt
¼ teaspoon dried red pepper flakes

Heat the olive oil in a large skillet over medium heat. Add the scallions and pine nuts and sauté a few minutes, until scallions are soft and pine nuts are lightly browned. Stir in the rice and sauté an additional 5 minutes. Stir in the chicken stock, raisins, lime zest, salt, and red pepper. Reduce heat to low. Cover and simmer until all the liquid has been absorbed, about 15 to 20 minutes.

Remove pan from heat, fluff rice with a fork, and serve.

SERVES 4

Cinnamon Brown Rice with Raisins

2   tablespoons orange juice
3   tablespoons golden raisins
½   teaspoon cinnamon
2   cups cooked brown rice (use instant or long-cooking)
½   tablespoon butter or margarine

Combine the orange juice, raisins, and cinnamon. When rice is cooked, drain it well and return it to the cooking pot but not to the heat. Stir in the butter and then the orange-raisin mixture. Pour rice into a serving bowl and enjoy.

SERVES 3 TO 4

Butter Pecan Rice

3   cups hot cooked rice
3   tablespoons butter or margarine
2   teaspoons fresh lemon juice
¼   teaspoon ground black pepper
⅔   cup pecans, coarsely chopped
3   scallions, sliced
    Pecan halves for garnish

Cook rice and remove from heat. Drain off any excess water, if necessary. Stir in the butter, lemon juice, and pepper. Cover and let stand for about 5 minutes, until all liquid is absorbed. Stir in the pecans and scallions. Garnish with pecan halves, if desired, and serve.

SERVES 6

Bagged Rice & Black Beans

This dish uses instant boil-in-bag white rice. I developed this recipe one evening when I was short on time yet needed a quick, hearty side dish to complement my meal.

2   cups water
2   cups canned chicken broth
1   clove garlic, minced
1   teaspoon ground cumin
1   teaspoon dried thyme
1   teaspoon chili powder
½   teaspoon salt
1   2-cup bag boil-in-the-bag white rice
1   teaspoon olive oil
1   18½-ounce can black beans, rinsed and drained
2   tablespoons chopped fresh onion (uncooked)
2   tablespoons chopped fresh cilantro (or 2 teaspoons dried)

Place the water, chicken broth, garlic, cumin, thyme, chili powder, and salt in a 2-quart saucepan and bring to a boil. Add the unopened bag of rice. Submerge completely and boil vigorously for 10 minutes uncovered. When rice is done, remove the bag carefully from the boiling chicken broth mixture and allow the excess liquid to drain. Slit open the bag of cooked rice and pour it into a 2-quart serving or mixing bowl. While rice is still warm, stir in the olive oil, then add the beans, onion, and cilantro. Mix gently and serve at once.

SERVES 4

Recycled Chinese Rice

Every time we get Chinese food, I am left with a quart of white rice. I've always felt it a waste to allow it to hang about my refrigerator until its moldy demise. Here's something interesting you can do to turn it into a palatable side dish.

1	to 2 teaspoons butter or margarine
2	tablespoons sliced scallions
1	quart cooked Chinese-style white rice
$1/4$	to $1/2$ cup orange juice
$1/2$	teaspoon grated orange peel
$1/4$	cup water

In a 10-inch skillet melt the butter on medium-high heat. Add the scallions and sauté a few minutes, until softened. Add the rice. It will be sticky, so mash it down with the back of a large spoon to separate the granules. Stir in the remaining ingredients. Reduce heat to medium-low and cover for a few minutes, stirring occasionally, until rice is heated through. Add additional orange juice if rice seems dry.

SERVES 4

PASTA ON THE SIDE

Butter Mint Orzo

Orzo is rice-shaped pasta that's used in soups or as a side dish in lieu of rice. The buttery mint flavor of this side dish works with almost any meat or fish.

1	cup cooked orzo, drained but not rinsed
$1/2$	teaspoon salt
1	tablespoon butter
$1/2$	teaspoon dried mint (or 2 teaspoons chopped fresh)

Cook orzo per package directions, adding salt to water. Drain, but do not rinse. Pour it into a serving dish and stir in the butter and mint. Serve at once.

SERVES 3 TO 4

Lemon Linguini

8	ounces linguini
1	tablespoon butter or margarine
2	tablespoons chopped fresh parsley
1	teaspoon grated lemon peel
$\frac{1}{2}$	teaspoon pepper
2	tablespoons lemon juice
2	tablespoons grated Parmesan cheese

Cook the linguini in boiling salted water until tender but firm to the bite. Lightly drain but do not rinse the pasta and return it to the cooking pot, but not to the heat. Stir in the butter, parsley, lemon peel, and pepper until the butter is melted and ingredients are mixed. Pour into a serving bowl, sprinkle with Parmesan cheese, and serve.

SERVES 4

Basil Linguini

1	pound linguini
2	tablespoons butter or margarine
1	teaspoon dried basil (or 1 tablespoon minced fresh)
$\frac{1}{8}$	teaspoon black pepper

Cook linguini in boiling, salted water until just tender but firm to the bite. Lightly drain, but do not rinse. Place linguini in a pasta-serving bowl. Stir in the butter, basil, and black pepper until the butter melts. Serve.

SERVES 6 TO 8

Twister Pasta Salad

3	cups spiral pasta, cooked, drained and rinsed ($\frac{1}{2}$ pound uncooked pasta)
$\frac{1}{4}$	cup chopped scallions
$\frac{1}{4}$	cup canned corn, drained
$\frac{1}{4}$	cup black beans, drained and rinsed
$\frac{1}{4}$	teaspoon ground cumin
1	teaspoon dried cilantro
1	tablespoon chopped fresh oregano leaves (or 1 teaspoon dried)
	Pinch black pepper
$1\frac{1}{2}$	teaspoons salt
1	teaspoon lime juice
2	tablespoons olive oil
2	tablespoons wine vinegar

Place the pasta in a large mixing or serving bowl. Mix in the scallions, corn, and beans. Add the remaining ingredients and stir gently to mix. Cover and chill at least 1 hour before serving.

SERVES 3 TO 4

RECIPE FOR KEEPING FIT

Get plenty of rest—naps are good

Pump iron to keep your metabolism moving

Dance your pants off to Richard Simmons

Exercise in tights in front of a mirror

Donate your fat clothes to Goodwill

Pretend that carrot is a piece of chocolate

VEG OUT

Vegetables are good for you, but they don't have to taste like medicine. There are plenty of ways to spruce them up, so they decorate a meal and enhance the flavor of the main entrée. Be creative with color contrasts—white potatoes are perked up by green beans or orange carrots—and you'll find you've automatically balanced the meal nutritionally. Mix crunchy and smooth, spicy and bland. Intrigue your guests with the unexpected (then run for cover if they don't like it).

Those wolf whistles aren't for you . . .

The day I was in town with my two young daughters—eleven and thirteen—and turned around to glare at the source of a whistle, I couldn't have been more embarrassed. It was intended for my daughters, not me. It was then that I realized that I wasn't "pretty" anymore and that a few things were beginning to go south. When this revelation occurs, we can take it lying down, or we can fight the uphill battle to keep ourselves youthful and attractive. Like happiness, attractiveness and youthfulness are not only external. They are generated from within us.

Now, I'm not saying you'll always look like a spring chicken. Time and the environment are natural agers, but you can remain young by thinking young. Stay active.

Go back to school and take up a subject that has always interested you—you may not have had the time or money to do this when you were raising children. Don't be afraid of making friends with those who are not in your age bracket; people will gladly accept you and enjoy your company as long as you keep up with the times. Many of our best friends are ten to twenty years younger than my husband and I. Mimic the way younger people think, and you will find yourself more readily accepting new ideas and being more willing to go places and have new experiences.

Learn from your children. Throw out the old-folk magazines and buy *Glamour*, *Self*, or even *Cosmopolitan* to keep up on styles, makeup, health, and trends. Look at the fashions. What colors and styles are "in"? Update your wardrobe with a modern piece of jewelry or a hip new belt. Notice the shoes. Get rid of those old-fashioned dress boots and get some with pizzazz. Avoid tiny flowers and namby-pamby colors unless they characterize your personal style—only the very young can carry them off without looking matronly. Spend money on skin care. You wear your face every day. Cosmetics and skin care products found in pharmacies have many of the same ingredients as department-store cosmetics at half the cost.

Last, but never least, choose an exercise program you can stick with. More and more studies are pointing to the benefits of moderate to active exercise at least 30 minutes a day. Your body is like a piece of equipment. If you don't keep the parts oiled and moving, they'll rust. Loss of muscle tone breeds fatigue. Increased circulation keeps everything in your body humming. Your skin will look better for the activity and your body will be fit. Wouldn't you prefer to wake up with a few aches from weightlifting to stiff joints from inactivity? With regular exercise, you'll substitute activity for aspirin and will feel increasingly alive with improved well-being. Exercise squeezes excess water out of your system, as do diuretics, so if you are menopausal, here's your no-pill solution to bloating.

Another great side effect of exercising is a svelte figure. Fight that spreading middle with tummy exercises and aerobics. Do chest lifts for those drooping boobs and keep that butt tight with leg exercises. The increased activity will raise your metabolism, so you can eat more without gaining weight. Too tired to exercise? Until you motivate yourself to get going, you won't realize the energy boost you've been missing. Exercise activates your mind as well, giving you a feeling of strength, well-being, and self-confidence. It will help you to think positively and reach for challenges in other areas of your life.

You'll sleep better. Sleep is another problem we oldsters encounter. Early to bed, early to rise, and several trips to the bathroom throughout the night is a typical scenario. Do you plop in front of the TV each night and veg out? Are you yawning about 8 o'clock, trying to stay up until 9:30 so you can go to bed? Are you tired or just bored? If you go to bed early, chances are when 5 AM rolls around you'll be ready to start your day. We all need to relax, and I'm not saying you shouldn't do that at night, but I ask you not to make it a habit. Habits—settling in—are typical of old age, and you must fight it with challenge. Extend your day by working on a project after supper for a bit. Plan an activity you enjoy. Take a night class. You don't need rest. You just need excitement. Nothing brings on a better night's sleep than a day filled with accomplishment. The bathroom trips, which may increase if you exercise, you'll have to deal with until you rid yourself of excess water.

VEGETABLE & FRUIT SIDE DISHES

Whenever possible, I cook vegetables in the microwave. They will cook in minutes, while retaining their color, flavor, and moisture and, since I can cook them in their serving dishes, are ready to go on the table right from the microwave oven.

MIXED VEGGIES

Oregano Garden Vegetables

½ cup fresh green beans
½ medium zucchini, sliced thin
1 scallion, chopped
½ fresh tomato, chopped
2 teaspoons fresh oregano (or ½ teaspoon dried)
2 tablespoons water
Salt and pepper to taste

Mix all ingredients in a microwave-safe serving casserole. Cover and microwave on high for 5 to 7 minutes or until vegetables are cooked, yet firm. Serve as a side dish.

SERVES 3 TO 4

Lemon Roasted Vegetables

1 teaspoon lemon peel, finely shredded
¼ cup lemon juice
3 tablespoons olive oil
½ teaspoon salt
¼ teaspoon pepper
¼ teaspoon fennel seed
8 baby new potatoes, halved (or 4 small, quartered)
3 medium sweet red, yellow, and green peppers, seeded and cut into bite-sized pieces
2 squash, zucchini and yellow, cut up
1 medium onion, cut into wedges
2 fennel bulbs or 4 stalks celery, sliced
3 cloves garlic, minced
⅓ cup pitted ripe olives

Preheat oven to 400°. In a large mixing bowl or plastic bag combine the lemon peel, lemon juice, oil, salt, pepper, and fennel seed. Add in all of the vegetables and remaining ingredients and mix to coat well. Pour vegetable mixture into a shallow 15 x 10 x 2-inch baking pan in a single layer. Roast in a 400° oven for about 40 minutes, until all the vegetables are cooked. Stir and turn vegetables occasionally to brown evenly.

SERVES 8 TO 10

cooking on the stovetop, cover the pan and steam 5 to 10 minutes, until vegetables are tender-crisp.

To microwave: cover and cook for 3 to 5 minutes or until vegetables are done. Serve at once with a meat or fish entrée.

SERVES 3 TO 4

Pineapple-Ginger Vegetables

Crystallized ginger is really a candied form of fresh gingerroot. I bought some for a recipe and invented this combination while trying to find other uses for the ginger. If you don't have crystallized ginger, use ¼ teaspoon ground ginger plus ½ teaspoon sugar for a similar flavor.

1   head broccoli, florets only
2   cups sliced carrots or baby carrots
1   cup pineapple chunks, juice reserved
¼   cup reserved pineapple juice
1   teaspoon crystallized ginger
¼   teaspoon salt
    Pinch black pepper

Place the broccoli, carrots, and pineapple in a 1½-quart saucepan or microwave-safe serving casserole. Stir in the reserved pineapple juice, ginger, salt, and pepper. If

Zucchini Medley

2   small zucchini squash, sliced
⅓   yellow pepper, cut into thin strips
3   tablespoons chopped onion
1   teaspoon dried basil
½   teaspoon balsamic vinegar
1   tablespoon olive oil

Mix all ingredients together in a 1-quart casserole dish. Microwave on high for 5 to 10 minutes or until squash is tender-crisp.

SERVES 3 TO 4

Grilled Garden Vegetable Packets

No pots to clean! Be creative and create your own combinations of vegetables. I usually place the prepared packets on the grill while it is preheating. By the time the meat or fish is cooked, they are ready, too.

	Heavy-duty aluminum foil
3	medium potatoes, sliced into 1/8-inch-thick circles
1/2	yellow pepper, julienne cut
1/2	small zucchini, julienne cut
1/2	Vidalia or other mild onion, quartered and then cut into 1/8-inch slices
1/4	cup chopped fresh basil leaves (or 1 tablespoon dried)
1	tablespoon butter or margarine
	Salt and pepper to taste

Make individual portion packets or one large one. Cut 2 squares of foil per person, one square for the base and the other for the lid. Distribute the vegetables and seasonings on the bottom pieces of the foil in the order listed. Dot each packet with 1/3 tablespoon of the butter. Cover with the top layer of foil and fold over each edge twice to seal it. Do not pierce with fork. Cook packets on the grill for 10 to 15 minutes, turning once with a large metal spatula, and being careful not to tear the foil. When you turn the packet to its second side, pierce it to ventilate the steam.

Test for doneness by piercing. Remove packets carefully onto a waiting platter, using one or two spatulas to support the base.

SERVES 3

GREEN VEGGIES

Broccoli Dijon

1/4	cup water
1	tablespoon butter or margarine, cut up
1	teaspoon Dijon mustard
1/2	teaspoon salt
	Pinch black pepper
1	head broccoli, trimmed and cut into spears

Mix the water, butter, mustard, salt, and pepper in a small heatproof cup or saucepan. Heat the mixture in the microwave or on the stovetop until the butter mustard mixture to coat spears. Cover and cook on high until broccoli is just tender. Stir partway through, if desired. Use the same procedure to cook on stove.

SERVES 4

Microwave Herbed Broccoli

Nice light taste.

1   large head broccoli, cut into spears
1/2   teaspoon salt
1/4   teaspoon ground marjoram or dried marjoram leaves
3/4   teaspoon dried sage leaves
    Pinch black pepper
1   tablespoon water
1   teaspoon butter or margarine, cut up into small squares

Place all ingredients except the butter in a zip-lock plastic bag. Turn bag several times to mix. Pour contents of bag into a 2-quart casserole. Dot with butter cubes. Cover and microwave about 5 minutes or until cooked yet crisp. Stir once, and then serve immediately.

Note: For asparagus, substitute 2 tablespoons of orange juice for the water.

SERVES 4

Rosemary Asparagus

1   bunch asparagus spears, trimmed
1   to 2 tablespoons water
    Salt and pepper to taste
1/4   teaspoon dried rosemary leaves
1/2   teaspoon dried parsley

Place all ingredients in a shallow skillet. Bring to a boil. Cover and simmer 4 to 8 minutes, stirring frequently until asparagus is tender. Serve at once. Do not overcook.

SERVES 4

Lemon Sage Green Beans

1 1/2   cups fresh green whole beans (or 1 10-ounce package frozen whole green beans)
1/2   teaspoon sage leaves (or 1 1/2 teaspoons chopped fresh sage)
1   tablespoon water
1/8   teaspoon salt
    Pinch black pepper
1   teaspoon fresh lemon juice

Place all ingredients except the lemon juice in a 1-quart microwave-safe casserole dish. Cover and microwave on high about 5 minutes or until beans are cooked. Stir in the fresh lemon juice and serve at once.

SERVES 2 TO 3

Oregano Green Beans

1/4 teaspoon dried oregano

1/2 pound fresh green beans (or 1 10-ounce package frozen beans)

1 clove garlic, smashed but left whole

1 teaspoon butter or margarine, cut up in chunks

Salt and pepper

2 tablespoons water

Place all ingredients in a microwave-safe casserole. Cover and microwave on high until beans are cooked. Do not overcook. Stir before serving. Add additional water if using saucepan on stovetop.

SERVES 2 TO 3

Minted Peas

A fresh tasting accompaniment to meat or fish. Particularly good with lamb.

1 10-ounce package frozen peas

1/2 teaspoon dried mint (or 1 teaspoon fresh chopped mint)

Salt and pepper to taste

Steam all ingredients in a covered saucepan with about 1/2 inch of water or use the microwave oven. To microwave, place all ingredients in a one-quart microwave-safe casserole dish. Cover and cook on high for a few minutes, until peas are defrosted and hot. Serve.

SERVES 2 TO 3

YELLOW & ORANGE VEGGIES

Microwave Glazed Carrots

6 carrots, scrubbed and sliced (or 4 cups whole baby carrots)

4 scallions, sliced

1/3 cup orange juice

3 tablespoons brown sugar

1 teaspoon salt

1/8 teaspoon black pepper

Place all ingredients in a 1 1/2- or 2-quart microwave-safe casserole dish. Mix well. Cover tightly and microwave 5 to 8 minutes on high or until carrots and tender. Stir once halfway through cooking. Mix well. Serve with a slotted spoon.

SERVES 3 TO 4

Spiced Acorn Squash

1 medium acorn squash peeled and cut up
  into chunks
1/4 teaspoon ground nutmeg
  Pinch ground cloves
1/4 teaspoon ground coriander
1 tablespoon butter or margarine, cut up
1/4 cup water

Place all ingredients in a microwave-safe
serving dish. Cover and cook on high until
squash is tender. Stir well, mashing squash
with a fork, and serve.

SERVES 3 TO 4

Baked Tomatoes Provençal

How I love those garden tomatoes!

6 medium ripe tomatoes
  Salt and black pepper to taste

ITALIAN CRUST:
1/4 loaf stale Italian or French bread,
  cut into cubes
1 small clove garlic, minced
1 teaspoon dried oregano
1 teaspoon dried basil
2 tablespoons chopped fresh Italian parsley
  (or 3 tablespoons dried)

1 1/2 teaspoons grated Parmesan cheese
2 tablespoons frozen or well-chilled butter
  or margarine
  Salt and pepper to taste

Preheat oven to 350°. Prepare the tomatoes
by them cutting in half horizontally and
seasoning to taste with salt and pepper. Lay
the tomato halves in a single layer on a
foil-lined cookie sheet or shallow baking
pan.

To make the topping: Using a food
processor or blender, whirl the bread cubes
and garlic until crumbs form. Add the
oregano, basil, parsley, and Parmesan
cheese. Cut the butter up into small pieces
and add them gradually to the food processor, while it is running. Blend only until
the crumbs begin to stick together.
Distribute prepared topping evenly among
the tomato halves. Bake for 10 minutes or
until tomatoes are cooked and topping is
browned. Serve hot.

SERVES 6

Microwave Mushrooms

Save washing a dirty skillet by microwaving mush-rooms in their serving dish.

1 10-ounce package mushrooms, sliced
2 tablespoons soy sauce
2 tablespoons butter or margarine, cut into
   1/2-inch cubes
   Salt and black pepper to taste

Place the mushrooms in a 1-quart microwavable casserole dish. Stir in the soy sauce. Dot with the butter. Cover and microwave on full power for 2 to 5 minutes or until mushrooms are cooked. Stir once halfway through the cooking cycle. Serve warm.

SERVES 3 TO 4

Mount Gay Onions & Mushrooms

2 tablespoons butter or margarine
2 Vidalia or other mild onions, sliced
8 ounces sliced mushrooms
1 teaspoon dried parsley
   Salt and pepper to taste
1/4 cup Mount Gay or other dark rum

In a 10-inch skillet heat the butter over medium-high heat. Add the onions and sauté for a few minutes. Add the mushrooms. Sprinkle with parsley, salt, and pepper. Cover the pan and cook the vegetables until they begin to soften. Stir in the rum and continue to cook uncovered until the onions and mushrooms are browned and pan juices are reduced. Serve as a side dish with steak.

SERVES 4 TO 6

Caramelized Onions

Nice served over roast beef or pork or potatoes.

3 tablespoons butter or margarine
3 medium onions
1 cup chicken stock
1 teaspoon sugar

In a 10-inch skillet melt the butter over medium heat. Add the onions and cook until golden brown, about 30 to 40 minutes, stirring occasionally. Add the chicken stock and sugar and continue to cook on medium heat an additional 10 minutes, until almost all the liquid is absorbed. Serve at once or cover and refrigerate. Reheat gently.

MAKES 1½ CUPS

Glazed Cranberries and Onions

A festive addition to a holiday dinner. Cook in the oven along with your roast or pop it in the microwave for a few minutes for the final "bake."

1 tablespoon butter or margarine
1 large Vidalia or other mild onion, sliced in rings and then quartered
2 tablespoons sugar
1½ cups fresh cranberries
  Pinch salt
  Pinch pepper
½ teaspoon grated orange peel
3 tablespoons orange juice

Preheat oven to 400°. In a large skillet heat the butter over medium-high heat. Sauté the onions until lightly browned, about 10 minutes. Add the sugar and toss to coat. Stir in the cranberries, salt, pepper, orange peel, and orange juice. Mix well, scraping any browned bits from the bottom of the skillet. Transfer the mixture to a buttered 1-quart casserole dish and bake at 400° uncovered for about 30 minutes, until the onions and cranberries are tender and bubbly.

MAKES 1½ CUPS

SPECIAL SIDES

Cinnamon Fruit

1   14-ounce can spiced apple rings, lightly
    drained
2   29-ounce cans pears, drained
1   16-ounce can apricot halves, drained

Place all the ingredients in a heatproof
casserole. Stir to mix and then cover and
heat either in the microwave or in a 350°
oven until hot. Serve warm.

SERVES 8

Ginger-Pear Cranberry Sauce

*We made this zippy variation of fresh cranberry sauce one
Thanksgiving, and we agreed the recipe was a keeper.*

1   cup sugar
1   cup water
2   tablespoons crystallized ginger
1   fresh pear, peeled, cored and chopped
1   package fresh cranberries

Microwave method: Combine the sugar
and water in a large microwave-safe bowl.
Microwave on high for 2 to 4 minutes,
until boiling. Stir every minute. Stir in the
ginger, pear, and cranberries. Microwave
for 2 to 5 more minutes, until fruit is soft

and sauce thickens enough to coat a spoon
and becomes glossy. Stir every 2 minutes
until done. Sauce will thicken further as it
cools. Refrigerate.

Stovetop method: Combine the sugar and
water in a saucepan and bring the mixture
to a boil. Stir in the ginger, pear, and cranberries and boil for 10 to 15 minutes, until
the pear and cranberries are soft and sauce
is done as described above.

MAKES 1½ CUPS

Roasted Chestnuts

1   to 2 pounds chestnuts

Soak the chestnuts in water for an hour to
soften their skins. Drain the water off the
nuts. With a sharp knife, make a small
slice in the skin, as you would a baking
potato, to allow steam to vent as the chestnuts cook. Preheat oven to 350°. Place
nuts in a single layer in a shallow pan. Add
a thin layer of water to the pan to keep
chestnuts moist while they are cooking.
Bake for 20 to 30 minutes. The chestnuts
are done when they are tender. Test for
doneness by breaking a chestnut apart. The
center should be meaty and juicy. If they
are dry, add a bit more water to the baking
pan and continue cooking. Check nuts at
5-minute intervals. Serve hot.

RECIPE FOR COMFORTING LOVED ONES

Celebrate small successes

Get to know the real person

Relive old times

Surround them with things they love

Share your everyday life, so they can enjoy it through you

Tell them you love them

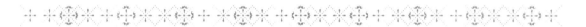

SALADS TO TOSS

Italians eat backwards. We enjoy our salads at the end of the meal, rather than at the beginning. My mom said it aids digestion, maybe so. But I've always felt a salad makes a nice transition between the main course and dessert or coffee. The truth is that salads taste good anytime. Some can even stand alone as a meal.

Life's not always a bowl of cherries . . .

Just when we think our life is under control, fate heaps on some sort of crisis to help us realize what is important. Maybe a cookbook is no place to bring up dealings with serious illnesses and deaths of loved ones, but they don't fit in anywhere. There's never a good time to deal with suffering. That's the trouble.

I was having a great life until my dad was diagnosed with cancer. My first instinct was to remain at his side through the whole ordeal, but he lived an hour and a half away. At first, I exhausted myself with frequent traveling. But fate has a way of stopping us short when we're too confused to do it ourselves. I became ill, and when I couldn't visit Dad for a while, I was forced to put things into perspective. I couldn't ignore my health or forsake my husband and children. They were important, too. I worked out a travel schedule I could live with and arranged for live-in help, so I could sleep nights knowing Dad was safe and cared for when I couldn't be there. This did nothing to ease the pain of his illness, but it provided me peace of mind.

That year, one of worst of my life, was one of the most enlightening times with my dad. I got to know him, and I learned what a strong-minded, heroic person he was. I treasure those afternoons we spent in his living room watching Zorro (or "Zero," as Dad called him) and his other favorite TV shows. We shared a chuckle and chatted in between. In the spring, we monitored the progress of a robin's nest that had formed in a yellowed, forgotten Christmas wreath outside his living room window, rejoicing as each chirping baby flew from its nest. (Maybe I need to learn a lesson from that robin.)

I was on constant search for anything that could make Dad smile. I loaned him a stuffed animal to cuddle, and instead of spending money on a Christmas present he might never use, I gathered pictures of our happy times and made up an album he could thumb through whenever he was lonely. I brought him dumb stuff: a twirling sippy straw for his juice to use instead of a hospital straw; a few bright-colored leaves, crisp with the smell of autumn; some pretty shells from the beach that smelled of the ocean. I made homemade soups and breads with ingredients he could eat, and perked up his appetite with forbidden treats, like fast-food burgers with fries and chocolate sundaes with real whipped cream. It gave me untold pleasure to watch him enjoy a single bite.

Pretending that things were "normal" was difficult. Dad was stubborn and refused to talk about his feelings. So we talked about our memories, recounting good times at family picnics and holidays. When Dad died, I was relieved of the pain of watching him suffer, but how I miss him. Yet I will be eternally grateful for every minute of that special time with him. I learned that wearing large dangling earrings, obsessing about my attire, or spending money on fancy trips was not nearly as crucial as love, family, and good health. The kids were grown up, and I am proud of them. When I tried to shield them from seeing him on the last bad days, they insisted on being there. I took comfort in their presence and found out what strong, wonderful adults we had reared.

Is all this sad? I hope not. Because as we get older, it's inevitable that at some point our parents or someone we love will begin to fail, and we must take care of them, just as some day we expect our kids to care for us. I'm thinking of getting it in writing.

*   *   *

I guess it was opening this can of black olives that led me back to my dad. He taught us to put one at the end of each finger and wiggle our hands, or maybe it was slicing these oranges. Dad could pare a mean set of orange-peel eyeglasses. I can't cut up a summer tomato without remembering how he loved to garden. I think of Dad when I cook because, like me, he always worried about what he was going to eat for dinner. It must run in our family.

TOSSED GREENS
& DRESSINGS

When I was growing up, and well into my adulthood, I was fortunate to have access to a garden from which I could pick all kinds of leafy greens to add to our salads. Butter crunch lettuce, romaine, escarole, Swiss chard, dandelions, and fresh herbs. You name it. We grew it. Today's fancy name for a mixture of greens is "mesclun." I've come to enjoy the prewashed, prepackaged salad mixtures now available at the supermarket because of the convenient and smaller portions available. I'm not into quantity cookery anymore, remember?

I was spoiled with garden tomatoes—big beefsteaks, tiny red cherries, and early and long-keeping types. In the fall, my dad used to cut down tomato-laden vines from his garden at the first hint of frost and drag them to his basement. He carefully laid them out on a newspaper to ripen and had fresh tomatoes until Christmas. If you are stuck with hard, tasteless store-bought tomatoes, as we all are during the wintertime, set them on your windowsill or throw them in a brown bag for a few days, and they will continue to ripen and improve in taste. Once you refrigerate tomatoes they won't ripen anymore.

GREEN SALADS

Basic Garden Salad

Start with your favorite kinds of lettuce and a tomato or two. If you don't have a tomato, cut up a piece of fruit instead. An orange works especially well. Check your vegetable bin for anything interesting to add, and don't forget your canned goods. Artichokes, roasted peppers, olives, beets, and beans make great additions to a salad.

2   tomatoes or pieces of fruit
     Your choice: fresh peppers, mushrooms,
       onions, carrots, cucumber, squash,
       canned olives, artichokes, tuna,
       roasted peppers, beans, etc.
1   head lettuce or equivalent in greens

½   cup or equivalent "Wing It" Vinaigrette,
       p. 181

Cut the vegetables and tomatoes into bite-sized pieces and layer them at the bottom of a large salad bowl. Top with greens. If serving immediately, toss in the dressing, otherwise cover and refrigerate until ready to serve. If making salad in advance, place the heaviest and juiciest items at the bottom and your lettuce will remain fresh and uncrushed until you are ready to dress and serve it. If you put vinegar or prepared dressing on a salad too far in advance, it is liable to wilt the greens.

SERVES 4 TO 6

½ teaspoon salt
¼ teaspoon ground black pepper
   Dash hot sauce

"Wing It" Vinaigrette

Try this the old-fashioned way, without a recipe. Mix the dressing right on the salad, taste a few leaves, then adjust the flavor. Begin with a few swipes of olive oil, a few less "swipes" of vinegar (preferably the Italian brands), and season to your heart's content. If you're a novice at seasoning, season the salad with salt and pepper to taste, and then add sprinklings of oregano, parsley, and basil. Oregano is strong, so go easy with it. Everyone will want your recipe, but you can smile smugly and tell them there isn't one.

Tossed Mandarin Salad with Glazed Almonds

I've yet to meet a person who hasn't enjoyed the sweet-sour taste of this salad.

¼ cup sliced almonds
1 tablespoon plus 1 teaspoon sugar
½ head lettuce, torn into bite-sized pieces
2 stalks celery, sliced
2 scallions, sliced
1 can mandarin oranges, drained

MANDARIN DRESSING:
¼ cup olive oil
2 teaspoons sugar
2 tablespoons wine vinegar
1 teaspoon dried parsley

In a saucepan cook the almonds and sugar over low heat, stirring constantly until sugar is melted and almonds are coated. Once the sugar starts to melt, the process goes very quickly. Do not leave the pan unattended. Remove the glazed almonds to a waxed paper-lined, heatproof plate to cool. When cool, break apart and store at room temperature. (Hide these or they'll be eaten.)

Make the dressing by shaking all ingredients in a tightly covered jar. Place the lettuce, celery, scallions, and oranges in a large salad bowl. Top with sugared almonds and toss with the dressing. Serve at once.

SERVES 4 TO 6

Red Lettuce with Apples and Fennel

I developed this dressing when experimenting with coriander. Coriander is the English name for the plant we call cilantro. The seeds are always called coriander and may be found whole or ground. This recipe uses ground coriander, which has a very different taste from cilantro. If you don't have leeks, substitute scallions. If you are not going to dress and serve the salad right away, toss the apple slices in a bit of lemon juice so they won't turn brown.

2	Granny Smith apples or other tart apples, sliced
$1/2$	bulb fennel (anise), sliced
1	leek or half bunch scallions, sliced
1	head romaine lettuce, torn into bite-sized pieces
$1/2$	can black olives, pitted

CORIANDER DRESSING:

$1/2$	cup olive oil
3	tablespoons wine vinegar
3	tablespoons lemon juice
$1/4$	teaspoon ground coriander
$1/2$	teaspoon salt or to taste
$1/4$	teaspoon black pepper

In a small bowl mix the dressing ingredients. Put all salad ingredients in a large salad bowl and toss them with just enough dressing to coat, about $1/4$ cup.

SERVES 4 TO 6

Tossed Green Salad with Orange-Oregano Vinaigrette

Grate the peel from one of the oranges and then use the meat of the orange in the salad.

ORANGE-OREGANO VINAIGRETTE:

$1/4$	cup olive oil
2	tablespoons balsamic vinegar
1	tablespoon fresh orange juice
1	teaspoon grated orange peel
1	tablespoon finely chopped onion
1	teaspoon salt
1	dash hot sauce
1	tablespoon fresh oregano leaves (or 1 teaspoon dried)

1	navel orange, peeled and sliced into half circles
$1/2$	head romaine lettuce, torn into bite-sized pieces
$1/4$	cup chopped celery

To make the dressing: In a small bowl mix together the olive oil, vinegar, orange juice, orange peel, onion, salt, hot sauce, and the oregano leaves. Let stand at room temperature at least 30 minutes, allowing flavors to meld.

Place orange slices and celery in the bottom of a salad serving bowl. Set lettuce on top. Cover and chill bowl until ready to serve, or serve at once tossed with enough of the Orange-Oregano Vinaigrette to please your palette.

SERVES 2

blend well. Stir in the Parmesan cheese. If making ahead, refrigerate the bowl with the dressing. When ready to serve, add in the lettuce and the croutons and toss well.

SERVES 4

Caesar Salad

Yes, it has anchovies. That's what makes it taste so good, but they are mashed into the dressing so your guests won't see them and shriek. For two people, use half a head of lettuce and fewer croutons. Save the extra dressing for the next evening's salad. The leftover anchovies will keep refrigerated for quite a while. Use them in Osso Buco, p. 81.

1	clove garlic, peeled
1/4	teaspoon pepper
2	pieces anchovy
1	teaspoon Dijon mustard
1/2	cup olive oil
5	tablespoons wine vinegar
	Juice of 1 lemon
3	teaspoons Worcestershire sauce
1/2	cup Parmesan cheese
1	head romaine lettuce, torn into bite-sized pieces
1/4	cup purchased croutons or homemade French Bread Croutons

With a fork, mash the garlic with the pepper at the bottom of the salad serving bowl. Add the anchovies and mustard and mash again. Add the olive oil, vinegar, lemon juice, and Worcestershire sauce and

French Bread Croutons

Float these croutons in soup or cut rounds in quarters for salads.

1	loaf French bread, sliced into 3/4-inch rounds
1/4	cup olive oil
1	clove garlic, mashed

Toast bread rounds on a baking sheet in a preheated 350° oven for 10 minutes. Meanwhile, combine garlic and olive oil. Remove bread from oven and brush with garlic oil mixture. Return to oven for an addition 10 to 15 minutes or until lightly browned.

Baby Greens with Mustard Vinaigrette

3   cups mixed baby greens
1   small ripe tomato, sliced into wedges
1/2   cup artichoke hearts, quartered

MUSTARD VINAIGRETTE:
3   tablespoons olive oil
1 1/2 tablespoons wine vinegar
1   teaspoon Dijon mustard
1   teaspoon dried chives
1/2   teaspoon salt
    Pinch ground black pepper

Place the greens, tomato, and artichokes in a salad serving bowl. Add the olive oil, vinegar, mustard, chives, salt, and pepper. Toss salad and serve at once.

SERVES 2

Mixed Green Salad Platter with Walnuts and Blue Cheese

This salad is served on a flat platter with the ingredients layered and pleasingly arranged. It is bright and decorative and looks especially nice on a buffet table.

1   head red lettuce, torn
1   medium head radicchio
4   heads Belgian endive
1   bunch watercress, stems trimmed
1/2   cup chopped walnuts, toasted
1/2   pound blue cheese, crumbled

SHALLOT MUSTARD DRESSING:
2/3   cup olive oil
1/4   cup wine vinegar
1/4   cup finely chopped shallots
1   teaspoon dried oregano
2   teaspoons Dijon mustard
1   teaspoon sugar
1/2   teaspoon salt
1/4   teaspoon black pepper

Line a large platter with the red lettuce. Layer the radicchio evenly around the platter, approximately 1 inch inside the rim. Layer endive shoots in a star formation out from the center. Top with watercress. Sprinkle walnuts and blue cheese evenly over top of the greens. Mix the dressing ingredients and drizzle over all or serve on the side.

SERVES 10

Red Lettuce with Pears

LEMON CHIVE DRESSING:

1/2	cup olive oil
1	teaspoon finely chopped walnuts
1	tablespoon chives
1/2	teaspoon salt
1/8	teaspoon pepper
3	tablespoons lemon juice
4	teaspoons balsamic vinegar

1/4	cup toasted walnut halves
1	16-ounce can sliced pears, drained (or 3 fresh pears, peeled, cored, sliced, and dipped in 1 teaspoon lemon juice)
1	head red lettuce, torn into bite-sized pieces
2	stalks celery, sliced
1/2	cup crumbled Feta cheese

Make the dressing: Mix all dressing ingredients in a small glass jar or microwave-safe bowl. Microwave for 30 seconds on full power. Allow to cool while preparing remainder of the salad. Toast the 1/4 cup walnuts in a 350° oven for a few minutes, until aroma is released. Set aside.

Place salad ingredients, including walnuts, in a large salad bowl in the order listed. Toss with cooled dressing and serve.

SERVES 8

Strawberry Ginger Tossed Salad

STRAWBERRY GINGER DRESSING:

1/4	cup olive oil
2	tablespoons balsamic vinegar
1	tablespoon orange juice
1/2	teaspoon peeled and diced fresh gingerroot
1/2	teaspoon salt
1/8	teaspoon black pepper
1/4	cup diced fresh strawberries

1	head dark green lettuce, such as romaine, torn into bite-sized pieces
2	scallions, sliced
6	to 8 fresh strawberries, sliced
1/2	cup artichoke hearts, drained and sliced in half (do not use marinated artichokes)

Make the dressing: In a small, microwave-proof mixing bowl combine the olive oil, vinegar, orange juice, gingerroot, salt, and pepper. Add the diced strawberries, mashing them into the mixture with a fork. Microwave 10 seconds on high to release the ginger flavor. Set aside.

Place the lettuce or spinach in a salad bowl. Add the scallions, strawberries, and artichoke. Toss gently with as much of the dressing as you wish. Serve at once.

MAKES 3/4 CUP DRESSING

SERVES 2

Mixed Greens, Grapes, & Almonds with Lime Vinaigrette

I started experimenting with spices one year after vacationing in Grenada, where spices are grown. Spices such as cinnamon, nutmeg, and ginger that we normally reserve for desserts permeate all the Grenadian dishes, giving them a distinctive island flavor.

$1/4$ head lettuce, torn into bite sized pieces
1   cup fresh mesclun mix (premixed greens assortment)
$1/2$ cup white or red seedless grapes
$1/4$ cup sliced almonds

LIME VINAIGRETTE:
$1/4$ cup olive oil
1   clove garlic, minced fine
3   tablespoons lime juice
1   tablespoon wine vinegar
$1/8$ teaspoon nutmeg
$1/4$ teaspoon salt or to taste
       Pinch black pepper

Place the lettuce, mesclun mix, and grapes in a medium salad-serving bowl. Prepare the lime vinaigrette by mixing all the ingredients in a small jar. When ready to serve, sprinkle the sliced almonds over the greens mixture and then add the vinaigrette. Toss well.

MAKES ¼ CUP VINAIGRETTE

SERVES 3 TO 4

Pineapple Tossed Salad

For a modern twist try this with mesclun mix or baby spinach. These are available washed and bagged at the supermarket.

PINEAPPLE BALSAMIC DRESSING:
2   tablespoons pineapple juice
2   tablespoons balsamic vinegar
$1/4$ cup olive oil
$1/4$ teaspoon fresh minced ginger
$1/4$ teaspoon salt
       Pinch black pepper

$1/2$ cup canned pineapple chunks, drained and juice reserved
4   cups mixed greens, torn into bite-sized pieces
2   scallions, sliced
$1/2$ cup pitted black olives

To make the dressing: In a small bowl mix the pineapple juice, vinegar, olive oil, ginger, salt, and pepper.

Place the pineapple chunks, mixed greens, scallions, and olives in a salad bowl. Toss with dressing and serve at once.

SERVES 3 TO 4

Holiday Tossed Salad

Try this colorful, festive salad any time.

ALLSPICE HONEY DRESSING:

1	teaspoon grated orange peel
1/4	cup orange juice
1/3	cup wine vinegar
3	tablespoons olive oil
1 1/2	tablespoons honey
3/4	teaspoon allspice
1/2	teaspoon salt or to taste
1/8	teaspoon ground black pepper

2	heads lettuce (or 2 bags prepared greens)
3/4	cup dried cranberries
2	firm, ripe pears, sliced (or one 28-ounce can pear slices, well drained)
1/4	cup slivered almonds

Mix the orange peel, orange juice, vinegar, olive oil, honey, allspice, salt, and pepper to make the dressing. If using fresh pears, dip slices in the orange juice beforehand to prevent browning. Just before serving, place the lettuce, dried cranberries, pears, and almonds in a large salad bowl. Toss with dressing and serve.

SERVES 10 TO 12

Red Lettuce Salad with Orange Balsamic Dressing

ORANGE BALSAMIC DRESSING:

1	tablespoon grated onion
1/2	teaspoon grated orange peel
1	tablespoon orange juice
3	tablespoons olive oil
1/2	teaspoon thyme
1/4	teaspoon salt
	Pinch black pepper

1	navel orange, peeled and cut up
1/2	cup pitted black olives
1/2	cucumber, sliced
2	scallions, sliced
1/2	head red lettuce, torn up

In a small cup mix the dressing ingredients. To make the salad, place the orange, olives, cucumber, scallions, and lettuce in a serving bowl. Toss with the dressing just before serving.

SERVES 2 TO 4

VEGETABLE & COMBINATION SALADS

Antipasto

This salad belongs at the beginning of a meal. Serve it as a first course or a meal in itself. Layer the different ingredients in such a way that one could lift a portion containing a little bit of everything.

1	head lettuce
1/2	pound prosciutto or other peppered ham, deli-sliced
1/4	pound Genoa salami, deli-sliced
1/2	pound sharp provolone cheese, sliced into wedges
2	to 3 ripe tomatoes, sliced in rings
1	jar marinated artichokes, drained
1	jar roasted peppers, drained
1	can Italian olives in olive oil (or black olives, drained)
1	can tuna, drained (optional)
	Olive oil
	Wine vinegar
	Salt and pepper

Select a large, round serving platter. Tear off enough lettuce leaves to line the bottom of the platter and then layer the ingredients in a circular fashion in the order given above. Allow one "set" for each person. Place olives in the center of the platter.

Drizzle with oil, then with vinegar. Season with salt and pepper.

SERVES 10

Tomato-Cucumber Salad

Most flavorful when made with fresh garden tomatoes. Decorate cucumber slices by running the tines of a fork up and down the length of a peeled cucumber before slicing it. Because of the acidity in the tomatoes, this is one salad that does not need vinegar. Dunk some bread in the juice left at the bottom of the salad bowl. Delicious!

1	cucumber, peeled and sliced
3	ripe tomatoes, sliced
1	teaspoon oregano
1	clove garlic, minced fine
3	tablespoons olive oil

Mix all ingredients and refrigerate until ready to serve.

SERVES 4

Multi-colored Tomato Salad

1   clove garlic, minced
½   teaspoon salt
¼   teaspoon black pepper
¼   cup olive oil
2   yellow tomatoes, sliced
6   plum tomatoes, sliced (or 3 medium
     red tomatoes, sliced)
¼   cup chopped fresh basil leaves (or
     1½ tablespoons dried)

Mash garlic into the salt and pepper in a
salad serving bowl. Stir in the olive oil.
Add the tomatoes and the basil. Toss well.
Refrigerate at least 30 minutes before
serving.

SERVES 4

Broccoli-Orange Salad

1   head broccoli florets, cut into bite-sized
     pieces
½   sliced Vidalia or other mild onion
2   large navel oranges, peeled and sliced

ORANGE MINT DRESSING:
½   cup olive oil
¼   cup wine vinegar
¼   cup orange juice
1   tablespoon minced onion (optional)
1   teaspoon dried mint (or 2 tablespoons
     chopped fresh)
½   teaspoon salt or to taste
⅛   teaspoon black pepper

Combine the broccoli florets, onion, and
oranges in a salad bowl. Add the oil, wine
vinegar, orange juice, minced onion, mint,
salt, and pepper. Toss well and refrigerate
for at least 30 minutes before serving.

SERVES 4 TO 6

Broccoli-Vidalia Salad

If you wish, add other garden vegetables, such as cucumbers or tomatoes, to this salad.

1   head broccoli, cleaned and cut into florets
2   tablespoons or more of water for steaming
1/3 cup sliced Vidalia or other mild onion

BASIC VINAIGRETTE DRESSING:
1   tablespoon olive oil
2   tablespoons balsamic vinegar
1   small clove garlic, minced fine
1   teaspoon salt
1/4 teaspoon ground black pepper
1/2 teaspoon dried oregano
1   teaspoon dried basil

Place florets and water in a microwave-safe container and cook on high for 2 to 3 minutes, or steam lightly on stovetop until cooked but still crisp. Meanwhile, slice the onion.

Prepare the vinaigrette in the salad/serving bowl by combining all the dressing ingredients; add the onion. When broccoli is steamed, drain off excess water and allow it to cool to room temperature before combining it with the onion and dressing in the salad bowl. Chill at least 30 minutes before serving.

SERVES 4

Orange-Fennel Salad

1/4 bulb fresh fennel (anise), trimmed and sliced
2   navel oranges, peeled and sliced

ANISE DRESSING:
1   tablespoon olive oil
1   tablespoon wine vinegar
1/4 teaspoon anise seed or anise extract
1/4 teaspoon salt

Place the fennel and oranges in a medium salad serving bowl. Add the dressing ingredients and toss to mix thoroughly. Chill at least 30 minutes before serving, allowing the flavors to meld.

SERVES 2

Orange-Olive Salad

8   navel oranges, peeled and sliced
½   cup pitted black olives, halved
1½ red onions, sliced
2   tablespoons olive oil
2   tablespoons lemon juice
1   teaspoon cumin
½   teaspoon salt
    Pinch black pepper

Put the oranges, olives, and onions in a large mixing bowl. In a measuring cup, whisk together the oil, lemon juice, cumin, salt, and pepper to make the dressing. Toss the dressing with orange mixture and turn into a serving bowl.

SERVES 8

Fresh Orange Salad

The first time I tasted this simple combination was at a family picnic when my uncle took an orange from the fruit bowl, peeled and sliced it into a paper bowl, and then stirred in a little olive oil and salt.

4   navel oranges, peeled and sliced in half circles
2   tablespoons olive oil
¼   teaspoon salt or to taste

Combine all ingredients in a medium salad bowl. Chill well before serving.

SERVES 4

Winter Fruit Compote

2   29-ounce cans pear halves, drained
1   29-ounce can sliced peaches, drained
1   14½-ounce can tart red pitted cherries, drained
⅓   cup Chambord raspberry liqueur

Combine all ingredients and heat in a covered, heatproof serving dish.

SERVES 8 TO 10

Celery & Olive Oil Dip

This, too, is a traditional family treat. At the end of a big meal, out would come the plate of celery. Before long, we'd fix up this little dipping sauce in a small custard cup right at the table for everyone to share. Good with fennel, too.

4	tablespoons olive oil
1½	teaspoons salt
¾	teaspoon black pepper
1	head celery, washed and trimmed

Place the olive oil, salt, and pepper in a small dipping cup. Stir with a stalk of celery and chomp. (Double-dipping is a no-no unless it's just the family.)

Marinated Garbanzos

Mix up and refrigerate beans in a covered container. Serve a spoonful as a side dish, or add some to your salads.

1	20-ounce can garbanzo beans (chickpeas)
4	tablespoons wine vinegar
1	tablespoon olive oil
2	sprigs of fresh oregano leaves (or 1 teaspoon dried)
½	teaspoon salt
⅛	teaspoon black pepper

Mix in a covered container and refrigerate until well chilled. Store in refrigerator for no longer than 2 weeks.

MAKES 2¼ CUPS

Herb Vinegar

I love to make this herb vinegar in the summer with fresh herbs from the garden and use it all winter long. Add it to a salad with olive oil and a little salt and pepper for an easy dressing. Experiment with different vinegar and herb combinations. This keeps indefinitely and makes a nice gift.

4	sprigs oregano
5	sprigs sweet basil
3	sprigs Italian parsley
1	tablespoon black peppercorns
1	medium clove garlic
1	quart wine vinegar (4 cups)
2	additional sprigs of herbs for garnish

Place the oregano, basil, parsley, peppercorns, and garlic in a 2-quart saucepan. In a separate pan heat the vinegar to boiling. Remove from heat and pour over into the herbs and seasonings in the 2-quart pan. Let steep at room temperature until completely cool. Strain the vinegar into two 2-cup decorative bottles. Place a sprig of fresh herbs in each bottle for garnish. Does not need to be refrigerated, as vinegar is a natural preservative.

MAKES 1 QUART

RECIPE FOR INDULGING YOURSELF

Take a long drive alone

Go clothes shopping without looking at the tags

Let Caller ID screen your calls

Go to sleep without removing your makeup and brushing your teeth

Forgo your workout—and order that hot fudge sundae

THE BREAD

Another one of my little indulges during these empty-nest days was the purchase of an electric bread maker. Loaves of bread piled up on my counter until I realized that two of us could never consume so many loaves. You see, electric bread making is so easy and fun that it can become an obsession. I'd plan my next loaf while the bread machine was working on the first of the day. My husband became so tired of awakening to the whir of the bread maker that he threatened to banish it to the basement. Eventually, I learned to temper my obsession, and to freeze extra loaves for future use. My bread maker lives at my daughter's house now, but every so often I have to urge to smell fresh bread baking.

All the cookies are yours . . .

All the cookies in the cupboard are yours, and so is the "dough." When that last child no longer needs your financial support, it feels as if you've been given a raise—no more school clothes to buy or mouths to feed. Maybe you still have payments to make on your car and your home, but life is good. What will you do with all that extra money?

You half-heartedly put some away for your retirement, which seems so far away that you can't get motivated. You consider making investments, buying a condo in

Florida, splurging on that boat you've been eyeing for years and could never afford. It feels so good not to pinch that penny hard that you splurge on an outrageously pricey diamond ring for your husband and make reservations for Europe. You've earned all this. Spoil yourselves!

When the kids were little we never strayed far from home. It was too expensive and such a hassle. Car trips were nightmarish. Between the radio and the giggling and poking in the back seat, I usually arrived at our destination with a throbbing headache and a crick in my neck from turning around to scold the kids. By the time we packed ourselves, along with our luggage and everyone's favorite toys, nothing short of a shoehorn would wedge us all out of the car for road stops. Hotel stays and meals for five on the move, even at the double arches, were a stretch on the trip budget. Flying would've been a bargain by comparison.

It wasn't until our kids grew to adulthood that we could enjoy vacations with them. Our finances had improved and, as the kids took jobs, they were able to buy most of their own clothes and pay for their entertainment. We flew us all to Florida for Christmas and went sailing in the Caribbean. And then, like "Figment," the little purple guy at Disney World, our vacations together were gone—new careers with no vacation time, impending marriages, and company relocations. It became nearly impossible to get everyone together. We learned to settle for a weekend here and there and an occasional evening out, but our lives became excruciatingly separate.

This morning, I am waking up in a luxury, air-conditioned suite. This feels almost surreal, like a fulfilled vision—just the two of us with all this extra cash to spend on ourselves. When we first began vacationing without the kids, I couldn't shake the feeling I'd left some luggage behind, and then I realized that I had—the remnants of our parenthood. Today, I'm not a mother. I'm a wife. I look over at my husband, still a long, lumpy heap under the covers, and realize I've been calling him "Dad" just like the kids. He's not my father, I remind myself. I duck back under the covers and give him a hug and a big smooch. He's still adorable.

We order champagne brunch in our hotel room, and then forgo the sightseeing to spend our day lounging on a glistening white beach, reading books and nursing frosty piña coladas. We make reservations at a romantic restaurant and feast on lobster, cooked tableside under the stars. We savor the wonder of it all—the total lack of responsibility and, for the first time in years, each other.

It's wonderful what changes a little extra money in your pocket can bring about. Not all of us choose to travel. We may decide to go back to school, invest in a piece of property, or start a new business. Having ready cash buys us the flexibility to fly to

California or Chicago and to visit our children or good friends, or to foot the bill for the kids' trips home. We develop a new pattern of spending and can support our family needs in ways we choose. All the cookies are ours now, and we only have to share them when we want to.

Breads & Breakfast

Yeast-based breads

The recipes in this section demand that you own or borrow an electric bread maker, although if you're good with yeast I see no reason why you couldn't mix these recipes by hand or in the food processor. Although a bread maker will bake the loaf as well as mix it, I get a fluffier, more "normal" shaped loaf if I remove the bread dough from the mixer for its last rise, shape it, and then bake it in my own oven. To do this, set your bread maker on its manual mode, and remove the dough once it has completed rising, but before the bake cycle begins. Be sure to use bread flour. King Arthur's is a good choice, because it can be used for bread as well as other baking. The yeast must be fresh, unless you plan on making hockey pucks. Read the instructions below before inaugurating your first loaf. Once you see how easy it is, you'll want to make more, and more, and more.

Electric bread basics

It is important to measure accurately. Level off dry ingredients and do not pack down flour. Check the dough for consistency after it has been kneading for a few minutes. If it is forming a dry-looking ball, add more water, one tablespoon at a time. If it stays sticky and is not pulling away from the sides of the mixer bowl and forming a ball, add more flour, one tablespoon at a time. Air temperature and humidity levels influence the consistency of the dough.

Place yeast in the bread maker bowl first, always in one outside corner as the manufacturer suggests. Add the remaining dry ingredients in the order listed. Then add the wet ingredients, saving the water for last.

All milks, butter, eggs, and the like must be brought to room temperature before adding them to the bread maker mix. To speed up this process, lightly microwave butter, milk, or yogurt for about 10 to 20 seconds. Place eggs in warm water for a few minutes. Be careful not to cook or overheat ingredients, as too much heat will "kill" the yeast. Water should be the temperature of baby's bath water.

Add nuts, raisins, or other dried fruit during the last few minutes of the kneading cycle. (My bread maker beeps to signal when it is time to do this.) This prevents these types of ingredients from being pulverized into small bits during the long mixing and kneading cycles.

Shaping dough

Remove the dough from the bread maker by holding the bread basin upside down over a floured breadboard. Shake out dough, disturbing it as little as possible. Remove dough hook. Working quickly and without kneading to maintain the fluffiness of the risen dough, form it into a smooth ball and shape as it you wish.

Rising and baking

Allow dough to rise in a draft-free area. Place shaped dough on a lightly greased baking sheet or pan and cover it lightly with a dishtowel. Allow it to rise until doubled in size, approximately 30 to 60 minutes. The denser the bread, the longer the rise cycle. It helps if the room is warm. To release air before placing loaves into a preheated oven, make several slashes across the tops of risen loaves with a very sharp knife. As a rule, most loaves will bake at 350° and be done in 25 to 30 minutes. Bread is cooked when you thump it on the underside and it sounds hollow.

To freeze, store, or reheat

Wrap cooled bread tightly in foil. Place it in the refrigerator or freezer as soon after baking as possible. Defrost loaves completely before rewarming. Heat them, uncovered, in a 350° oven and they will taste fresh baked. If bread is a bit stale, wrap it in foil and heat it for about 10 minutes, until warmed through. To crisp the crust, remove the foil and continue heating the bread for a minute or two more.

Yeast Breads

French Bread

I make this recipe most often. To achieve a crustier loaf, knead the bread for an extra cycle in the electric bread maker. Do this by simply shutting the machine off after the first knead and then re-starting it. Shape the loaves and bake them on perforated French bread pans, available at kitchen shops, or on a cookie sheet. Don't be afraid to let this bread rise high.

3 teaspoons active dry yeast or bread
  machine yeast
3¼ cups white bread flour
1½ teaspoons salt
1½ tablespoons sugar
1½ cups warm water

Add the ingredients to the bread maker in the order listed. Set the machine on "manual" (white bread). Once the first knead is completed, turn the machine off and then reset it to give the bread an extra kneading cycle. After the first rise, remove the dough from bread maker. Place dough on a floured board. Cut it in half and stretch pieces into two 12-inch loaves. Set loaves in the wells of a greased, perforated loaf pan or place them lengthwise, a few inches apart, on a baking sheet. If using a perforated pan, set the pan on top of a baking sheet to avoid having a draft underneath. Cover top and sides of loaves lightly with a dishtowel and allow them to rise in a draft-free area until they have doubled in size,

about 30 to 60 minutes. With a sharp knife, make a few slashes along the length of the loaves to allow air to escape. Bake loaves in a preheated 350° oven for 20 to 25 minutes or until bread sounds hollow when thumped on the underside. Let cool about 20 minutes before serving.

MAKES 2 LOAVES

Seeded Onion Bread

This spicy bread is even better than garlic bread. Try it with a steak dinner or a robust stew. Use dried minced onions for best results. I keep a large jar of them on hand just for this recipe. The poppy seeds will be less expensive if you buy them in bulk from a health-food store.

3 teaspoons active dry yeast or bread
  machine yeast
3¼ cups bread flour
1½ teaspoons salt
2 tablespoons brown sugar
½ cup dried onions
1 teaspoon poppy seeds
1 teaspoon black pepper
2 tablespoons butter or margarine
½ cup lukewarm milk
¾ cup warm water

Add the ingredients to the bread maker in the order listed. Set machine on "manual" (white bread). Watch the bread carefully while it's in the knead cycle. Dried onions sometimes absorb too much of the water and the mix may be dry. If this is the case, add water, a tablespoon at a time, until the dough's consistency improves.

After the first rise, remove the dough from the bread maker. Place it on a floured board. Cut dough in half and shape it into 2 round or oval loaves or, if desired, 1 large loaf. Set the loaves on a greased baking sheet a few inches apart. Cover and let rise until doubled in size, approximately 30 to 60 minutes. Bake in a preheated 350° oven for about 25 to 35 minutes or until the bread sounds hollow when thumped on the underside. The crust will be a light color. Let cool about 20 minutes before serving. To freeze or store, wrap cooled bread tightly in foil. Defrost completely. Re-warm uncovered in a 350° oven.

MAKES 1 LARGE OR 2 SMALL LOAVES

Marmalade Bread

This light, soft loaf complements fish or chicken. It also makes great sandwiches.

3 teaspoons active dry yeast or bread machine yeast
3 cups white bread flour
1½ teaspoons salt
1 tablespoon sugar
2 tablespoons butter or margarine, at room temperature
¼ cup orange marmalade, at room temperature
1 tablespoon lemon juice
1 tablespoon lime juice

⅛ teaspoon grated fresh lemon peel
½ cup lukewarm milk
¼ cup plus 2 tablespoons warm water

Add ingredients to the bread maker in the order listed. Set the machine on "manual" (white bread). After first rise, remove dough from bread maker. Place it on a floured board. Cut dough in half and shape it into oval or long loaves. If desired, shape or braid into 1 large loaf. Set loaves on a greased baking sheet. Cover and let rise until doubled in size, about 30 to 60 minutes.

Bake in a preheated 350° oven for about 25 to 30 minutes or until bread sounds hollow when thumped on the underside. The crust will be a naturally light color. Let cool about 20 minutes before serving. To freeze or store, wrap cooled bread tightly in foil. Defrost completely before rewarming uncovered in a 350° oven.

MAKES 1 LARGE OR 2 SMALL LOAVES

Dried Cherry Bread

Serve toasted with cream cheese for breakfast, or use it for sandwiches. Great with ham or turkey. Buy the cherries from a health-food store or from Williams-Sonoma. Braid the dough or fashion it into a wreath for the holidays.

3	teaspoons active dry yeast or bread machine yeast
3	cups white bread flour
1¼	teaspoons salt
1	tablespoon brown sugar
¼	cup unsweetened applesauce
¼	cup cherry yogurt
¾	cup warm water
¾	cup dried cherries

Add the ingredients except for the dried cherries to the bread maker in the order listed. Set the machine on "manual" (white bread). Add the dried cherries during the last few minutes of the final knead cycle. After the first rise, remove the dough from the bread maker. Place the dough on a floured board. Cut it in half and shape pieces into 2 oval or long loaves. Set the loaves on a greased baking sheet. Cover and let rise until doubled in size, about 30 to 60 minutes.

Bake in a preheated 350° oven for about 25 minutes or until bread sounds hollow when thumped on the underside. Let cool about 20 minutes before serving. To freeze or store, wrap cooled bread tightly in foil. Defrost completely before rewarming uncovered in a 350° oven.

MAKES 1 LARGE LOAF OR 2 SMALL LOAVES

Brioche

Serve these at a fancy meal.

2	teaspoons active dry yeast or bread machine yeast
3¼	cups white bread flour
1½	teaspoons salt
3	tablespoons sugar
2	eggs at room temperature
4	tablespoons butter at room temperature
1	cup milk at room temperature

EGG GLAZE:

1	egg, beaten
1	tablespoon sugar

Place the ingredients in the bread maker in the order given and according to the manufacturer's directions for your machine. Machine setting should be on "manual" (white bread), so that it will not bake the bread. Once the dough has completed its kneading and first-rise cycles, remove it from the machine and place it on a breadboard that has been dusted with flour.

Divide dough into 12 large balls. From each large ball, pinch off a small amount of dough and roll it into a ball. Place the large balls of dough into a lightly greased muffin tin. Make a dent in the center of each large ball and press a small ball of dough into the groove, making the traditional brioche. Cover with a towel and let rise for about 40 minutes in a draft-free spot until doubled in size. Meanwhile, preheat the oven to 375°. Mix the beaten egg and sugar in a small cup and brush it onto the tops of the brioches. Bake for 15 to 20 minutes or until cooked.

MAKES 12

about 30 to 60 minutes. Bake in a preheated 350° oven for about 25 minutes or until the bread sounds hollow when thumped on the underside. Let cool for 20 minutes before serving. To freeze or store, wrap cooled bread tightly in foil. Defrost completely before rewarming uncovered in a 350° oven.

MAKES 1 LARGE OR 2 SMALL LOAVES

Sunflower Bread

The sunflower seeds add a nutty taste. Do not use processed seeds, as the shells will be tough and spoil the texture of the bread. This bread is nice for sandwiches.

3   teaspoons active dry yeast or bread machine yeast
2$\frac{1}{2}$ cups white bread flour
$\frac{3}{4}$ cup wheat bread flour
$\frac{1}{2}$ teaspoon salt
2   tablespoons butter or margarine
3   tablespoons honey
$\frac{1}{2}$ cup lukewarm milk
$\frac{3}{4}$ cup warm water
$\frac{1}{2}$ cup lightly salted sunflower seeds

Add the ingredients except for the sunflower seeds to the bread maker in the order listed. Set machine on "manual" (white bread). Add sunflower seeds during the last few minutes of the final knead cycle. After the first rise, remove the dough from the bread maker. Place the dough on a floured board. Cut it in half and shape pieces into 2 oval or long loaves. Set the loaves on a greased cookie sheet. Cover and let rise until doubled in size,

Pumpernickel Bread

This is a stiff dough, so your bread maker may thump a bit. Stay in the area while this is kneading. My bread maker hopped off the counter the first time I made this recipe. I've prevented that problem from recurring and reduced the noise level in my kitchen by placing the machine on a rubber mat in a deep corner of the countertop.

3$^1/_4$ teaspoons active dry yeast or bread machine yeast

1$^1/_2$ cups plus 2 tablespoons white bread flour

$^1/_2$ cup wheat bread flour

1 cup rye flour

$^1/_4$ cup cornmeal

1$^1/_2$ teaspoons salt

2 tablespoons brown sugar

2$^1/_2$ tablespoons cocoa powder

2 tablespoons butter or margarine, at room temperature

3$^1/_2$ tablespoons molasses, at room temperature

$^3/_4$ cup lukewarm, brewed coffee*

$^1/_2$ cup lukewarm milk

2 teaspoons caraway seeds (optional)

Place all the ingredients except the caraway seeds in bread maker in the order given and according to the manufacturer's directions for your machine. Machine setting should be on "manual" (white bread) so that it will not bake the bread. Start machine. Once your machine has completed its first knead, stop it, reset it, and then restart the machine to create an extra knead cycle. This method produces a fluffier, crustier loaf. Add the caraway seeds during the last few minutes of kneading to avoid crushing them. Once the dough has completed its kneading and first-rise cycles, remove it from the machine and place it on a breadboard dusted with cornmeal. Shape into loaves and place a them few inches apart on a lightly greased baking sheet. Cover loaves with a towel and set away from draft for second rise, approximately 1 hour and 20 minutes, until doubled in size. Be patient. This is a heavy bread and takes a while to rise. Bake at 350° for 25 to 30 minutes or until bread sounds hollow when tapped lightly on the underside.

Remove loaves from oven and cool 20 minutes before serving, or wrap them tightly in aluminum foil and freeze until needed.

To reheat: Unwrap frozen loaf and thaw completely. Heat in 350° oven for 5 to 10 minutes until heated thoroughly. Serve warm with Orange Honey Butter.

* * Substitute ½ teaspoon instant coffee plus ½ cup warm water for brewed coffee.*

MAKES 1 LARGE OR 2 SMALL LOAVES

Easter Bread

As far back as I can remember, a log of fruited egg bread signaled Easter morning at our house. My grandmother used to fashion a braided circle out of citron-fruited dough with several colored eggs placed in its crevices to hard cook with the bread. Usually, I associate my mother's raisin egg bread with Easter. I'd slice at it for days after Easter, adding more butter to each slice as the bread staled, and I was always sorry when the last bit was gone. My attempts at recreating my mother's bread by hand produced dense, brick-like loaves that my children avoided like the flu. I like to think that my electric bread maker is responsible for resurrecting our Easter Bread tradition by enabling me to produce this sophisticated, fluffy loaf that I've updated with today's dried fruits.

3	teaspoons active dry yeast or bread machine yeast
3¹⁄₄	cups white bread flour
1¹⁄₂	teaspoons salt
¹⁄₂	teaspoon grated lemon peel
1	teaspoon vanilla extract
2	eggs, room temperature
3	tablespoons honey
¹⁄₄	cup lukewarm milk
³⁄₄	cup warm water
¹⁄₄	cup golden raisins
¹⁄₂	cup mixed dried cherries, cranberries, blueberries (or other mixed dried fruit of your choice)
¹⁄₄	cup toasted almonds

COINTREAU GLAZE:

1	tablespoon honey
1	teaspoon lemon juice
1	tablespoon Cointreau or Triple Sec (or other orange-flavored liqueur)

Add the ingredients to the bread maker in the order listed, except for the dried fruits and almonds. Add the dried fruits and nuts during the last 5 minutes of the final knead cycle. After the first rise, remove the dough from the bread maker. Place it on a floured board.

To shape into two braids: Divide dough in half. Working with one half of the dough, make 3 ropes about 6 inches long. Pinch ropes together at one end, braid, and pinch together at the other end to secure. Repeat for second loaf. Set loaves on a greased baking sheet. Cover and let rise until doubled in size, about 30 to 60 minutes.

Bake in a preheated 350° oven for about 30 to 35 minutes or until bread sounds hollow when thumped on the underside.

To make the Cointreau Glaze: In a small cup combine the glaze ingredients.

Brush the glaze on the hot bread. Let cool about 20 minutes before serving. Serve with Orange Honey Butter.

To freeze or store, wrap cooled bread tightly in foil. Defrost completely before rewarming uncovered in a 350° oven.

MAKES 2 BRAIDED LOAVES

2   eggs
1¼ cups flour
½   teaspoon salt
1   teaspoon sugar
1   cup milk
1   tablespoon melted butter

Orange Honey Butter

Good on any of the breads in this chapter.

1   cup butter, softened
⅓   cup honey
1   tablespoon freshly grated orange peel

Blend and store in refrigerator until ready to spread.

MAKES 1 CUP

Preheat oven to 475°. Either grease muffin tins or insert foil cupcake liners. Don't use paper liners, as they will stick to the batter as it cooks. Place the eggs in a blender or food processor and whirl until beaten. Add the remaining ingredients and whirl to blend thoroughly. Stop the blender and scrape the sides with a rubber spatula part-way through. Fill prepared muffin tins half full with the blended batter. Bake for 15 minutes at 475°, then reduce the oven temperature to 350°. Continue to bake for an additional 15 to 20 minutes, until popovers are browned.

MAKES 12

QUICK BREADS & COFFEECAKES

I've always thought the designation "quick bread" was quirky until I realized that if you don't mix baking powder–based breads "quick," you won't get that much-coveted light, tender texture. As a rule, always whisk the dry ingredients together and then add the liquids all at once. Stir until barely blended.

Popovers

I've used this recipe for years. Popovers are a welcome change from standard bread when served with a heavy meal. While these rolls puff up impressively, they are not difficult to make. The trick to crusty popovers is the change in oven temperature.

Garlic Bread

An old standby to serve with pasta, steak, or whenever you need an easy-to-make starch to complete a meal. Save leftovers to reheat again.

1   loaf purchased Italian or French bread
4   tablespoons butter or margarine
2   cloves garlic, crushed and minced
1/2 teaspoon dried oregano

Sliced the bread lengthwise to make 2 long pieces. Combine the butter, garlic, and oregano in a small saucepan or microwave-safe bowl and heat until butter is melted. Lay bread halves on a large piece of aluminum foil, crust side down. Using a pastry brush, spread the butter mixture evenly over the cut bread halves. If bread is fresh and at room temperature, broil the top sides until they sizzle and begin to brown. If you are using chilled or not-so-fresh-bread, put halves together to reassemble the loaf and wrap tightly in the foil. Bake at 350° for about 15 minutes or until the bread is heated through. Remove the bread from the oven and turn on the broiler. Open the halves and top brown. Serve hot.

SERVES 6 TO 8

Cheese Bread

Serve this with cocktails, or offer with soup, chili, or stew.

4   tablespoons butter or margarine
2   cloves garlic, crushed and minced
1   tablespoon dried parsley
1   loaf French bread
1/2 cup Havarti (or any soft) cheese, shredded
1/2 cup cheddar or Monterey Jack cheese, shredded

Preheat oven to 400°. In a small saucepan add the butter, garlic, and parsley and heat on low until the butter is just melted. You may also do this in a microwave. Slice bread in half lengthwise and place on an aluminum foil–lined baking sheet. Brush the cut sides of bread with the butter mixture. Combine the cheeses and distribute evenly over the top of the buttered bread. Bake for about 10 minutes, until cheese is melted. Cut into wedges and serve hot.

MAKES 1 LOAF

Zucchini Bread

We made this recipe in desperation the summer we had an overload of zucchini in our garden. Delicious as it continues to be, it (sigh) only uses one or two squash—not nearly enough when you've got green "baseball bats" rotting in your garden. We finally solved the problem with a family project. We canned sixty jars of zucchini pickles that summer.

2	cups flour
2	teaspoons baking soda
1	teaspoon salt
$1/4$	teaspoon baking powder
1	tablespoon cinnamon
3	eggs, beaten
1	cup vegetable oil
$1^1/2$	cups sugar
2	teaspoons vanilla
2	cups grated zucchini, pressed and drained well
1	cup chopped nuts
	Powdered sugar for garnish

Preheat oven to 350°. Grease loaf pans or muffin tins. Sift flour, baking soda, salt, baking powder, and cinnamon together into a mixing bowl or onto a piece of waxed paper. In a large mixing bowl combine the eggs, vegetable oil, sugar, and vanilla. Stir in the zucchini. With a wooden spoon fold in the flour mixture $1/2$ cup at a time until well blended. Gently fold in the chopped nuts. Pour the mixture into two $7^1/2$ x $3^1/2$ x $2^1/2$-inch loaf pans or fill $3^1/2$-inch muffin tins three-fourths full. Bake loaves for 40 to 45 minutes or muffins for 20 to 25 minutes. Bread is cooked when a toothpick inserted in the center comes out clean. Sprinkle with powdered sugar, if desired. Keeps well. May be frozen.

MAKES TWO LOAVES OR 6 JUMBO MUFFINS

"Crack 'O Dawn" Muffins

When my husband was on his health kick, I made these healthy jumbo muffins for his breakfast. I would make up a batch and freeze them, individually wrapped, so he could take one to work each day. Place frozen muffins in the microwave for 40 seconds to defrost and heat them. Like fruitcake, the flavor improves as these age. If you don't have wheat and oat flours, it's okay to use all white flour.

2	cups grated carrots (about 2 large)
$1/2$	cup cored, peeled and shredded apple (1 small)
1	8-ounce can crushed pineapple, juice reserved
$3/4$	cup raisins
$1/2$	cup pecans or walnuts, chopped
1	cup sugar
1	cup white flour
1	cup whole wheat flour
$1/4$	cup oat bran
1	tablespoon cinnamon
2	teaspoons baking soda
$1/2$	teaspoon salt
3	eggs, the equivalent in egg substitute, or 6 egg whites
$3/4$	cup vegetable oil
1	teaspoon vanilla
2	tablespoons oat bran for garnish

Preheat oven to 350°. Spray jumbo 3½-inch muffin tins lightly with oil. Prepare and grate the carrots and apple. Drain the pineapple. Combine carrots, apple, and pineapple in a mixing bowl and then stir in the raisins and nuts. In a separate mixing bowl whisk together the sugar, white and wheat flours, oat bran, cinnamon, baking soda, and salt. Mix in the carrot-fruit mixture until coated with dry ingredients. In a third bowl whisk together the eggs, oil, vanilla, and the reserved pineapple juice. Add this liquid mixture all at once to the flour-fruit mixture in the large bowl. Stir gently to just mix. Fill prepared muffin tins to the brim. Sprinkle with oat bran and bake for 25 minutes in a preheated 350° oven. Cool muffins and then wrap them individually in plastic wrap or store in an airtight container. Refrigerate or freeze until ready to serve.

MAKES 12 JUMBO MUFFINS

Blueberry Pear Cobbler

Try this no-batter coffeecake when time is short.

4 pounds ripe pears, peeled, cored, and sliced
2½ tablespoons fresh lemon juice
½ cup sugar
1 12-ounce package frozen blueberries
2 tablespoons cornstarch
1 package regular-sized refrigerated buttermilk biscuits
4 tablespoons melted butter or margarine
¼ cup granulated sugar

Preheat oven to 350°. Butter a 9 x 13 x 2-inch baking pan. In a mixing bowl combine the pears, lemon juice, sugar, blueberries, and cornstarch. Pour the mixture into the prepared pan. Open the package of biscuits and separate them. Dip each biscuit top first in the melted butter and then in the sugar. Arrange them on top of the fruit in a single layer. Bake the cobbler in a 350° oven for about 50 minutes, until fruit bubbles and is tender and the biscuits are golden brown. Serve with vanilla ice cream.

SERVES 8

RECIPE FOR A SWEET LIFE

Show kindness to those who are less fortunate

Ride the middle road

Have no regrets

Give for the joy of it

Find the good in everyone and everything

Eat chocolate

JUST DESSERTS

People don't eat desserts like they used to. The problem this presents is that when you have a party, the leftovers sit on your counter for days afterwards, haunting you. And, if you look at the sweets long enough they'll wind up on your hips. Cookies, cakes, and pies—despite our need to avoid them—still make our world go 'round. They celebrate our finest occasions, entertain our dearest guests, and pick us up when we are down.

Make mine decaf . . .

Coffee is my surrogate dessert. I actually find it satisfying at the end of the meal, especially if it is a flavored brew like chocolate raspberry or hazelnut vanilla. Although I never drank coffee until long after the kids were born, it has come to my rescue more times than I could imagine. I learned to escape into a cup of coffee whenever I needed to put order in my life. I still love the feel of a warm cup in my hand; it's reassuring. When the kids come to visit, we make our own coffee klatch, like we used to when they lived at home. I save up heaps of catalogs for these occasions and we sit around the kitchen table in our robes, drinking coffee and deciding what to buy. We got a substantial telephone order placed to Victoria's Secret before church one Easter Sunday.

Yet, sweets have always been my downfall. My husband may forget about a luscious whipped cream cake after one satisfying slice, but the remainder of that cake will call out to me wherever I am—in the car driving home, sorting laundry, or working on the computer. It nags at me like a fishwife until I'm standing over the sink wolfing down a big hunk. I used to bake when the kids were little—cookies for snacking, cupcakes for school birthdays, and fancy cakes and pies for holidays. But there's no one home to eat that stuff now, except chubby me. It takes all the willpower I can muster to dump leftover whipped cream down the garbage disposal or wash a mixing bowl and beaters without first running my fingers around their inner surfaces, scraping them clean.

But, the temptation is always there. When we go out to dinner, I steel myself to avert my eyes when the server comes by with the dessert tray. She can barely hear me hiss, "I'll have just a cup of coffee, decaf."

Great coffee!

Off-the-shelf canned coffee was good enough for me until the day my daughters introduced me to a bag of gourmet coffee beans and an electric grinder. It was then that I became hooked on "good" coffee. Everything has its price, though. While indulging in gourmet coffee is decadence, to do it "right" means making a separate stop at a coffee shop that does its own roasting and paying double the price of canned brands like Maxwell House and Folgers. But you now have both the time and the bucks to do this, so go ahead and spoil yourself. Begin your quest by deciding on the type of coffee, flavored or nonflavored, and then choose from an overwhelming array of varieties with exotic names, like Sumatra Mahandling and Mocha Java.

Making a good cup of coffee, I've found, is an art that begins with using whole beans. Because there are fewer surfaces exposed to the air, whole beans retain the coffee's freshness and flavor longer than beans that have been ground. Coffee aficionados swear that ground coffee and coffee beans retain their best flavor when stored in an airtight container in the freezer and used within two to four weeks. As loss of moisture and exposure to air are two means of flavor deterioration, this makes sense.

It's in the grind

A food processor will work as well as an electric coffee grinder, as long as you time the grinding cycle to obtain the desired coarseness. When grinding coffee beans, the rule of thumb is that the faster the brew method, the finer the grind. For example, a very finely ground coffee is used for espresso, which brews in seconds, while coarsely ground coffee works best for a French press, which needs to steep for a few minutes. Here are some guidelines to get you started:

Espresso   Extra-Fine Grind: 20 seconds
Automatic Drip   Fine Grind: 15 seconds
Manual Drip   Medium Grind: 12 seconds
Percolator or French Press   Coarse Grind: 9 seconds

Experiment until you determine the coarseness that gives you a smooth-tasting, balanced cup of coffee. If the coffee tastes weak, try grinding it a little finer. If it seems bitter, grind it more coarsely next time.

Brewing tips

Use your favorite pot—we all have our preferences. The electric drip coffeemaker is preferred by many because it's almost foolproof. Next, use good-tasting water. If your tap water is imbued with chemicals, such as chlorine, you may want to use filtered or bottled water to avoid transferring the off-taste to your precious coffee. Some say cold water contains more oxygen, so it's best to start a pot with cold water; and that the brewing temperature of water in the pot should be between 195 and 205 degrees. Use a paper or "gold" filter in the coffeemaker basket for all except a French press (which hasn't a basket).

Measure the grounds using a tablespoon or a coffee scoop, which equals 2 tablespoons. Until I researched this further, I hadn't realized that I had been drinking imperfect gourmet coffee all these years.

Good coffee: 1 tablespoon ground coffee per cup for each 8-ounce cup of water
Great coffee: 2 tablespoons ground coffee per cup for each 6-ounce cup of water

When I checked with two well-known coffee companies, they were unanimous in claiming that one scoop (2 tablespoons) of ground coffee should be used per cup of water; i.e., 10 scoops per 10-cup pot. (What? I'd been using half that amount!) And worse, they consider a cup 6 ounces, not the customary 8 ounces, which means a greater than one on one ground to coffee ratio. While this seems excessive, they say using less coffee will "under extract" the flavor. Should coffee brewed this way be too strong, one fellow added, it can be "weakened" to taste without losing the flavor by adding some hot "tea" water.

I tried it their way and to my surprise the coffee wasn't too strong; it was delicious—rich and creamy enough to be a dessert. (Bear in mind that coffee this concentrated needs more lightening, so I did add a hefty amount of cream. Also, it contains twice the caffeine of traditional coffee, so unless you are drinking decaf you'll be super wired with fake energy.) Now my coffee habit's going to cost me even more, because I'm no longer satisfied with a "good" cup of coffee. I want it to taste *great!*

CAKES

Spiced Banana-Nut Cake

¹/₂   cup butter or margarine, softened
1¹/₂ cups firmly packed brown sugar
3   eggs
1¹/₃ cups mashed bananas (2-3 medium
      bananas)
¹/₄   cup buttermilk*
1   teaspoon vanilla extract
2¹/₄ cups flour
2   teaspoons baking powder
1   teaspoon baking soda
1¹/₂ teaspoons cinnamon
³/₄   teaspoon nutmeg
¹/₄   teaspoon ginger
¹/₂   teaspoon salt
1   cup chopped walnuts

Preheat oven to 350°. Grease and flour two 8-inch cake pans or one 9 x 13 x 2-inch baking pan. In a large electric mixing bowl cream the butter and sugar. Add the eggs, bananas, buttermilk, and vanilla and beat well. In a separate mixing bowl whisk together the remaining ingredients, except the nuts. Add the dry ingredient mixture to the banana mixture and blend on medium speed for 30 seconds, scraping bowl constantly, and then beat on high speed for another 3 minutes. Stir in the nuts. Pour the batter into baking pans and bake for 35 minutes or until a wooden toothpick comes out clean when inserted in the center of the cake. Cool 10 minutes and then remove from the pan. Place layers on a baking rack to cool completely before frosting them.

To make a buttermilk substitute: Add 1 teaspoon of vinegar to the milk (reduce the quantity of the milk by 1 teaspoon) and let the mixture sit at room temperature for about 15 minutes, until milk begins to curdle.

MAKES ONE 9 x 13 x 2 INCH SHEET CAKE
OR TWO 8-INCH LAYERS

Food Processor Frosting

Enough to frost one layer cake or one sheet cake.

¹/₂   cup vegetable shortening
¹/₂   cup margarine, cut up into cubes
4   cups powdered sugar
1   teaspoon vanilla
2   teaspoons cold milk

Blend the shortening, margarine, powdered sugar, and vanilla in a food processor. Add the milk to the processor while it is running and continue to process until all ingredients are smooth and well blended.

Sponge Cake with Kirsch Cream

With a little care, this cake will come out perfect and light every time. Be sure to beat the eggs long enough. For a simple dessert, sprinkle the layers with powdered sugar and cut into wedges. Serve with coffee or afternoon tea. Fancy fare? Ice the layers with Kirsch Cream. Yummy.

5   eggs
1¼ cups sugar
1   cup cake flour
⅛ teaspoon salt

KIRSCH CREAM:
1   cup heavy cream
½ cup Kirsch or other cherry-flavored
      liqueur

Preheat oven to 350°. Grease two 8-inch cake pans. In a large mixing bowl, beat the eggs with an electric mixer for several minutes until they become frothy. Add the sugar, ¼ cup at a time, beating after each addition. Continue to beat the eggs until batter is thick and lemon colored. In a separate bowl whisk the flour and salt. Gently fold the flour mixture into the egg batter with a rubber spatula until blended. Pour batter into the cake pans and bake at 350° for about 20 minutes or until cake springs back when touched lightly in the center. Cool completely and frost with Kirsch Cream, if desired.

To make the Kirsch Cream: Beat heavy cream until foamy. Slowly add Kirsch and continue beating until soft peaks form.

MAKES TWO 8-INCH LAYERS

Pies & Tarts

Apple season is piemaking time

Fall is apple season in Glastonbury, Connecticut, where orchards abound with fresh-off-the-tree varieties. This is when I buy apples by the bushel—more than I can ever use. But apple pie is a welcome treat at almost any occasion, so I use the apples to make a batch of pies. I label and double wrap the pies and freeze them unbaked. (Fruit pies can be frozen unbaked, while custard pies should be baked before freezing.)

The variety of apples you choose for pie is important. Look for a firm, tart apple that will hold its shape while baking—Wolf Run, Baldwin, Ida Red, and Rome, to name a few. Less crisp apples, such as Macintosh or Delicious, will turn to applesauce in your pie. Make the task of pie-making more manageable by breaking it into smaller segments, like I do. *Stage one:* Peel and slice apples and store them in one-pie portions in zip-lock plastic bags. To avoid brown apples, add about ¼ cup orange or lemon juice to each bag and smoosh the apple slices around to coat them. The apples will keep in the refrigerator for a few days. *Stage two:* Prepare the crust, mix the apple filling, and assemble the pies for either freezing or immediate baking.

Easy peeling

Apple peeling used to be a gargantuan task that I bribed the kids to do when they lived at home. Once they moved out, I convinced my husband to help peel the apples. (I told him I wasn't baking pies if I had to peel the apples alone.) When I received a manual apple-peeling machine as a gift, I thought I was in heaven. This wonder machine not only cored and peeled the apples, but it sliced them, as well. Ah . . . the slicing. The apple peeling machine sliced the apples much thinner than I did by hand, causing them to turn brown and disintegrate when stored. Also, the slices became mushy when baked in the pies. I resolved this problem by giving the peeler away and investing in one that would allow me to deactivate the slicing mechanism. Problem solved. I slice the apples by hand, but the peeling machine doest the rest.

The crust?

Well, my experience with piecrust making is akin to making yeast breads by hand—total failure. With such good refrigerated piecrust dough available from supermarkets, it makes sense for those of us who can't produce that coveted flaky crust to take the shortcut to Crustdom. Buy it ready to roll out and be prepared to receive compliments on your wonderful pies. Few who taste it will realize that the crust hasn't been made from scratch.

Classic Apple Pie

1   package refrigerated piecrust dough

APPLE PIE FILLING:
10   cups pie apples, peeled and sliced
3/4   cup sugar
1 1/2   tablespoons tapioca
1   teaspoon cinnamon
1/2   teaspoon nutmeg
1/2   teaspoon vanilla
1   teaspoon grated lemon or orange peel
2   tablespoons butter, cut into 1/2-inch cubes

CINNAMON SUGAR TOPPING:
1/2   teaspoon granulated sugar
    Pinch cinnamon

Preheat oven to 425°. Prepare pastry by rolling out each layer to fit a 10-inch deep-dish pie plate. Place bottom layer in plate, allowing it to overhang about an inch all around. In a large bowl combine the apples with all the remaining ingredients except the butter. Pile the mixture into a pie plate lined with pastry. Distribute butter cubes evenly over top. Cover with top layer. Roll edges and pinch in towards pie to seal. Prick top with a fork to vent. Mix the sugar and cinnamon to make the topping and sprinkle on top of pie. Bake at 425° for 50 to 60 minutes, until the crust is browned, apples are tender, and juices bubble. If the edges get too brown, cover them lightly with foil. Should the top crust become too brown before the pie is done, reduce the oven temperature to 350° and lay a piece of foil lightly over the top.

To freeze: Cover unbaked pie with plastic wrap and then overlay this with aluminum foil. For best results, defrost the pie completely before baking it.

MAKES ONE 10-INCH PIE

Praline-crusted Apple Pie

This pie is certain to be devoured quickly. Use the same recipe as Classic Apple Pie for the crust and filling.

1	baked double-crusted apple pie
1/4	cup butter or margarine
1/2	cup firmly packed brown sugar
2	tablespoons half and half
1/2	cup chopped pecans

Preheat oven to 425°. In a small saucepan over medium heat melt the butter. Stir in the brown sugar and half and half. Slowly bring to a boil. Remove the pan from heat and stir in the pecans. Spread topping evenly over the baked pie. Place the pie on a cookie sheet. Put the pie in the oven to bake for 5 minutes or until the topping bubbles. Cool at least an hour before serving.

MAKES ONE 10-INCH PIE

Apple Pie with Dried Cranberries and Currants

A festive change from the traditional apple pie. As usual, I cheat on the crust. If you wish to make the crust from scratch, mix the lemon and nutmeg right into the dough.

APPLE, DRIED CRANBERRY, & CURRANT FILLING:

9	cups sliced McCoun or tart pie apples, peeled and cored
2/3	cup sugar
1/2	cup dried currants
1/2	cup sweetened dried cranberries (or 3/4 cup chopped fresh*)
3	tablespoons quick cooking tapioca
1 1/4	teaspoons ground cinnamon
2/3	teaspoon ground nutmeg
1	tablespoon butter or margarine

QUICK LEMON NUTMEG CRUST:

1	package refrigerated piecrust dough
1	teaspoon grated lemon peel
1/2	teaspoon nutmeg

Preheat oven to 400°. In a large mixing bowl combine the apples, sugar, currants, cranberries, tapioca, cinnamon, and nutmeg. Mix well and set aside.

Prepare piecrust from refrigerated dough: Unfold dough onto a floured pastry cloth or a piece of waxed paper. Sprinkle half the lemon zest and half the nutmeg evenly over the bottom crust. Cover with another sheet of waxed paper and roll spices into the dough with a rolling pin. Repeat procedure for top crust, using the remaining lemon zest and nutmeg.

Assemble pie: Carefully lay bottom crust in pie plate and tamp it in place. Trim the edges of the crust, leaving ³/₄ to 1 inch of overhang. Pour in the filling, distributing it evenly and gently packing it down. The apples should be heaped at the center of the pan. Dot with butter, and then lay the top crust over all. Use your fingers to roll up and seal the edges. Crimp with fork if desired. Poke holes or a slit into the top crust to vent steam. Bake pie until crust is golden brown, apples are tender, and juices bubble, about 1 hour and 10 minutes. Cool about 20 minutes. Serve warm with Real Whipped Cream or ice cream.

  * *If using fresh cranberries, add 1 more tablespoon of sugar.*

MAKES ONE 10-INCH PIE

Mile-High Lemon Meringue Pie

I crave a light, sweet dessert around June, when the weather warms. If you're in a rush, substitute packaged lemon pie filling for the homemade. Pie should be served well chilled. Does not freeze well.

1   package refrigerated piecrust dough

LEMON PIE FILLING:
2   cups sugar
6   tablespoons cornstarch
3   cups cold water
6   egg yolks
    Grated zest of 2 lemons
¹/₂ cup lemon juice
2   tablespoons butter or margarine

MERINGUE TOPPING:
8   egg whites
¹/₄ teaspoon cream of tartar
¹/₄ teaspoon salt
³/₄ cup sugar

Roll one piecrust thin enough to fit a 10-inch pie pan. Lay the crust in the pan and poke holes in it to vent steam. If you wish, lay a 9-inch foil pan inside the crust when baking it to help keep its shape. Bake according to package directions. Allow crust to cool.

To make the lemon filling: In a large saucepan, combine sugar and cornstarch. Gradually stir in water until smooth. Stir in egg yolks. Cook over medium heat, stirring constantly until filling comes to a boil. Boil one minute or until filling thickens. Remove from heat and stir in the lemon zest, lemon juice, and margarine. Cool.

To microwave filling: Whisk together the sugar and cornstarch in an 8-quart microwave-safe bowl. Gradually stir in the water, then the egg yolks. Cover bowl and microwave on high for about 5 minutes, until mixture boils and begins to thicken. Stir and check every 2 minutes until done. Stir in the lemon zest, lemon juice, and the butter. Cool.

Prepare meringue topping: Preheat oven to 350°. In a large mixing bowl beat the egg whites with an electric mixer until foamy. Add the cream of tartar and the salt and beat until soft peaks form. While continuing to beat the eggs, gradually add the sugar until stiff peaks form and the meringue becomes glossy.

Assemble pie: Pour lemon filling into baked piecrust, filling to top of pie plate. Spread prepared meringue over lemon filling, covering it completely and sealing the meringue to the inside rim of the crust. Bake the pie at 350° for about 15 minutes or until the meringue is golden brown. Let cool, then refrigerate. Serve well chilled.

MAKES ONE 10-INCH DEEP DISH PIE

Mount Gay Pumpkin Pie

Try this new twist on an old favorite. Few can guess that this pie's rich flavor comes from the dark rum. If you plan to make this pie ahead and freeze it, bake it first.

1   unbaked piecrust

PUMPKIN FILLING:
4   cups solid packed pumpkin (two 16-ounce cans)
1   cup dark brown sugar, packed
1/2   cup granulated sugar
2   tablespoons flour
2   teaspoons ground cinnamon
1 1/2   teaspoons salt
1   teaspoon mace
1   teaspoon ginger
1/2   teaspoon allspice
1/2   teaspoon cloves
6   large eggs
2 1/4   cups whipping cream
1/4   cup Mount Gay rum (or other dark rum)
1 1/2   teaspoons vanilla extract

Roll out the crust and place it in a 10-inch pie plate. Set aside. Preheat oven to 425°.

Prepare filling: Put the pumpkin, sugar, flour, cinnamon, salt, mace, ginger, allspice, and cloves into a large mixing bowl and stir by hand or on low speed with an electric mixer until blended. Add in the eggs, cream, rum, and vanilla and mix well. Pour the filling into the crust. Bake pie for 10 minutes at 425° and then reduce the oven temperature to 350°. Continue baking for another 40 to 50 minutes or until filling no longer moves in center when dish is shaken. Filling will rise slightly and begin to crack when it is done. Remove the pie from the oven and cool it completely. Tastes best when chilled. Serve with Real Whipped Cream.

MAKES ONE 10-INCH PIE

Real Whipped Cream

1   quart heavy cream
3   to 4 tablespoons sugar

Place mixing bowl and beaters in the freezer for about 10 minutes, and be sure the cream is well chilled. Pour the cream into the mixing bowl and beat until it begins to thicken. Add the sugar. Continue beating until cream stands in stiff peaks. Do not overbeat the cream or it will begin to separate and you will have made butter!

Strawberry Pie with Amaretto Crust

A springtime favorite.

6   cups fresh strawberries, hulled and sliced
1   20-ounce can pineapple chunks, drained
2/3 cup sugar
2   tablespoons tapioca
1   teaspoon freshly grated orange peel

AMARETTO CRUST:
1   package refrigerated piecrust
2   teaspoons amaretto or other almond-flavored liqueur
4   tablespoons sliced almonds

Preheat oven to 425°. Make filling by combining the strawberries, pineapple, sugar, tapioca, and orange peel in a medium mixing bowl.

Prepare the bottom and top piecrusts: Using refrigerated piecrust dough or homemade pie dough, roll out top and bottom crusts to fit a 9-inch pie plate. Brush the dough with the amaretto and sprinkle the almonds evenly over both crusts. Place a piece of waxed paper over the dough and press the almonds into the piecrust dough with a rolling pin.

Assemble pie: Lay the bottom crust in the pie plate. Fill crust with strawberry filling and then lay on the top crust. Seal edges and make slits in top crust to vent. Bake pie for 45 to 50 minutes. If crust gets too brown, place a piece of foil lightly over the top for the latter part of the cooking process.

MAKES ONE 9-INCH PIE

Fresh Fruit Tart

Excellent flavor. Tastes as if it took more work than it does to make. Especially nice in the summer when berries and other fresh fruits are readily available. Use your choice of fruits—I've even mixed canned fruit with the fresh. Apples, pears, bananas, and any other fruit that tends to brown when exposed to the air should be first tossed in the orange juice before layering on the tart. Also try the crust and filling variations.

1	package refrigerated piecrust dough
1	8-ounce package cream cheese, softened
3	tablespoons granulated sugar
1/2	teaspoon vanilla extract
3	fresh peaches, sliced
1	to 2 tablespoons orange juice
1	pint fresh strawberries, hulled and cut in half
1	pint fresh blueberries (or 1 package frozen)
1/4	cup orange marmalade
1	tablespoon water

Preheat oven to 450°. Line a 15 x 10 x 1-inch cookie sheet with the 2 piecrusts in the package. Lay both crusts in the pan with edges slightly overlapping the pan rim. Cut the excess dough away with a knife and use to fill in any empty spots. Press the dough gently around edges and bottom of the pan to cover it and make a rectangular crust. Poke a few holes in the crust with the tines of a fork, and bake it at 450° per package directions. Cool.

Prepare filling: In a small bowl beat the cream cheese, sugar, and vanilla with an electric or hand mixer until the mixture is fluffy. Spread over the cooled crust. In a separate bowl mix the peaches, orange juice, strawberries, and blueberries. Pour the fruit into a colander to drain excess juices. Arrange the fruit attractively over the top of the filling. Combine the marmalade and water and brush over the top of the fruit. Refrigerate the tart at least 1 hour before serving. Cut into squares.

FRUIT TART VARIATIONS:

Cookie dough crust: Preheat oven to 375°. Slice 1 package refrigerated sugar cookie dough as directed on package. Arrange "cookies" in a single layer on the bottom of a 15 x 10 x 1-inch baking pan. Press them evenly into the bottom of the pan. Bake crust at 375° for 16 to 20 minutes, until golden brown. Cool.

Ricotta cheese filling variation: In lieu of the cream cheese mixture, combine 1 1/2 cups ricotta cheese, 3 tablespoons granulated sugar, 1/2 teaspoon vanilla, and the grated rind of one lemon.

SERVES 8

Baked Amaretto Pears

Simple and elegant. Especially good in the fall when pears are in season.

4	ripe pears, peeled but left whole
1	tablespoon fresh lemon juice
1/2	cup Marsala wine
2	teaspoons butter, cut into chunks
4	teaspoons brown sugar
1/8	teaspoon cinnamon
1/2	cup crushed amaretto cookies or macaroons

Preheat oven to 350°. Peel the pears, leaving stems on. Brush the pears with lemon juice and then set them upright in an 8 x 8 x 2-inch baking pan. Pour the Marsala wine over the pears and then scatter the chunks of butter over them. Mix the sugar, cinnamon, and amaretto crumbs. Sprinkle the crumb mixture evenly over the pears. Bake pears uncovered for 50 to 60 minutes or until pears are soft. Serve at room temperature with whipped cream or ice cream.

SERVES 4

BARS, COOKIES, & CANDY

Hazelnut Brownies

What I like best about this recipe is that it doesn't require special chocolate. A bag of chocolate chips is usually in my cupboard awaiting a spur-of-the-moment batch of cookies or to be eaten plain during a chocolate binge.

1	12-ounce bag semi-sweet chocolate chips
4	tablespoons butter or margarine
1	cup sugar
2	eggs
1/2	cup flour
1/4	teaspoon baking powder
3	tablespoons Frangelico or other hazelnut liqueur
1/2	cup chopped hazelnuts

Preheat oven to 350° and grease a 13 x 9 x 2-inch baking pan. Melt butter and chocolate chips together over low heat in a saucepan or in the microwave oven for 3 minutes at 50 percent power. Set aside.

In a large mixing bowl combine the sugar, eggs, flour, baking powder, and Frangelico and beat with an electric mixer on medium speed until well blended. Add the warm chocolate mixture and continue beating until well blended. Pour into the prepared pan and bake the brownie batter in a 350° oven for 25 minutes or until it begins to pull away from pan. Do not overcook. Allow to cool for 30 minutes and then slice into squares.

MAKES ABOUT 28 BROWNIES

Molasses Cookies with Orange Butter Icing

After all these years, this old family recipe is still my Christmas favorite over gingerbread cookies. Grab a few with a glass of milk and you'll be hooked, too. I cut the cookie dough into stars, bells, trees, etc. and ice them once they are baked. I sometimes adorn them with nuts or sprinkles.

4	cups flour
1	teaspoon salt
1½	tablespoons baking powder
½	teaspoon cloves
½	teaspoon cinnamon
½	teaspoon mace
1	teaspoon ginger
½	cup (1 stick) margarine, melted
1	egg
1	12-ounce bottle Br'er Rabbit Molasses*

ORANGE BUTTER ICING:

1	pound confectioners' 10x sugar
½	cup butter or margarine, softened
3	tablespoons plus 1 teaspoon fresh orange juice

In a large mixing bowl combine the flour, salt, baking powder, cloves, cinnamon, mace, and ginger. Stir in the melted margarine. Add the egg and mix well. Add molasses and mix well. Dough will be loose and sticky. Pat flour on top of the dough and then divide it into 4 sections. Scoop dough onto a floured piece of plastic wrap and wrap tightly to form a flattened ball. Chill about 1 hour or until dough becomes firm enough to shape.

To bake: Preheat oven to 350°. On a floured board roll firmed dough to ¼-inch thickness. Use cookie cutters to make shapes. Place cookies on a greased cookie sheet about 2 inches apart and bake for 8 to 10 minutes or until lightly browned on the underside. Allow cookies to cool before decorating them.

To make the Orange Butter Icing: In a large bowl combine the sugar, butter, and orange juice and beat with an electric mixer until it is creamy. If necessary, add more sugar or orange juice to achieve a desirable spreading consistency. Spread a thin layer of icing on each cookie and decorate as otherwise desired. Allow icing to dry. Store cookies between layers of waxed paper in a tightly covered container. May be frozen.

*My mom always insisted this brand of molasses worked best in this recipe, so I use it whenever I can find it.

MAKES ABOUT 3 DOZEN

Molasses Nut Biscotti

My dad enjoyed this variation of Molasses Cookies (previous page)—a biscotti-like confection that he would hoard for dunking in his homemade wine all winter long. I used to make a double recipe of Molasses Cookies (8 cups of flour!) and save about one quarter of the dough to make these for him.

Preheat oven to 350°. Knead $1/4$ cup chopped walnuts into 1 quarter of the chilled molasses cookie dough. Cut the dough into thirds and roll it into 3-inch-wide loaves, using your hands. Place the loaves on a greased cookie sheet and bake in a 350° oven for 15 to 20 minutes, until they are browned and crusty and a toothpick placed in the center comes out clean. Remove loaves from the oven. Reduce oven temperature to 300°. Using a sharp knife, slice hot loaves into $3/4$-inch-piece biscotti-shaped cookies and them lay them flat on the cookie sheet. Return cookies to the oven for an additional 10 to 15 minutes. Bake until cookies are dry on top. Let cool completely. Store in an airtight container.

MAKES ABOUT 2 DOZEN COOKIES

Orange Chocolate-Chip Cookies

$1^1/4$ pounds butter (1 stick), softened
$1/2$ cup granulated sugar
$1/3$ cup dark brown sugar, packed
2 tablespoons orange juice
1 teaspoon fresh grated orange peel
$1/2$ teaspoon vanilla
1 egg
$1^1/2$ cups flour
$1/2$ teaspoon baking soda
$1/4$ teaspoon salt
6 ounces chocolate chips

Preheat oven to 325°. Place the butter, sugars, orange juice, orange zest, vanilla, and egg in a large mixing bowl and beat with an electric mixer until creamy. In a separate bowl, whisk together the flour, salt and baking soda. With the electric mixer running, add half the flour mixture to the large mixing bowl and beat until blended, then beat in the remaining flour mixture. Use a rubber spatula to scrape the bowl occasionally. The batter will be stiff. Fold in the chocolate chips. On an ungreased cookie sheet, drop teaspoonfuls of the batter (to form small mounds) about 2 inches apart. Bake cookies in a 325° oven for 7 to $8^1/2$ minutes or until lightly browned on the underside. Remove cookies to a wire rack or onto a piece of waxed paper to cool. Store covered. Note: If substituting margarine for the butter, bake cookies at 350°.

MAKES $3^1/2$ DOZEN 2-INCH COOKIES

Joy's Jumbles

1	cup sugar
1/2	cup plus 3 tablespoons shortening
1	egg
1/3	cup milk
1	teaspoon vanilla
2 1/4	cups flour
1/2	teaspoon salt
1	teaspoon cream of tartar
1/2	teaspoon baking soda
1/2	cup golden raisins
3/4	cup chopped walnuts

CINNAMON-SUGAR TOPPING:

1/4	cup sugar
1/2	teaspoon ground cinnamon

Preheat oven to 350°. In a large mixing bowl combine the sugar, shortening, egg, milk, and vanilla and beat with an electric mixer until well blended. In a separate bowl blend the flour, salt, cream of tartar, and baking soda using a fork or wire whisk. Add this mixture to the sugar mixture and beat until well blended. Stir in the raisins and walnuts. Mix the cinnamon and sugar in a small cup or bowl to make the topping. Drop dough by the tablespoonful onto an ungreased cookie sheet, placing cookies about 2 inches apart. Sprinkle evenly with about half of the cinnamon-sugar topping. Bake in a 350° oven for 12 to 15 minutes or until cookies are lightly browned. Remove cookies from the oven and immediately resprinkle them with the remaining cinnamon topping. Gently lift cookies off baking sheet and place them on a wire rack to cool. Store in an airtight container.

MAKES 3 DOZEN 2½-INCH COOKIES

Secret Fudge

The story is that Grandma Smith's aunt weaseled this recipe from the chef at a famous candy company. When I first read the recipe, my "Fear of Candy Making Syndrome" kicked in as I recalled previous experiences with "hard ball"—which is not a sport, but a basic of candy making. Despite this, my first attempt resulted in a gloriously smooth, rich fudge. (Yours will too—and you didn't have to sleep with the cook.) Fudge makes a great hostess gift and is nice to put out on a small plate at a dinner party. Despite the calories, people still love it.

4½ cups sugar
1   12-ounce can evaporated milk
3   6-ounce packages chocolate chips
½   cup unsalted butter
1   15-ounce jar marshmallow creme
1   teaspoon vanilla
2   cups chopped walnuts

In a large, heavy saucepan heat the sugar and the evaporated milk to boiling. Continue boiling about 10 minutes, until it reaches the hard ball stage (see below), stirring often with a long-handled wooden spoon. Remove from heat. Add the chocolate chips, butter, and marshmallow creme and continue stirring until the chips are melted and the ingredients are well blended. Mix in the vanilla and the walnuts and pour at once into a buttered 9 x 13 x 2-inch Pyrex dish. Work quickly to spread fudge to fit the pan. Allow the fudge to cool and then refrigerate it. Cut into 1-inch squares and keep it chilled. Serve cold. This fudge freezes beautifully.

MAKES 5 POUNDS

ACHIEVING "HARD BALL"

The cooking pot should hold 4 times the volume of the liquid to avoid overflow as mixture boils up. This mixture will be extremely hot, so be careful. When it is almost done, it will be clear with brownish clumps. Drop a spot of it into ice water. Fish the candy clump out of the water and rub it between your fingers. It should be thick and rubbery in texture, like a hard ball.

Microwave Brittle

You don't need a candy thermometer to make this brittle. Proceed cautiously, and use pot holders to handle the bowl when removing it from the oven. Mixture becomes extremely hot. Experiment with different kinds of nuts—cashew, almonds, hazelnuts, or peanuts; even canned cocktail nuts will work in this recipe.

Butter
1 cup roasted nuts, coarsely chopped
1 cup granulated sugar
1/2 cup light corn syrup
1/4 teaspoon salt (omit if nuts are salted)
1 tablespoon butter
1 teaspoon vanilla
1 teaspoon baking soda

Grease a cookie sheet with butter and set aside. To avoid boilovers, make brittle in a 2-quart microwave-safe bowl or a glass measuring cup with a spout. Put the nuts, sugar, corn syrup, and salt in the bowl and stir. Microwave on high uncovered for 6 to 8 minutes, stirring every 2 minutes, until mixture is light brown. Remove the nut mixture from the oven and stir in the 1 tablespoon butter. Continue to microwave on high for an additional 1 1/2 to 2 minutes until the mixture turns caramel-colored.

Remove the mixture from the microwave and stir in the vanilla and baking soda, working quickly until mixture is light and foamy. Immediately pour brittle onto the prepared baking sheet and spread it out using the back of a spoon. Mixture will thicken almost immediately, so it's important to work quickly. When cool, break brittle into chunks. Store in an airtight container. Keeps about 2 weeks (if you hide it).

MAKES 15 OUNCES

EPILOGUE

Shucking the vestiges of parenthood is like shedding a skin that no longer fits. It's constraining and then feels old and used as it falls off in heaps, and we emerge fresh and new. Our life is fuller now than it's ever been. We may be pursuing a new career or simply basking in the simplicities of our lives. With less responsibility, we can follow our dreams and our whims. We haven't lost our family. We've gained some new sons-in-law and daughters-in-law who spoil us to tears and promise us grandchildren. Our children open up their homes to us and welcome us like royalty. We've never had it so good. The best of both worlds is ours.

Well, I have to get packed. We're catching a flight to Raleigh at noon. It's hot there in the summer, so I'll gather shorts and a sundress or two in case we go out to dinner. My husband is honking the horn in the driveway. It's time to leave. I grab my cooler bag and ease in the pan of frozen lasagna and a container of homemade pasta sauce. I toss in a bottle of chilled champagne and drop in a plastic container of homemade brownies. We'll be there mid-afternoon. I can't wait to see the kids!

Measurements, Conversions & Substitutions

When I was working on these recipes, I had many opportunities to figure out equivalents. Substitutions are my game. I found these to be the most common exchanges. Pencil in any information you find is missing and you'll end up with your own customized conversion chart and never again have to wonder if you guessed right.

Teaspoons
10 drops = dash
⅛ teaspoon = a few grains
3 teaspoons = 1 tablespoon
8 teaspoons = 1 ounce

Tablespoons
1 tablespoon = ½ fluid ounce
2 tablespoons = 1 fluid ounce or ⅛ cup
4 tablespoons = ¼ cup or 2 ounces
16 teaspoons = 1 cup or 8 ounces
64 tablespoons = 1 quart

Cups
⅛ cup = 1 ounce or 2 tablespoons
⅜ cup = 6 tablespoons
⅓ cup = 5 tablespoons + 1 teaspoon
½ cup = 8 tablespoons or 4 ounces
2 cups = ½ pint or 8 ounces
2 cups = 16 ounces or 1 pound
4 cups = 1 quart

Dry Volumes
½ cup = 1 pint
2 cups = 1 pint
2 pints = 1 quart
4 quarts = 1 gallon

1 Pound Equivalents
2 cups butter
4 cups all-purpose flour
3½ cups powdered sugar
2⅓ cups brown sugar
2 cups milk
3½ cups nuts

Liquid Measures
1½ ounces = 1 jigger
1 quart = 2 pounds
1 tablespoon = ½ fluid ounce
1 cup = 8 ounces
1 quart = 32 ounces
1 quart = 64 tablespoons

Butter

1 pound = 32 tablespoons
1 pound = 2 cups
¼ pound = 1 stick
1 stick = 4 ounces or ½ cup

Cheese

1 pound = 4 cups grated
1 pound cottage cheese = 2 cups
½ pound cream cheese = 1 cup
½ pound cream cheese = 8 ounces

Eggs

1 whole = 2 whites
2 large = ½ cup
3 medium = ½ cup
6 medium = 1 cup

Fruits

1 lemon = 2 to 3 teaspoons juice
1 lemon = 2 teaspoons zest or peel
1 lime = 1½ to 2 teaspoons juice
1 orange = 6 to 8 teaspoons juice
1 orange = 2 to 3 teaspoons zest or peel
1 banana = ½ cup
1 pound bananas = 3 to 4 med. bananas
1 pound apples = 3 cups sliced

Starches

1 cup uncooked macaroni = 2 to 2½
   cups cooked
1 cup uncooked noodles = 1¼ cups
   cooked
1 cup uncooked rice = 2½ cups
   cooked
1 pound potatoes = 2 cups mashed

Temperature Conversions

0 degrees centigrade (Celsius) = 32
   degrees Fahrenheit, which is the freezing point of water.

100 degrees centigrade = 212 degrees
   Fahrenheit, which is the boiling point
   of water.

To convert centigrade (Celsius) to
   Fahrenheit: multiply the centigrade
   degrees by 9, then divide by 5 and add
   32.

To convert Fahrenheit to centigrade:
   Subtract 32 from Fahrenheit degrees,
   multiply by 5, and then divide by 9.

Oven Temperatures

Below 300 degrees F. = very slow, low heat
300 degrees F. = slow
325 degrees F. = moderate
350 degrees F. = moderately hot
400–425 degrees F. = hot
450–475 degrees F. = very hot
500 degrees F. or higher = extremely hot

Substitutions

Dairy

1 cup buttermilk = 1 cup plus 1 tablespoon milk + 1 tablespoon vinegar. Let stand 5 minutes. It will thicken and begin to curdle.

1 cup milk = ½ cup evaporated milk + ½ cup water; or 5 tablespoons dry milk + 1 cup water

1 cup light cream = 1 cup evaporated milk, 1 cup half and half, or 1 cup nondairy creamer

1 cup sour cream = 1 cup plain yogurt + ⅓ cup butter

1 ounce chocolate = 3 tablespoons cocoa + 1 tablespoon butter

6 ounces semisweet chocolate chips or squares = 6 tablespoons unsweetened cocoa powder + 7 tablespoons granulated sugar + ¼ cup shortening

Flours

1 tablespoon flour = ½ teaspoon cornstarch

1 tablespoon flour = 2 teaspoons quick-cooking tapioca

1 cup sifted cake flour = ⅞ cup sifted all-purpose flour

1 cup all-purpose flour = 1 cup + 2 tablespoons cake flour

Other

1 small onion = ¾ teaspoon onion powder

1 small clove garlic = ¼ teaspoon garlic powder

1 pound fresh mushrooms = 6 ounces canned

2 tablespoons chopped celery = 1 teaspoon dried celery flakes

1 tablespoon fresh ginger = ¼ teaspoon ground ginger

1½ tablespoons balsamic vinegar = ¼ cup wine vinegar

1 tablespoon jerk sauce = 1 tablespoon A1® Bold Steak Sauce or 1 tablespoon regular A1® Sauce plus ⅛ teaspoon hot sauce

Equal Alternatives for Herbs and Spices

¼ teaspoon ground herbs = ¾ teaspoon dried herbs = 2 teaspoons fresh herbs

basil = oregano

caraway = anise

celery seeds = minced celery

chervil = parsley, tarragon

fennel = anise, tarragon

oregano = marjoram

sage = thyme

allspice = equal parts cinnamon, cloves, and nutmeg

chili peppers = cayenne

nutmeg = mace

INDEX